RHETORIC IN ANTIQUITY

Laurent Pernot

RHETORIC IN ANTIQUITY

Translated by W. E. Higgins

The Catholic University of America Press
Washington, D.C.

Originally published in 2000 as *La Rhétorique dans l'Antiquité* by Librairie Générale Française in the series "Antiquité" edited by Paul Demont.

The paper used in this publication meets the minimum requirements of American National Standards for Information Science—Permanence of Paper for Printed Library materials, ANSI Z39.48-1984.

∞

LIBRARY OF CONGRESS CATALOGING-IN-PUBLICATION DATA
Pernot, Laurent.
   [Rhétorique dans l'Antiquité. English]
   Rhetoric in antiquity / Laurent Pernot ; translated by W. E. Higgins.
     p. cm.
   "Originally published in 2000 as La rhétorique dans l'Antiquité by Librairie générale française in the series "Antiquité edited by Paul Demont"—T.p. verso.
   Includes bibliographical references and index.
   ISBN 13: 978-0-8132-1407-8 (pbk. : alk. paper)
   ISBN 10: 0-8132-1407-6 (pbk. : alk. paper)
   1. Rhetoric, Ancient.   2. Speeches, addresses, etc., Greek—History and criticism.
3. Speeches, addresses, etc., Latin—History and criticism.   4. Oratory, Ancient.
I. Title.
   PA3038.P46 2005
   808′.00938—dc22

2004012526

Contents

Translator's Note

All ancient sources have been rendered into English based on the translations found in the Loeb Classical Library, when available, and on others, identified as they occur, when there is no Loeb volume. The initials WEH indicate those I have done myself. I have also noted where I have modified existing translations, Loeb or others, in order to suit the tenor of Professor Pernot's argument better or to foster, in my opinion, a contemporary reader's livelier understanding. I have also translated any French in addition to Professor Pernot's.

In translating Greek and Latin technical terms, I have been guided by the solutions of other translators and scholars of ancient rhetoric. I hope this will facilitate the ability of the non-specialist reader or the reader without Greek and Latin to use and cross-reference this volume with other books on the topic. The reader should note, however, that standard or "canonical" translations for each and every term do not exist in English, so some variety is inevitable, mirroring the variety and nuance of the ancient writers.

As for the spelling of Greek names in English, I have generally preferred to rescue them from the practice of making them look like Romans in disguise, but I cannot claim complete consistency in solving this perennial problem, especially where the most widely known names are concerned. So I am content to live with a happy eclecticism that can tolerate both "Socrates" and "Isokrates."

A translator necessarily serves two masters, a parlous state about which no less an authority than Sacred Scripture warns us. The fact that the work translated here deals in part with the intricacies of translation as well as with the requirements of style only compounds the inherent riskiness of the situation. So it is with more than formulaic courtesy that I add my own acknowledgments to those of Professor Pernot below. I thank David McGonagle, director of the CUA Press, for his support and willingness to free me from some of the tasks associated with preparing this volume. My editor at the Press, Sarah Donahue, made helpful suggestions improving my English and the book's format. Gerald Heverly, Classics librarian at New York University, facilitated my work by introducing me to resources available at the Bobst Library. I must also personally thank Pierre Zoberman for bringing this project to my attention. A translator himself and *bilingue extraordinaire*, he lavished time and insight on major and minor points of the translation and helped to make it better than it otherwise would have been. All gaffes, however, remain my responsibility.

Introduction

The word "rhetoric" comes from the ancient Greek *rhētorikē,* which means "art of the spoken word." Right off, etymology indicates the role the ancients played in the subject of the present work. If Greco-Roman antiquity by itself did not invent the art of speaking—other, more ancient civilizations could lay claim to this honor—it did develop it in a special way and conceptualize it with an unprecedented rigor and richness. This art has occupied an important place in the history of Western culture, and it continues to exert a genuine influence, although less visibly present than before, on the modern world's forms of expression and modes of thought.

But in bequeathing us the art of the spoken word, antiquity also left us with a fear of it. Some among the ancients advertised their mistrust of rhetoric, and still today the noun and the adjective "rhetoric" and "rhetorical" may remain pejorative in accepted usage, where they can designate empty or deceitful words. As with "literary," "prosaic," "sophistic"—all terms with which it is connected—the word "rhetoric" sometimes carries a sense of hesitation and suspicion, which corresponds to a very deep-seated anxiety about the power of language, its autonomy in relation to things and ideas, and the risks of its misuse.

Here the aim is to go beyond this appearance, to get past the anxiety, and to try to understand better an essential and controversial object.

First of all, what is rhetoric? We can look for an answer to this question in the treatise of Quintilian on the education of the orator, which devotes a chapter to different definitions proposed in antiquity (*Institutio Oratoria* 2.15: first century A.D.). The most widespread opinion defined rhetoric as "the power of persuading" *(vis persuadendi).* Generally, this definition signified that the orator is someone whose speeches can win the assent of the listener and that rhetoric is the means of achieving this. It is the spoken word that brings about this persuasion and not, for example, mere actions or money or drugs or trustworthiness or authority. Persuasion's principal realm is public discourse, where its specific application is to political and civic issues, that is, those where the interest of the city and the citizens is at stake. Yet it can also have a place in dialogues and private conversations.

Instead of "the power" many preferred to speak of "the art" (in Greek *tekhnē,* in Latin *ars*). This word's ancient meaning does not stress what moderns understand by artistic creation so much as it does the idea of a reasoned method, a system of rules meant for practical use, a technical production, and a craft. Others used words like "the virtue," "the science," or—pejoratively—"the routine." Quintilian, for his part, winds up with a different definition: rhetoric as "the science of speaking well" *(bene dicendi scientia).* The substitution of "speaking" for "persuading" aims at enlarging the field of rhetoric by extending it to virtually all forms of discourse, whatever their aim and effect. As for the adverb "well," it has an intended ambiguity, since it can encompass at the same time grammatical correctness, aesthetic beauty, moral value, and the speech's practical effectiveness. This last definition is the most general and the most inclusive.

This brief rehearsal of rhetoric's different definitions offers in itself an overview of the subject. To start with, there is persuasion: the enigma of persuasion. How do we explain this phenomenon, at once frequent and mysterious, which consists in bringing someone else, without apparent force, to think something he previously was not, or not yet, thinking? Rhetoric was invented to answer this question. Fundamentally, it looks to understand, produce, and regulate persuasion.

In these terms, rhetoric is a technique aiming at effectiveness, a way to produce persuasive speech based upon a certain know-how and even on recipes. Behind this know-how, there is a knowledge, a science if you will, in any case a profound and systematic reflection on the nature and functioning of the spoken word. This knowledge and this know-how are objects of instruction. Furthermore, rhetoric is deployed in precisely datable political and institutional frameworks and ideological configurations. Rhetoric is anchored in society, and consequently it has a history that develops in relation to the general history of ancient societies. Rhetoric also aims for beauty and is bound up with taste and aesthetics. Finally, in every age the moral and philosophical problem arises of the validity of rhetorical discourse, its conformity to truth and virtue. In every age as well, the problem arises of the extension of rhetoric, with reference to other forms of discourse and other aspects of language, and of its relations with linguistics and with literature.

To be precise, we are taking the word "rhetoric" in its full sense. In contemporary language, rhetoric, considered in outline, has two uses: a restrained use, which designates only the theory of discourse (in this case, "rhetoric" is opposed to "eloquence," as theory is to practice), and a wider use, which covers theory and practice together. Since this terminological fluidity is a source of confusion, it is important to remove the ambiguity. In contrast to some other books on ancient "rhetoric," which in effect restrict themselves to theory, the present work looks at rhetoric throughout its extension, encompassing both the theory and the practice of discourse; that is, it looks at treatises, manuals, and abstract discussions, as well as at oratorical compositions, addresses, legal pleadings, panegyrics, and so on. It seems to me that this approach, in fact, is the most attuned to ancient thought and the most fruitful for modern consideration of the subject. The full sense was the ancients' sense. For them rhetoric was a productive science, a body of specific knowledge and rules permitting an effective verbal performance. Decoupling theory and oratorical practice separates two aspects that were in constant dialogue, mutually influencing each other. It risks misprizing both, by changing theory into bookishness detached from reality, and by dissolving professional practice into "literature." It bypasses what is special about the phenomenon of rhetoric: precisely its attempt to consider the activity of discourse as a complex totality, proceeding from intellectual problem to social act. In reality, theory and practice are two sides of an identical art, even if among the representatives of this art some can be more theorists and others more practitioners. A Cicero, at once an author of treatises and speeches, delineated the perimeter of rhetoric in its totality, and this is the perimeter to be explored.

The exploration will be diachronic. Since rhetoric is tied to historical settings, to social, political, and intellectual conditions, and since it evolved with these conditions, it is essential to mark out the major trends and stages: the six chapters of this work retrace, therefore, the history of rhetoric throughout antiquity, from Homer up to the end of the pagan Empire (eighth century B.C. to third century A.D.). The singular in the title, *Rhetoric,* postulates the coherence of the subject across its historical and geographical changes and variations. Since the history of rhetoric is a relatively new discipline, research on a number of points is still ongoing, and the time has not yet come, should it ever, for presenting accepted truths like a manual. Accordingly, I have not hesitated to draw attention to difficulties arising in the sources, to put forward interpretations, and to write, when necessary, a problematic history. Excursuses inserted at different points of the book's development highlight controversies or significant examples. The Conclusion opens up paths to the heritage of Greco-Roman rhetoric in Christianity and in the modern world. Finally, the Thesaurus, devoted to the system of ancient rhetoric, gives the synchronic approach its due, presenting concepts and classifications which existed in different periods and which belong to the long term (many are still in use today).

The present edition of this book contains a certain number of changes to the French text of the original. Minor modifications have been introduced here and there. The Conclusion contains supplementary references on the study of rhetoric in Europe and in the United States. The Bibliography has been reworked to respond to the needs of an English-speaking public and to take account of the most recent books and articles. There are in total around one hundred new titles, for the most part works in English published in the last few years.

A work like this is rooted not only in research, but also in teaching. That is why I dedicate these pages in friendship to the colleagues and students who have participated in my seminars on rhetoric at the Ecole Normale Supérieure in Paris and at the University of Strasbourg. I thank my colleagues and friends Jean D. Moss, Thomas M. Conley, Lawrence D. Green, Craig W. Kallendorf, Thomas A. Schmitz, and Pierre Zoberman who have all shown an interest in the English version of this work, as well as David J. McGonagle, who accepted the book for the Press he directs. My heartiest thanks go to William Higgins who put at the service of this translation his exceptional knowledge of ancient and modern languages and who throughout the translating fostered a fruitful and friendly dialogue.

FIRST EXCURSUS

✿ *Rhetoric of . . .*

Books and articles dealing with antiquity, using a title something like "Rhetoric of . . . ," have multiplied these last years, notably in English, but also in other languages. Here are some examples (the list does not mean to be exhaustive):

D. G. Battisti, *La retorica della misoginia (la satira sesta di Giovenale)*, Venosa, 1996.

M. Cahn, "The Rhetoric of Rhetoric: Six Tropes of Disciplinary Self-Constitution," in *The Recovery of Rhetoric*, London, 1993.

G. B. Conte, "La retorica dell'imitazione come retorica della cultura: qualche ripensamento," *Filologia antica e moderna* 2 (1992).

P. DuBois, "Violence, Apathy, and the Rhetoric of Philosophy," in *Rethinking the History of Rhetoric*, Boulder, 1993.

J. Farrell, "Towards a Rhetoric of (Roman?) Epic," in *Roman Eloquence*, London, 1997.

S. M. Flaherty, *The Rhetoric of Female Self-Destruction: A Study in Homer, Euripides, and Ovid*, Yale Univ. dissertation, 1994.

J. Hesk, "The Rhetoric of Anti-Rhetoric in Athenian Oratory," in *Performance Culture and Athenian Democracy*, Cambridge, 1999.

N. G. Kennell, "Herodes Atticus and the Rhetoric of Tyranny," *Classical Philology* 92 (1997).

M. Mariotti, "Sul contrasto di modelli nella retorica dell'aegritudo: 'consolatio per exempla' e 'fletus immodicus' in AL 692 R. e Petron. 115.6–20," *Materiali e discussioni* 38 (1997).

G. W. Most, "*Disiecti membra poetae:* the Rhetoric of Dismemberment in Neronian Poetry," in *Innovations of Antiquity*, New York, 1992.

E. Oliensis, *Horace and the Rhetoric of Authority*, Cambridge, 1998.

P. Rose, "Cicero and the Rhetoric of Imperialism," *Rhetorica* 13 (1995).

D. Sullivan, "Kairos and the Rhetoric of Belief," *Quarterly Journal of Speech* 78 (1992).

S. C. Todd, "The Rhetoric of Enmity in the Attic Orators," in *Kosmos. Essays in Order, Conflict and Community in Classical Athens,* Cambridge, 1998.

Y. L. Too, *The Rhetoric of Identity in Isocrates,* Cambridge, 1995.

Y. L. Too and N. Livingstone, eds., *Pedagogy and Power: Rhetorics of Classical Learning,* Cambridge, 1998.

R. Webb, "Salome's Sisters: the Rhetoric and Realities of Dance in Late Antiquity and Byzantium," in *Women, Men and Eunuchs,* London and New York, 1997.

G. B. Wittmer, *Isocrates and the Rhetoric of Culture,* Univ. of Pittsburgh dissertation, 1991. ❧

Twenty or thirty years ago one might have written in a number of cases "Theory," "Codes," "Ideology," "Poetics," "Politics." Today one writes "Rhetoric" (sometimes even in an abusive manner): a sign of the times. Rhetoric appears as a critical tool indispensable for the study of forms of expression and frameworks of thought, not only in strictly rhetorical texts, but also beyond that in the realm of poetry, philosophy, religion, history, and so forth. This phenomenon is a barometer of the present-day development of studies in ancient rhetoric.

Two principal reasons explain this development. First, it is part of an overall progress in ancient studies that has intensified research in all areas with contemporary means and requirements and has encouraged the methodical exploration of this aspect, among others, of ancient culture. Previously left a little by the wayside and still incompletely known, the history of rhetoric is a new angle of approach to understanding antiquity better. Second, ancient rhetoric by its very nature chimes with the preoccupations of modern and postmodern thought, with, for example, structuralism, formalism, intertextuality, the language of the arts, the history of *mentalités,* the new literary history, ethics, and politics: hence its current favor (we will come back to this theme in the Conclusion). The favoring of rhetoric, moreover, is not limited to ancient studies; it can be observed in other periods as well. From this point of view, ancient rhetoric has the privileged status of source and model.

RHETORIC IN ANTIQUITY

Chapter One

Rhetoric before "Rhetoric"

Homer

From the time of the Homeric poems, which are the first literary Greek texts, the spoken word and persuasion occupy an important place. I. J. F. de Jong has calculated that in the *Iliad*, speeches in direct discourse, by number of verses, represent 45 percent of the entire length of the poem. The epic, therefore, joins narrative and speech in an almost equal partnership by having the characters whose adventures it relates speak in a direct manner. Even in the midst of battles and dangers, the "winged words," as a formulaic expression calls them, constitute an essential dimension of Homeric poetry.

It is worth emphasizing this dimension, because it is not self-evident: other choices could have been possible. Consider, for example, the celebrated scene in the *Odyssey* where Odysseus introduces himself to Nausikaa. A stranger tossed up by the storm in Phaiakia, Odysseus needs the young girl's help, but he is afraid his repugnant appearance will terrify her. So he deliberates with himself: should he grasp Nausikaa's knees in supplication, or should he stand still, without advancing, and content himself with addressing "winning words" to her? Should he have recourse to gesture or word? Odysseus chooses the spoken word, and "at once he made a speech both winning and crafty" (*Od.* 6.148). A long address by Odysseus follows, at once flattering, urgent, and subtle, which will achieve its aim. Among the multiple points of interest which such a scene entertains (adventures in a strange land, role of the gods, allusions to daily life, social ties, erotic atmosphere), the poet has obviously chosen to put the use of the spoken word to the fore. It shows the attention he accords to speech.

This attention is immediately noticeable in the structural frameworks of epic poetry, the formulas and archetypal scenes. A good number of formulaic verses serve to introduce verbal undertakings: "Then, glowering at him, he said . . ."; "Sagely, he begins to speak and says . . ."; "Then he groaned, his eyes raised to the broad heavens . . ."; "Telemakhos looked at her calmly and said . . ." A goodly number of scenes or sequences built along traditional outlines are devoted to remarks or exchanges of remarks, such as scenes of deliberation, a guest's reception, festivals, prayers, and so on. Thus the spoken word is present in the most basic and primitive elements of epic diction, the inherited elements that the poet plays with and refashions.

In the *Iliad* as in the *Odyssey,* the characters both human and divine begin to speak in all sorts of situations induced by the plot, and their speeches reflect all the imaginable forms of verbal exchange: monologue and dialogue, question and answer, narrative, enumeration and catalogue, order, promise, challenge, insult, rodomontade, prediction, consolation, transaction, and so forth. Often the desire to sway the person addressed is clear and pronounced, as in prayer scenes and scenes of request and supplication. Alongside these exchanges between individuals, speech situations of an institutional nature occur in which the spoken word is used for persuading and for counseling. Such is the case with the frequent assembly scenes, where the participants express themselves publicly in order to have their opinion prevail (cf. "the many-voiced assembly," *Od.* 2.150). Regulated use of the spoken word is also to be found in diplomatic mission scenes (at Achilles's tent, *Il.* 9), in the exhortations before battle, or in the ritual use of lamentation (over Hektor, *Il.* 24). There is a depiction of a courtroom argument on the shield of Achilles (*Il.* 18.497–508). Finally, the Homeric poems allot a large space to the deceitful word, to tricks and doubletalk, whether it be the speech of the Dream to Agamemnon, itself followed by Agamemnon's calamitous ruse before the assembly (*Il.* 2), or the false narratives which Odysseus multiplies, passing himself off as a Cretan, in the second half of the *Odyssey.*

Among the characters who all speak and whose speech depicts them, some distinguish themselves by an oratorical aptitude peculiarly their own, like Nestor, speaker of sound advice in the councils, or like Odysseus. Impudent or inappropriate talk, by contrast, discredits others, like Thersites or Iros. Thus, epic presents, as it were, a gallery of orators.

But it is most remarkable that Homer is not content just to make his characters speak: he describes and judges the very way they go about speaking. Homeric epic not only makes regular use of speech, it also reflects on speech. First of all, Homeric language admits of numerous terms designating the action of saying and speaking, the words, the discourse, and the different ways of speaking. For example, clustered around the idea of "expressed opinion," terms can be found like, among others, *boulē* (counsel), *paraiphasis* (encouragement), *ephetmē* (behest), *mēdea* (plans), *sumphrazesthai* (to consult together), *keleuein* (to exhort, to order). The richness and suppleness of the vocabulary thus permit a precise and nuanced description of the varieties of discourse. Moreover, the fact that the characters' speeches are inserted into a narrative thread induces a critical distancing. Sometimes it is another character who judges the speech that has just been delivered; sometimes the action itself, by the course of events, is responsible for showing if a speech was accurate or not, appropriate or not. There are likewise cases where several characters by turns deliver a speech on the same subject, implicitly prompting a comparison among their divers forms of eloquence, for example, the three parallel speeches of the ambassadors (*Il.* 9) or the two paired addresses of Hektor and Ajax (*Il.* 15).

The poet's express assertions leave no doubt as to his critical awareness with regard to discourse, as some quotations show:

1. "So true is it that the gods do not give gracious gifts to all alike, not form, nor mind, nor eloquence. For one man is inferior in looks, but the god sets a crown of beauty upon his words, and men look upon him with delight, and he speaks on unfalteringly with sweet modesty, and is conspicuous among the gathered people, and as he goes through the city men gaze upon him as a god. Another again is in looks like the immortals, but no crown of grace is set about his words." (*Od.* 8.167–75)

2. [Agamemnon to Nestor] "Once again, old sir, you surpass in speech the sons of the Achaeans. I wish, Father Zeus and Athene and Apollo, that I had

ten such counselors among the Achaeans: then would the city of king Priam immediately bow its head, taken and sacked by our hands." (*Il.* 2.370–74)

3. "But let us even now consider how we may make amends [to Achilles] and persuade him with kindly gifts and gentle words." (*Il.* 9.111–13)

4. "Then among them rose up Nestor, sweet of speech, the clear-voiced orator of the men of Pylos, he from whose tongue speech flowed sweeter than honey." (*Il.* 1.247–49)

5. "But when they began to weave the web of words and of devices in the presence of all, Menelaos to be sure spoke fluently, with few words, but very clearly, since he was not a man of lengthy speech nor rambling, even though in years he was the younger. But whenever Odysseus of many wiles arose, he would stand and look down with eyes fixed on the ground, and his staff he would move neither backwards nor forwards, but would hold it stiff, like a man of no understanding; you would have thought him some sort of churl and nothing but a fool. But when he projected his great voice from his chest, and words like snowflakes on a winter day, then could no man rival Odysseus; then we were not so astonished at Odysseus's appearance." (*Il.* 3.212–24)

6. "He [Odysseus] made the many falsehoods of his tale seem like the truth." (*Od.* 19.203)

7. "And he [Odysseus] spoke and addressed her [Athene] with winged words; yet he did not speak the truth, but checked the word before it was uttered, always revolving in his breast thoughts of great cunning." (*Od.* 13.253–55)

8. "Glib is the tongue of mortals, and words there are on it many and various, and of speech the field is wide on this side and that. Whatever word you speak, such could you also hear." (*Il.* 20.248–50)

9. "Telemakhos, surely the gods themselves are teaching you a lofty style, and to speak with boldness." (*Od.* 1.384–85)

10. [Phoinix to Achilles] "For this reason he [your father] sent me to instruct you in all these things, to be both a speaker of words and a doer of deeds." (*Il.* 9.442–43)

The first quotation shows that oratorical ability is as much a quality of the hero as beauty and intelligence (to which it is, moreover, connected). Counsel and diplomacy are two realms using this skill (numbers 2 and 3). The poet characterizes the heroes from this point of view, underlining the sweetness of Nestor's words (number 4) and ascribing to Antenor a probing comparative critique of the oratorical talents of Menelaos and Odysseus (number 5). Furthermore, the speech of Odysseus, in the *Odyssey,* is often described as lying (numbers 6 and 7), which leads to a more general reflection on language's fundamental shiftiness (number 8). The two following passages show that eloquence is an aptitude that can be taught, whether by the gods (number 9) or by a man, as in the case of Phoinix, Achilles's tutor (number 10). Eloquence for Homer is something to be taught, whether by gods or men, just like medicine (which Kheiron taught to Achilles), or hunting, horsemanship, warfare, or the singer's craft. Better put, it forms part of a general education, which prepares at the same time for speaking and doing. The text of number 10 uses two key words in Greek, the verb *didaskein* (to teach) and the noun *rhētēr* (orator), which will remain in use throughout the history of the Greek world, even in Modern Greek, with this single difference that the form *rhētōr* has won out over the form *rhētēr.*

The ancients themselves remarked on the role of the spoken word in Homer. They cited Nestor and Odysseus in discussions on the proper practice of speech (Aristophanes, *Clouds* 1057; Socrates according to Xenophon, *Memorabilia* 4.6.15). Antisthenes interpreted the Homeric epithet *polutropos* (of many turns), applied to Odysseus, as referring to the flexibility and cleverness of the hero's speech (fragment B XIX 10, in Radermacher, *Artium scriptores;* in fact this epithet refers to Odysseus's numerous voyages or, as was also said in antiquity, to his resourceful and deceitful character).

The theorists developed, moreover, the theme of "Homeric rhetoric" by maintaining that Homer practiced rhetoric and practiced it magisterially, both in the narrative, where he speaks in his own voice, and in the speeches of the characters he portrays. He established the rules, as much by example, thanks to the unsurpassable models he presented, as by theoretical suggestions implicit in his work. This conception of Homer as master of rhetoric was incorporated in the more general idea of Homer as model and lawgiver for all the arts and all wisdom. Many subscribed to this conception, for example, Telephos of Pergamon (second century A.D.), who composed a treatise, now lost, *On Rhetoric According to Homer.* The ancient rhetoricians made an industry of finding in the Homeric poems the ideas, the distinctions and the rules of contemporary rhetoric. For example, quotations 4 and 5 above, when combined, were interpreted as the first attestation of the system of the three stylistic genres *(genera dicendi),* which distinguishes the simple style as represented here by Menelaos, the middle style, by Nestor, and the high style, by Odysseus (Quintilian, *Institutio Oratoria* 12.10.64; Aulus Gellius, *Attic Nights,* 6.14.7). In these terms, Menelaos would prefigure Lysias, Nestor would prefigure Isokrates, and Odysseus, Demosthenes (Anonymous, in Spengel, *Rhetores Graeci,* III, pp. 152–53). Or again, Homer would have limned, in Odysseus, the very definition of oratorical "virtuosity," *deinotēs* (Hermogenes, pp. 370– 71, Rabe ed.).

Whatever the liveliness and precision with which the ancients developed the theme of "Homeric rhetoric," there is surely no question for us moderns of following their path. We must be wary of a retrospective interpretation, overlaying *a posteriori* the art of rhetoric onto texts still unaware of it. But the facts no less remain: the presence of speech, the consciousness of speech. What conclusions are to be drawn?

On the whole, from an anthropological perspective, one can place the Homeric use of speech between "magico-religious speech" and "dialogue-speech" (concepts of M. Detienne), and nearer the latter than the former. Certain passages are related to the notion of an empowered speech, in the full sense of the term, a speech endowed with an intrinsic efficaciousness, the speech of the "masters of truth," who are also masters of deceit. Yet Homer uses speech more often as a means of exchange between individuals or within a group. In this case, it does not possess "immediacy" but a temporal dimension; it is not action in and of itself, but prepares, provokes, or comments on the action of the heroes. This dialogue-speech is fraught with thought, but also with emotion or trickery, making use of arguments and stylistic and structural effects. It does not have, however, codified forms (in the way that the forms of rhetorical discourse will be codified later).

This use of speech has a documentary interest, to the extent that it is possible to deduce evidence about society from the Homeric poems. This must be understood in a broad sense, since, as is known, Homer does not describe a particular society of a definite date. The "world of Homer" is a fictional composite, combining features belonging to several different eras; and there are, moreover, differences separating the *Odyssey* from the *Iliad*. Still, these reservations notwithstanding, one can say that the Homeric poems from the beginning of the first millennium—across the Mycenaean, Dark, and Geometric Ages—exhibit a practiced use of the spoken word and that they accord an importance to discourse, notably to public discourse held in assemblies.

But the Homeric epic is like the chevalresque song cycle in Victor Hugo's description: "It is history eavesdropping on legend" (preface to *La Légende des siècles*). Beyond the issue of historical evidence, there is the problem of epic's heroic scale and values. Looking at the Homeric poems from this angle, we can see that, in the poet's value system, verbal skill is just as much a part of the hero's superhuman dimension as might in combat and skill in surmounting trials. Highly prized, eloquence is an element of prowess, and the epic is its showcase. The pleasure for the listener consists in savoring the noble speeches that the verse of epic language serves up to him, just as he savors the noble exploits. Subtle arguments and striking formulations will be particularly appreciated, or, inversely, simple and direct remarks, and most especially the extreme and paradoxical moment when discourse shows itself to be more useful than action and achieves what force could never have achieved. Such is the meaning of Odysseus's conduct before Nausikaa, as we saw, or Priam's before Achilles when he came to claim the body of Hektor (*Il.* 24), or Thetis's before Zeus (*Il.* 1).

It is necessary to read history in the right direction. Homer did not anticipate the laws of rhetoric, but he established, in accord with the ideas of his own time, the importance of the spoken word. Homer's influence, which will be immense, will bear upon this point as well. It will contribute, along with many other factors, to the prestige of rhetoric in the ancient world.

From the Homeric World to the Classical World

In the long period extending from the Homeric to the Classical world (eighth to fifth centuries), we will keep to a few milestones. Persuasion *(Peithō)* occupies a significant place in the Greek thought of the era, represented in literary texts and on vase paintings not only as a literary and intellectual concept, but also as a personification of a human power and a goddess complete with a mythological genealogy and cult status in sanctuaries (at Athens, Megara, Argos, Sikyon, Thasos, etc.). Sometimes it symbolizes seduction and trickery, sometimes the refusal of violence and the search for good social order. In a parallel way, poetry after Homer carries on its representation of speaking through the discourses of the gods, mortals, and the poet himself. It also continues to reflect on the ambiguous powers of the spoken word, capable at once of truth, justice, and mendacity, as the beginning of Hesiod's *Theogony* and the *Homeric Hymn to Hermes* show. But at this point a new literary vehicle of expression appears: prose. From the sixth century, philosophical and historical works in prose begin to spread, whereas up to then Greek literature had been exclusively in verse. This development of literature without meter was a necessary condition for the later recognition of the dignity and worth of rhetorical discourse.

From an institutional viewpoint, the fundamental characteristic of the period is the advent of the city-state *(polis),* which offers a new context for public speaking. In the Dorian city-states, the oligarchic regime does not exclude deliberation within assemblies, councils, and boards of magistrates. In Athens the gradual development of the democracy multiplies the circumstances for the citizens to express themselves in the form of a speech. One by one the institutions that I will describe later when we discuss the Classical period begin to be established. The notion of *isēgoria,* which means in its first sense "freedom of speech," and as a consequence political equality in its totality, makes clear the link between the use of discourse and political institutions. One hears mention of statesmen who will have been great orators (Themistokles).

Literature goes hand in hand with the oratorical dimension of the Athenian democracy, by promoting or transposing it. Solon's elegies (beginning of the sixth century) are true political speeches in verse, in which the author explains his action and exhorts his fellow citizens. Tragedy puts on the stage speeches and debates, the *Eumenides* of Aiskhylos offering a remarkable example in the trial of Orestes (458

B.C.). Also in Aiskhylos, the king of the Pelasgians is presented as a political orator who wins the decision of the Argive people thanks to "the persuasive, subtle windings of his speech" (*Suppliants* 623, Loeb modified).

These examples show that by the middle of the fifth century B.C., public discourse had acquired civic status, particularly at Athens. Herodotos provides a last landmark and at the same time leads us to the following stage, the sophists. Indeed, he includes speeches and debates in his *Histories,* notably in the last books, where he orchestrates a council scene (7.8 ff.: Xerxes consulting before deciding to invade Greece), and scenes of diplomacy (7.157 ff.; 8.140 ff.). He analyzes and judges an address of Themistokles, which appears excellent to him (8.83). He relates a debate, supposed to have taken place in Persia, among conspirators who, after they had assassinated the usurper in power, deliberated on the choice of the best political regime, using an abundance of antitheses and subtle twists of argument (3.80 ff.). One suspects that the political themes and rhetorical forms that the sophists were developing, especially "antilogy" or the juxtaposition of contradictory speeches, could have influenced this famous text.

Chapter Two

The Sophistic Revolution

The "First Inventors"

Antiquity typically had recourse to the idea of "first inventor" *(prōtos heuretēs)* to describe the birth of different activities, arts, and techniques, in order to rationalize in some way their emergence, by attributing them to one individual's decisive action, whether a mortal's, a god's, or a hero's. Thus the invention of rhetoric was attributed either to Hermes—the god of crossroads and highways, of movement, passage, of communication in all senses of the term—or, as we have seen, to Homer, and finally to three men of the fifth century B.C., Empedokles, Korax, and Tisias.

Empedokles of Agrigentum, a celebrated philosopher and public figure, is spoken of as the inventor of rhetoric according to a tradition going back to Aristotle. Gorgias was said to be his student. But the texts say scarcely anything more.

As for Korax and Tisias, Sicilians as well, the sources are more expansive, but for the most part rather late. These two were looked upon as the first ever to have composed a treatise on rhetoric, whether it was two distinct works or a single work bringing together their teaching (Tisias was the student of Korax). According to Plato and Aristotle, they were particularly interested in the notion of "likelihood" *(eikos)*, which permits proposing arguments from probability at trials in the absence of established fact (Plato, *Phaidros* 267A, 273A ff.; Aristotle, *Rhetoric* 2.1402a18). An important piece of information on the historical setting of their work merits citation:

Thus Aristotle says that in Sicily, after the expulsion of the tyrants, when after a long interval restitution of private property was sought by legal means, Korax and Tisias the Sicilians, with the acuteness and controversial habit of their people, first put together some theoretical precepts.

(Cicero, Brutus 46, Loeb modified)

According to Cicero, who is referring to a lost work of Aristotle, Korax and Tisias would therefore have written their treatise to meet the needs of litigants after the fall of the tyrannies and the establishment of democracy in the different cities of Sicily, toward the middle of the fifth century. One might ask, following this reasoning, why comparable works had not already been composed sooner in other cities that had had experience of democratic institutions (Athens, for example) before those in Sicily. It hardly matters. What does matter is the judicial and democratic character of the new invention. Despite the problems it poses for establishing the text and interpretation, this passage allows us to see an essential link between rhetoric and politics.

Here is another echo:

A young man seized with a desire for rhetoric went to Korax and promised that he would pay him his usual fee, if he won his first case. They agreed, and when the youth was already displaying sufficient skill, Korax demanded his fee. But the other said "No." Both then took each other to court; and at the trial, it is said, Korax used for the first time an argument of this kind, to wit, that whether he won the case or lost it he ought to receive the fee: if he won, because he had won, and if he lost, because that was what they had agreed. For his opponent had agreed to pay him the fee if he won his first case, so that if he did win it, he was thereby bound to discharge the debt. The judges severally cried out "Just so!" when the young man began his speech in turn and used exactly the same argument: "Whether I win," he says, "or whether I lose, I don't have to pay Korax the fee: if I win, because I have won; and if I lose, because that is what we agreed. For I promised to pay the fee if I should win my very first case; but if I should lose, I shall not pay." The judges then, suspending judgment and utterly at a loss owing to the equal force of the rhetorical arguments, expelled both men from the court, crying: "Garbage in, garbage out!"

(Sextus Empiricus, Against the Professors, 2.97–99, Loeb modified. The same
anecdote appears in numerous Introductions to Rhetoric, where it is made clear that
the student is called Tisias: cf. Rabe, Prolegomenon sylloge, pp. 26–27, 52–53, 67, 272;
Walz, Rhetores Graeci, V, pp. 6–7)

In this unverifiable and probably spurious anecdote, Korax is presented as a professor of rhetoric who teaches for pay. He displays his cleverness in court, as in the former text, but this time in the context of private quibbling, not in political cases. Above all, this cleverness, whether of master or student, disdains morality and justice. Such a narrative expresses both wonder and worry about a certain use of rhetoric, even as it expresses satisfaction at seeing wiliness being turned back upon its author. Criticisms of the sophists take up these themes again, for example, in Aristophanes: the art of courtroom pleading which permits legally overturning the legitimate claims of creditors, in a word, the rhetoric which furthers nonpayment of debts, is precisely what Stepsiades seeks to do in the *Clouds*. A similar anecdote circulated concerning Protagoras and his pupil Euathlos. In short, Korax and Tisias appear here as sophists before the fact.

It is difficult to say what historical basis there may be in the material about the "inventors" of rhetoric. The references to Sicily prompt the thought that research could have been carried out particularly on this island, to be spread abroad through an intermediary like Thourioi, a Panhellenic settlement in southern Italy, or via the relations existing between Athens and Sicily. Be that as it may, the invention narratives are above all a way of thinking about our topic, and they highlight some of its essential aspects: its connection to philosophy, politics, and ethics; its intellectual subtlety; the importance of judicial speeches; the production of written treatises. These traits will reappear among the sophists.

The Sophists

A certain number of thinkers from the second half of the fifth century are traditionally grouped under the name "sophists" *(sophistai)*. They came from different parts of the Greek world, traveled, taught, gave lectures, and published works. They were not a school or an organized movement: others, both their admirers and their adversaries, coined them "the Sophists" and bestowed upon them a body of shared opinions to which they themselves would perhaps not have laid claim. Thus, the list of "the Sophists" was not fixed or invariable. The accepted list today includes Protagoras, Gorgias, Prodikos, Hippias, and some others; there is debate on doubtful cases, like Kritias. It is furthermore certain that the sophists were far more numerous than those now known to us. Most of their works are lost, and our information in the majority of cases derives from fragments and late *testimonia*. Finally, it is necessary to remember that the characterization of the sophistic movement as "Presocratic," that is, predating the death of Socrates in 399, is arbitrary and that sophists continued to exist after that. We are not going to linger any more on these historiographical problems; it suffices here to have noted them to remind ourselves of the prudence required in delineating the chief traits of sophistic thought on rhetorical matters.

Among the ideas the sophists advanced, several have a direct bearing on rhetoric. Two famous statements of Protagoras question the very existence of unchanging values and intelligible realities: "About the gods, I am not able to know whether they exist or do not exist" (fragment B4, Diels-Kranz, Freeman trans.); "Of all things the measure is Man" (frag. B1, Diels-Kranz, Freeman trans.). Beyond the religious problem, all standards are undermined here to the benefit of a phenomenalist and relativist conception of the world. The theme of "the critical moment" *(kairos),* often repeated by the sophists, expresses a similar intention and suggests a situational ethics. Such conceptions imply, as a logical consequence, that there is no truth or justice defined once and for all to which discourse has to conform. On the contrary, justice and truth are constructed in the moment, in each and every instance, in and through the discourse that gives them life. Hence the affirmation that "there are two contradictory arguments about everything" and that one can "make the weaker cause the stronger" (Protagoras, frags. A 20–21, B6, Diels-Kranz, Freeman trans.). In this vein Protagoras had written the *Antilogies,* a collection of contradictory arguments applied to the same topic. A small, anonymous work entitled *Double Arguments (Dissoi Logoi)* likewise expresses opposed ways of reasoning on ethical and political subjects. Experts in the reversibility of arguments, the sophists were said to be just as able to expand and collapse them at will: "[They] make small things seem great and great things small by the power of their words, and new things old and old things the reverse" (Plato, *Phaidros* 267A, concerning Tisias and Gorgias; likewise Isokrates, *Panegyric* 8). They were also said to be masters of a speech's duration, undertaking to speak either at length or concisely on the same issue (Plato, *Protagoras* 334E–335A; *Gorgias* 449C–D; *Phaidros* 267B).

Beneath these bold propositions lies a profound reflection on the use of the spoken word in all situations where truth has not been identified previously and from without, where the discussion is situated within the category of values and probabilities, not of axioms and scientific demonstrations. The sophistic movement shows its provocative character in postulating that situations of this latter type do not exist. Their claim is illustrated by, and in part based on, the situation of the courtroom, the archetypal stage for rhetoric, where speeches oppose one another and justice and truth are not preexisting, but only pronounced afterward, at the end of the debates that have evoked them. Political deliberation also exemplifies the same essential feature: persuasion goes hand in hand with antilogy, the juxtaposing of conflicting arguments. Rhetoric so conceived develops in the arenas of human activity that require discussion, negotiation, and exchange, at the other extreme from revealed truths and univocal thought. Behind its apparent cynicism and manipulation, the rhetoric of the sophists probably means to be a force for progress and liberty—that is one of the possible readings.

In combination with this fundamental conception, the sophists carried out research on the different aspects of discourse and language. They were interested in eristic, the art of refutation and verbal conflict. They discussed concepts, for example nature and law, or the definition of causality and responsibility, and they laid down the foundations of grammar. Protagoras was the first, it seems, to have distinguished the types of nouns and to have reflected on the correct use of language, while Prodikos made his specialty distinguishing synonyms, and Hippias conducted research about the letters of the alphabet, syllables, and rhythms.

Far from limiting themselves to theoretical considerations, the sophists were all teachers. In an era when education was focused principally on music, poetry, and physical exercise, they introduced a new type of instruction with an intellectual character, dispensed by traveling masters who were much in demand and often quite expensive, and who taught the rich young men of the city-states. Rhetoric played an essential role in this instruction, because it was simultaneously both subject and method. It was a subject to the extent that the sophist claims "to make one a clever speaker" (Plato, *Protagoras* 312D; *Gorgias* 449E)— an important objective which is closely bound up and goes hand in hand with the other aims of the sophistic endeavor: preparation for playing a role in private and public affairs, development of intelligence, education of the citizen, teaching of politics, indeed, of a certain form of virtue. To reach these objectives, the teaching itself takes the path of rhetoric. The sophists deliver lectures *(epideixeis)* that form the basis of their lessons; these lectures are of varying lengths, vary in price, and can treat of any theme. Sometimes—the height of virtuosity—they are improvised on a theme proposed by the audience. Protagoras also put in writing commonplaces, and Gorgias ways to develop arguments pro and con (Cicero, *Brutus* 46–47). Thus there were models that the students tried to imitate and replicate, as in the scene sketched by Plato at the beginning of the *Phaidros*.

Gorgias

Gorgias is the only sophist whose work we still possess. According to the sources, he was also the one who most devoted himself to rhetoric. A Sicilian, he was born in Leontinoi, to the north of Syracuse, in the 480s and he lived to be more than a hundred. In 427 he came to Athens, sent by his country as an ambassador, and his eloquence impressed the Athenians enormously. He taught and delivered orations in various Greek cities and in Thessaly. We have four of his works:

— The treatise *On the Nonexistent or On Nature* is a work of paradoxes which considers the concept of Being according to a demonstration with three points: (1) Nothing is or exists; (2) If something does exist, this something cannot be apprehended by man; (3) If this something can be apprehended, it cannot be communicated. Philosophy and rhetoric are indissolubly linked in the author's approach, as he undertakes at the same time a critique of ontology and a demonstration of virtuosic argumentation. The final thesis, that Being, even if knowable, could not be communicated to another, would seem to deny the very idea of communication and therefore undermine all rhetoric. In fact, it does not destroy language, but makes language relative by admitting that in the absence of a speech charged with truth, there exist discourses, multiple and variable.

— The *Praise of Helen* aims to justify the heroine against those who reproach her because her conduct made her responsible for the Trojan War and the great evils that ensued for the Greeks. After a brief encomium on the birth and beauty of Helen, Gorgias undertakes to excuse her by arguing that if she followed Paris, she could only have done so for one of these four reasons: (1) she obeyed the gods' commands; (2) she was carried off by force; (3) she was persuaded by speech; (4) she succumbed to love. In all instances she was not responsible, the author concludes, indicating at the end that his speech is a *jeu d'esprit* *(paignion)*. We take that to mean a tour de force in the handling of argument and paradox, but one that does not exclude serious intentions, particularly in the treatment of the third point, which occasions an analysis of the powers of *logos*.

— The *Defense of Palamedes* is an apology put in the mouth of the hero Palamedes, whom Odysseus had accused of conspiring with the enemy. In a fictional case, borrowed, like the preceding, from the legends of the Trojan War, Gorgias gives an example of courtroom pleading, focused on the examination of proofs and probabilities.

— Of the *Funeral Oration,* which belongs to the genre of public *epitaphios,* only one page is preserved. It praises the moral qualities of the deceased.

One sees in these four texts a coherent outline of a philosophical vision of the world and a theory of persuasion. The ontological critique questions reality and values, and it spotlights concepts of opinion, emotion, illusion, and the decisive moment. In these circumstances, the power of language assumes critical importance. As the *Praise of Helen* (8–14) describes it, this power consists in persuading. Language exerts a violent force on the soul, comparable to the action of drugs on the body and to the arts of sorcery and magic; it arouses or suppresses opinions and emotions; and it takes many forms, including poetry, incantations, speeches written "artfully" (the word *tekhnē* is used at 13) for delivery in debates, and philosophers' controversies. This very important passage of the *Helen* reveals a profound reflection on the nature and function of language in its relations with persuasion. Armed with these general principles, Gorgias concentrated on the technique of individual speeches, as the *Palamedes* shows for the judicial genre. His research was closely bound up with his pedagogic activity, which explains the noticeably didactic quality of his preserved works, their clear outline, clearly marked transitions, and explicit statements of theme, all betraying their intended use as models. Finally, in addition to being a theorist and professor, Gorgias was also an orator, as is evident from the funeral oration (even if it is uncertain whether it was ever actually spoken). The *testimonia* also confirm that he was an important politician in his own city, that he spoke as an ambassador at Athens, and that he delivered panegyrics at Olympia and Delphi, or, another example, a speech on the Eleans.

Gorgias was also celebrated for his style. Pursuing the idea that the *logos* is supposed to charm and bewitch, Gorgias wrote an artistic and highly artificial prose which aimed to rival poetry by compensating for the absence of meter and musical accompaniment with stylistic effects. The preserved texts are striking for their word jingles and their repetition and opposition of terms, as at the end of the fragment of the *Funeral Oration* (translation can only give a pale idea of the original):

[They were] men showing reverence toward the gods by their justice, piety toward their parents by their care, justice toward their fellow-citizens by their fair dealing, respect toward their friends by keeping faith with them. Therefore, although they are dead, the longing for them has not died with them, but immortal though in mortal bodies, it lives on for those who live no more.

(Frag. B6, Diels-Kranz, Freeman trans.)

The ancients stressed the "poetic" character of Gorgias's style (Aristotle, *Rhetoric* 3.1404a26). They noted his taste for metaphors, which led him to write "Xerxes, the Persian Zeus" or "vultures, living tombs" (Pseudo-Longinus, *On the Sublime* 3.2, Freeman trans.). They called "Gorgianic figures" an ensemble of procedures, comprising sentence components with parallel structure *(isokōla),* antitheses whether in content or expression *(antitheseis),* and similarly sounding words producing effects of assonance and alliteration *(paronomasiai)* and rhyme *(homoioteleuta)* (Diodoros the Sicilian 12.53.4; Dionysios of Halikarnassos, *Demosthenes* 4.4; 25.4). If Gorgias was not the first to use each of these procedures, or the coiner of the technical terms that subsequently denoted them, it really does seem that he intentionally multiplied them and so is entitled to his place in the history of rhetoric as the first creator of artistic prose and as the inventor of a style, the "Gorgianic," characterized by bold and showy effects.

The shock the sophists provoked—success and scandal—was profound in Athenian society. It is reflected in the literature of the era, notably in the plays of Euripides and Aristophanes. The former from the 430s, and the latter from the 420s, put on the stage the varied forms taken by the art of the spoken word, and they marvel at the power of speech and the recent innovations introduced in this realm. But using the words *sophos, sophisma, sophistēs,* they denounce speeches that are too clever and professors who split hairs. Some later texts, referring to the same period (the last third of the fifth century) bear similar witness: notably certain dialogues of Plato, in which Socrates converses on rhetoric with leading sophists, or a passage in Thucydides where Kleon in 427 says that the Athenians, smitten with word jousting and newfangled arguments, are bringing sophistic ways into deliberative eloquence and transforming the latter into political theater. They are a people "in thrall to the pleasures of the ear," who, when convened in the Assembly, are more "like men who sit as spectators at exhibitions of sophists than men who take counsel for the welfare of the state" (3.38.7). The pedagogical allure which the professors of eloquence exerted is conveyed by the *topos* of the visit to the sophist, wherein a prospective student is anxious to win the master's acceptance and eager to hand himself over entirely, provided the master teaches him how to speak (Aristophanes, *Clouds* 427 ff.; Plato, *Protagoras* 312).

The agreement of these texts, so different in their aims, attests to the extensiveness of the sophists' innovations. From then on, the sophistic movement and rhetoric will be forever joined in ancient thought, even if the movement is not simply equated with rhetoric and even if a number of orators refuse to be called sophists. Plato insists on this, not without malice: despite all the differences one can establish between the two categories, "sophists and orators are jumbled up as having the same field and dealing with the same subjects" (*Gorgias* 465C, 520A). And, in fact, the sophists did establish an autonomous discipline and theory of speech. The object "speaking" was isolated and became in itself a subject of reflection and art. This art encompassed theories on persuasion and the philosophical foundations of discourse, technical research (in the area of argumentation and style), and teaching. Some speeches began to be published and not only delivered orally. Athens, where the sophists stayed a relatively long time, was the crucible for these innovations.

A perfect example of this period is Antiphon (ca. 480–411 B.C.). Thucydides praised him as "a man who had proved himself most able (among the Athenians of his time) both to formulate a plan and to set forth his conclusions in a speech," but who "was under suspicion with the people on account of his reputation for rhetorical cleverness" (Thuc. 8.68.1, Loeb modified). The body of work attributed to him, dating from the last twenty or thirty years of his life, includes, on the one hand, three courtroom speeches pertaining to homicide cases, and on the other, school exercises entitled *Tetralogies*. These envision four different sets of arguments for the same case (two for the prosecution, two for the defense), to which a partially preserved treatise *On Truth* is attached, along with fragments of treatises and speeches. There is a question whether all these works were from the same man or if it is necessary to distinguish Antiphon the Orator from Antiphon the Sophist. Current scholarship tends to accept the unity of a work that combines oratorical practice, training in eloquence, and philosophical reflection.

Theorizing about courtroom eloquence was in full swing in late-fifth-century Athens. Plato in the *Phaidros* (266D–267D) drew up a long list of those masters of rhetoric (Theodore of Byzantium, Evenos of Paros, Tisias, Gorgias, Prodikos, Hippias, Polos, Lykimnios, Protagoras, Thrasymakhos of Khalkedon) who were composing treatises and promulgating rules on the design and parts of the courtroom speech, on the methods of argument, on style, and on the emotions.

The *History* of Thucydides is another prime source. Thucydides, as a matter of fact, considers that his subject matter is divided into two categories, deeds done and speeches spoken. The latter, accordingly, amount to half of his material (1.22). By virtue of this, his work provides a precious document on political eloquence (assemblies, diplomatic missions, debates and speeches of different sorts) as it was practiced in the Greek world, particularly at Athens, during the time of the Peloponnesian War. Thanks to Thucydides, we have an echo of the speeches Perikles delivered who was, according to his contemporaries, a very great orator, nicknamed "the Olympian." But Thucydides, as is known, rewrote the speeches of his historical characters, and that changes everything.

The historian is an orator. He displays through numerous speeches an unmistakable rhetorical ability nourished by contemporary advances in the discipline that he advances anew. These speeches are by no means digressions; they are an integral part of the historical enterprise, and it is that which makes for the profundity of Thucydidean rhetoric. Just as the historian conceptualizes and structures actions, transforming the clay of occurrences into an object of intelligible and rational narrative, so too he reshapes the speeches to put them at the service of building historical truth. For Thucydides the speeches permit the presentation of a given situation or a person's attitude as a synthesis; grouped to contrast, they allow him to present two opposing points of view and to serve a sense of impartiality. Finally, and above all, they are the means to clarifying action, to eliciting from it sense and setting, thus rendering deeds comprehensible. If the alternation between narrative and speech was traditional ever since the epic, Thucydides is the first to make the speech into an instrument of historical analysis. In that he also exemplifies the sophistic movement. The speech for him is not only a social reality and a literary form to be practiced but, much more, a way of truth.

The development of the *epideixis* or public lecture provides a final indication of the importance rhetoric assumed in this period. Different sorts of specialists, whether scholars or technical experts, used the *epideixis* to display their art to audiences narrow and wide. The texts were written down and published. The Hippocratic Collection preserves some examples of such lectures, namely the treatises *Concerning the Winds* and *On Art,* dating from the last quarter of the fifth century. They are really speeches of persuasion—the second is a polemic—in an ornate style. The display could just as well take the form of an antilogy, setting forth opposing opinions, with a debate in several rounds and stages of cross-examination.

SECOND EXCURSUS

❧ *The Birth of the Word* Rhētorikē

The word *rhētorikē,* used as a noun (and not as an adjective with the noun *tekhnē*), appears for the first time in Greek in two works from the beginning of the fourth century B.C.:

Alkidamas, *On the Authors of Written Speeches or On the Sophists* 2: "[I] suppose that those who spend their lives on this particular skill [speechwriting] have serious shortcomings in both rhetorical skill [*rhētorikēs*] and in philosophy, and [I] consider that they would much more justly be described as script-writers than as sophists." In the preceding paragraph, Alkidamas has already criticized "some of those who are called sophists . . . having acquired a very small part of an orator's ability *(tēs rhētorikēs dunameōs),* [and who] lay claim to the art as a whole" (Muir trans., modified).

Plato, *Gorgias* 448D–449A: "Socrates: For I see plainly from what he has said, that Polos has had more practice in what is called rhetoric [*tēn kaloumenēn rhētorikēn*] than in discussion . . . or rather, Gorgias, do you tell us yourself in what art it is you are skilled, and hence, what we ought to call you. Gorgias: Rhetoric [*tēs rhētorikēs*], Socrates." (The word *rhētorikē* appears numerous times in the rest of the dialogue.)

Editors date the text of Alkidamas around 390 (G. Avezzù, R. Mariss) and the *Gorgias* to 387–385 (E. R. Dodds), but these are only approximations. As for the dramatic date of the *Gorgias* (the time of the dialogue's setting), Plato does not fix it precisely, since the text freely brings together observations that go back to different moments from the last quarter of the fifth century.

Before these two texts, the words *logos* and *legein* are found in Greek ("word," "discourse," "to speak," "to discourse"), as well as the expression *logōn tekhnai* ("skills of speeches," *Double Arguments* 8: perhaps around 400 B.C.). The word *rhētōr* (we have seen that Homer used the word *rhētēr*) is used in the fifth century in the sense of "orator," and *rhētoreia* ("eloquence") is found around 390 in Isokrates's *Against the Sophists* (21). These terms will remain in use throughout the history of the Greek language, while *rhētorikē* continues its career in Plato, Aristotle and beyond.

These facts have sparked a discussion among scholars on two points:

1. *The first appearance of the word.* E. Schiappa has maintained that Plato deliberately invented the word *rhētorikē* in the *Gorgias* ("Did Plato Coin *Rhētorikē?" American Journal of Philology* III [1990]:457–70; cf. also the book by the same author, *The Beginnings of Rhetorical Theory in Classical Greece* [New Haven, 1999]).

2. *The first appearance of rhetoric itself.* E. Schiappa's thesis agrees with the work of T. Cole (*The Origins of Rhetoric in Ancient Greece* [Baltimore, 1991]), according to which rhetoric, properly so called, was invented by Plato and Aristotle, everything earlier being "pre-rhetoric" or "proto-rhetoric."

As for the first point, it is necessary to note that the idea of a Platonic creation only holds if one down dates the text of Alkidamas to place it after the *Gorgias,* and that is conjectural. The turn of phrase Plato uses ("what is called rhetoric," *tēn kaloumenēn rhētorikēn*) indicates, if one interprets it in the most natural way, that the word is considered current in the period of the dialogue (whatever one thinks this to be). This is precisely what the text of Alkidamas confirms, where the word does not appear to be a neologism. The large number of texts that have disappeared—notably the texts of the sophists—imposes, moreover, the most extreme caution. We will confine ourselves, therefore, to concluding that the word *rhētorikē* is attested in the preserved sources from about 390, and that it appears in a way that leads one to think that it was already in existence. Schiappa is right, nevertheless, to observe that its total absence from the preserved texts of the fifth century cannot be fortuitous. Without going so far as to say that the word was nonexistent, one can admit that it probably was rare. *Rhētorikē* was a technical word, specialized, a term of the trade, carrying an intellectual connotation because of its suffix—*ikos*. It is in this sense that Plato ironically puts it in the mouth of Gorgias: still a specialized usage, still (as we might say today) a "-tech" word, which can contain a whiff of charlatanism. Alkidamas, who belonged to the profession, is not bothered by the term. But others will be, for example Isokrates, who never uses *rhētorikē*, because he does not want to be reduced to the status of a mere technician and because he has higher aspirations to culture and philosophy. Thus this discussion permits defining better the exact nuances of the word, which was and forever remained a marked, technical term, liable for that reason to seduce or frighten.

As for the second point, it is essentially a definition problem: the question is to know if one should limit the use of the word "rhetoric" to the teachings of Plato and Aristotle on the matter (however one conceives of those teachings), or if one is justified in applying this term to the thought of the fifth century. Looking closely at the sources, it seems that the fifth century indeed began to explore rhetoric in the principal meanings of this term, whether in the most current senses (practice and theory of eloquence, thoughts on persuasion) or in the narrow sense of "a speaker's or writer's self-conscious manipulation of his medium with a view to ensuring his message as favorable a reception as possible on the part of the particular audience being addressed" (T. Cole, op. cit., p. ix; cf. also D. A. Russell in the *Journal of Hellenic Studies* 112 [1992]:185–86, and D. M. Schenkeveld in *Mnemosyne* 45 [1992]:387–92). The interest of the debate Cole opened lies in its stressing that the fifth century was only one stage and that the fourth century contributed much more to the history of rhetoric.

One can refer, for comparison, to the problem of the origins of philosophy and of the existence of philosophy before the word *philosophia,* as P. Hadot has set it forth in Part One of *What Is Ancient Philosophy?,* trans. M. Chase (Cambridge, MA, 2002). ❧

Chapter Three

The Athenian Moment

For the fourth century B.C., between those convenient reference points, the end of the Peloponnesian War (404) and the death of Alexander the Great (323), it is essential to focus on Athens. The sources are incomparably richer for this city than for the rest of the Greek world, and this is not a chance occurrence but results from the existence of practices, codifications, and constant discussions of what is now called rhetoric.

The Practice of Oratory

Very many situations, but first and foremost judicial and political settings, provided opportunities for the practice of oratory at Athens. In the courts, the parties had to plead their cases by themselves, without being able to have an attorney represent them. There was no public prosecutor's office, so that charges necessarily had to be brought by private individuals: in a private suit *(dikē),* by the injured party; in a public suit *(graphē),* by any citizen. Such a system supposed an active participation of the citizenry, as defenders and as prosecutors, in judicial life. Recourse to different sorts of help facilitated this involvement. When the litigant feared he might not be up to the task, he could seek the assistance of a relative or friend, who was then called a *"synēgoros,"* with whom he shared his allotted time for speaking. Or he could pay a professional speechwriter, called a "logographer," for a speech he himself would then learn by heart and recite before the jury. Prosecutions, in addition, were sometimes undertaken by "sycophants," professional accusers who systematically used their right of bringing a charge to attack the wealthy in order to pocket a reward (part of the fine) if they secured a conviction, or who practiced blackmail by threatening a prosecution if a target did not buy them off. Some measures were taken to try to check the scourge of sycophancy.

The courts were in session all year long, about two hundred days annually. Leaving aside the arbitration procedures used in private litigations and the judicial powers conferred on certain magistrates, verdicts were rendered by juries, chosen by lot at the beginning of the year from citizens (that is, free males of Athenian parentage) aged thirty and over, and assigned (again by lot) the very morning of each case. The juries comprised 201 or 401 members for private actions, 501 and sometimes more for public actions (there is a jury of 2,500 in Deinarkhos 1.52). The latter cases lasted an entire day (which left around three hours for each side to speak, prosecution and defense), and perhaps several days in certain exceptional instances, whereas private actions were shorter. Charged with multiple tasks, which extended from private disputes to criminal matters to administrative and political oversight, the courts of the people (and, in addition, the Areopagos court for certain special cases) constituted a very important arm of the State.

The principal institutions of the government were the Assembly *(ekklēsia),* which exercised executive power, voting decrees and choosing magistrates, and the Council *(boulē),* which prepared the Assembly's agenda. The Council, composed of 500 citizens over thirty years of age, held its sessions every working day in the Council Hall *(bouleutērion)* overlooking the agora; its deliberations were private. The Assembly, comprised of all adult citizens (18 was the age of majority), held sessions thirty or forty times a year on the hill called the Pnyx, in a site which was rearranged around 400 B.C. and which probably was provided with wooden benches, as well as a podium *(bēma)* for the speakers. Six thousand constituted a quorum, roughly one-fifth of the total number of Athenian citizens. The length of the sessions could not go past nightfall. On each item of the day's agenda, the herald proclaimed the ritual question: "Who wishes to speak?" (*Tis agoreuein bouletai:* Demosthenes, *On the Crown* 170); the debate consisted of a succession of speeches followed by a vote.

These, then, are the institutions themselves that encouraged rhetorical activity at Athens. Taking account of the frequency with which the assemblies and courts met, it was an almost daily activity and an activity that unfolded before a large public, given the extremely large numbers of listeners in each instance (several hundred to several thousand people). "Speaking to the people" in fourth-century Athens constituted a communications situation difficult to imagine today. It entailed making oneself heard by veritable crowds in uncomfortable physical conditions and acoustics, where the stakes were immediate and real. For the listeners, sitting in session and giving a hearing were serious activities, for which they received a stipend *(misthos),* and which were done under oath in the courts, and invested with religious ritual. They were clearly essential to the functioning of the city. For the speakers, the power to persuade was a necessity. In the courts, in fact, professional magistrates did not oversee the arguments, the concept of legal precedent did not obtain, and juries did not have the possibility of deliberating with each other before voting (Aristotle, *Politics* 2.1268b9–11). The impression produced by the pleaders, therefore, along with the preconceived opinions of the listeners, determined the verdict. Similarly, in the Assembly, where there were no political parties in the modern sense of the term and no party whip, the unfolding of events in the session and above all, the speeches delivered were what determined the votes.

In the Kerameikos, the Athenian cemetery, another oratorical ritual took place, the "funeral oration" *(epitaphios logos),* delivered as part of the national obsequies honoring Athenian soldiers who had died for their country. This oration was an official act, the orator being chosen by the people on the recommendation of the Council. Its content, dictated by custom, contained a eulogy of the dead and their ancestors as well as words of exhortation and consolation addressed to the living. In the ancestors, all Athens was celebrated: its history, its democratic government, its military exploits, its benefactions to other Greeks. By paying homage to the combatants, the city celebrated itself, created its own legend, and affirmed its own values. An institutional and civic oration, the funeral speech was a genre endowed with a powerful ideological message.

Athenians also delivered speeches in an official capacity outside of Athens, for example, the addresses of ambassadors before other cities or foreign rulers. Used for negotiating treaties, presenting demands, offering thanks or honors, these were a frequent type of speech, because the conduct of foreign policy in Greece depended on the sending of envoys. Speeches delivered outside of Athens also include those on the field of battle, in which generals exhort their troops before combat. Historians who report such speeches certainly lengthen and embellish them, but there is no reason to doubt that these orations, which were part of the general's duties, actually took place. They could, moreover, be spoken briefly or at a leisurely length some time before the actual fighting.

Men in the public eye wrote political discourses addressed to their fellow countrymen or to foreign governments, which were not meant to be delivered in official debates, but which were sent to their intended audience in epistolary form. They circulated throughout the Greek world through oral recitations and written copies. These works of pamphleteers, which only concerned their author and his friends, deliberately imitated the forms of public, institutional speeches. They multiplied in the second half of the fourth century, when everybody wanted to address the Macedonian kings.

Panegyrics, delivered, for example, at the Olympic or Delphic festivals, were directed toward a Panhellenic audience assembled for the occasion. They treated themes befitting the context: international relations and especially the relations among Greeks, as well as the values of political life in general.

We come finally to the speeches of all sorts delivered in private homes or in any type of non-public setting, which belonged to the genre of the lecture and dealt with various topics. Examples include courtroom pleadings put in the mouth of mythological or historical characters, essays, manifestoes, pamphlets, mock ("paradoxical") encomia (of salt, of pots, of pebbles, of death, of poverty, etc.), and *jeux d'esprit (paignia)* of every kind.

From this constant and varied practice, we have clearly only the written traces. The judicial speeches, whose content was prepared in advance, lent themselves more to being written down, which was anyway necessary when a logographer was involved. By contrast, the orations addressed to the Assembly, which placed a premium on improvisation as a function of the motions presented in session and the twists and turns of the debates, were written down later and then only rarely. The published texts did not necessarily reproduce verbatim the words actually spoken but were revised for artistic ends and to take account after the fact of the opposing side's arguments. Between "orality" and "literacy" there was a constant give and take in the Athenian rhetoric of the fourth century.

The two most important bodies of work, in quantity and quality, are those of Isokrates and Demosthenes. They illustrate the broad spectrum of Athenian rhetoric.

Isokrates

Isokrates (436–338), born in comfortable circumstances, was, it is said, a student of the sophists Prodikos and Gorgias. He devoted his life to rhetoric and was unique in that he did not deliver his own orations. Without either the good voice or the confidence necessary for speaking before a crowd, he did not appear before the public, and he abstained from all physical participation in political debate, contenting himself with reading his works in private groups and publishing written versions. We possess twenty-one speeches (one of which, *To Demonikos,* is probably spurious), extending from 403 to 339, as well as some letters.

The Peloponnesian War having ruined his family, he began by plying the trade of logographer for about a dozen years. Six court speeches or parts thereof attest to this activity (the celebrated *On the Team of Horses* for the son of Alkibiades is an example), and they deal with credit cases, inheritances, and assault and battery cases. Around 390, he forsook the courts and opened a school of rhetoric, which he was to keep going until his death. To mark the launching and program of this school, he wrote the orations *Against the Sophists,* the *Praise of Helen,* and *Busiris*. Isokrates here defines his own methodology, criticizes his rivals, masters of philosophy and masters of rhetoric combined, and shows he can conquer the sophists on their own turf—paradox. In 380 he published the *Panegyric*, a work he had mulled over for a long time. Ostensibly meant as a panegyric for the Olympic festival, it owes a great deal to the tradition of the *epitaphios logos*. In it he expresses his cardinal themes: in politics, the necessary uniting of the Greeks and the no less necessary war against Persia; in argumentation, the combination of praise and counsel; in style, the search for an elegant and artistic prose which makes use of "Gorgianic" figures but without reproducing the excesses of Gorgias himself. With the *Panegyric*, Isokrates found his calling: "Hellenic" and "political" orations, taking up major topics of general interest, of use to Athens and to all the Greeks. From then on he will no longer refrain from intervening but will actively participate in political life through intellectual debate.

In the years 370–360, he supports the kings of Salamis on Cyprus, a Greek dynasty but vassal to the Persian king *(To Nikokles, Nikokles, Evagoras)*, and opines on the affairs of Boiotia and the Peloponnesos *(Plataikos, Arkhidamos)*. The works of this period contain important research and rhetorical innovations, particularly an imaginary speech with a characterization of the orator (when Isokrates has the Spartan Arkhidamos speak) and the first praise of a contemporary in prose (the encomium of Evagoras), as well as prefaces dealing with theoretical problems in oratorical discourse *(Nikokles, Evagoras)*. In the 350s, Isokrates advises the Athenians on foreign and internal policy *(On the Peace, Areopagitikos)*. He also publishes the *Antidosis*, a huge apology in which he defends his life and works and sets forth his ideas about intellectual culture. In fact, the accusation to which the oration is ostensibly responding never occurred. This fictitious pleading is the rhetorical means Isokrates conceived to answer the criticisms leveled against him throughout his career and to undertake an autobiographical approach that was still novel in Greece. In the 340s, Isokrates directs his attention to Philip of Macedon, in whom he sees the sovereign capable of uniting the Greeks and fighting the barbarians *(Philip)*. Finally, in 339, almost a hundred years old, he completes his last oration, the *Pana-*

thenaikos. This is a complex and subtle work, where the author presents his cherished political and rhetorical ideas, using dissonances, deliberate ambiguities, calculated digressions, and the introduction of an anonymous opponent who gives to this oratorical testament an unexpected polyphonic character.

Demosthenes

The Demosthenic corpus, not counting the *Letters* and the *Prooemia,* contains sixty items, around two-thirds of which are assuredly authentic, with the rest either apocryphal or doubtful (speeches by other contemporary orators were inserted among those of Demosthenes). Putting aside the *Letters* and a curious and jesting work on love *(Erotic Essay)* whose authenticity is debated, as well as the collection of *Prooemia* written for use in assembly speeches, there are four categories of orations properly so called: the *Addresses,* delivered before the Assembly; the *Public Orations,* relating to legal cases in the people's name; the *Private Orations,* relating to private cases; and the *Funeral Oration.* Thus the work of Demosthenes fits easily within the institutional categories of Athenian public discourse and did not search for formal innovation. Its importance lies elsewhere, in its exceptional historical interest and in its author's oratorical talent, which can be at once pithy and supple, reasoned and passionate.

Demosthenes (384–322) lost his father when he was seven, and the family fortune was placed in charge of trustees who squandered it. When he reached legal majority, Demosthenes undertook to reclaim his money. He enrolled in the school of the great orator Isaios, who specialized notably in inheritance cases, and he sued his trustees, with, it seems, at least partial success *(Against Aphobos, Against Onetor).* He then embarked upon a speechwriter's career, which he continued to practice (in both private and public legal cases) even after becoming famous and after it had brought him riches and connections. He was simultaneously preparing himself, however, for a political career by reading Thucydides and by working to improve his oratorical delivery, that is, his manner of declaiming his speeches. Plutarch relates that he took lessons from an actor, fitted out an underground room where he practiced declamation, spoke with pebbles in his mouth to correct faults of pronunciation, and recited prose and poetry while running in order to strengthen his voice and breath control (*Life of Demosthenes* 7 and 11). It was to these stubborn efforts, undoubtedly, as much as to his temperament that he owed the fervent delivery which won the admiration of his contemporaries and which we must try, as much as we can, to recreate mentally so that the orations we possess do not remain dead on the page.

When he was thirty, Demosthenes delivered the first preserved of his addresses to the Assembly *(On the Symmories)*. He took some time to find his way, until the moment when he clearly recognized in Philip of Macedon the new protagonist of Greek politics and marked him out to his fellow citizens as Athens's principal menace. That was in the *First Philippic* (351), which reproaches the Athenians for their inaction and proposes a military and financial plan for warding off the danger. In 349–348, the three *Olynthiacs* develop the same line of argument and call energetically for defending the city of Olynthos, then under attack by Philip. When he was not heeded, Demosthenes supported the peace concluded between Athens and Philip in 346; in the following years this Peace of Philokrates occasioned the embassy trial, one of the most famous cases in Athenian history and also very instructive about the role of rhetoric in the political confrontations of the time. After 346, Demosthenes wanted to disassociate himself from the Peace which he and Aiskhines, with other colleagues, had just concluded. He enlisted a friend, Timarkhos, to accuse Aiskhines of malfeasance for his conduct on one of the embassy's missions that had negotiated the Peace. Aiskhines countered by accusing Timarkhos of having been a prostitute in his youth, cause for losing his citizen status; and Aiskhines won. Demosthenes let some time pass; then, in 343, he reopened the case against Aiskhines in his own name. Aiskhines was acquitted, but only by a thirty-vote majority. We possess the two orations of Aiskhines *(Against Timarkhos, On the Embassy)* as well as that of Demosthenes *(On the Embassy)*, in versions certainly revised for publication. These monuments of oratorical art show how speeches delivered in a certain context, born of motives of the moment and aiming at immediate effectiveness, are not only documents, historical evidence. They also can lay claim at the same time to the status of rhetorical models and works of literature through the quality of their language, style, argumentation, historical and political conceptions, their human truthfulness.

In the period 346–338, Demosthenes was one of those influencing Athenian policy by his oratorical activity, up until the battle of Khaironeia (338), when Philip finally defeated the Greeks. Demosthenes was chosen at that time to deliver the *epitaphios:* the speech so titled in the corpus has been suspected because it is so ordinary, but it is probably necessary to accept it as authentic and to recognize in it the weight of convention that this oratorical form entails. The last act of the rivalry between Aiskhines and Demosthenes then played out. When Ktesiphon, Demosthenes's friend, proposed that a crown be awarded to Demosthenes for his public service, Aiskhines immediately brought a charge against Ktesiphon for making a false and illegal motion. The case, begun in 336, was only settled in 330, when Aiskhines thought the situation favored him. He spoke against Ktesiphon; Ktesiphon replied with a brief defense, followed by a long oration of Demosthenes who intervened as a *synēgoros,* or friend of the defense. Ktesiphon was acquitted, while Aiskhines, having obtained less than a fifth of the votes, was fined and barred from intervening in the future with accusations of the same sort. This penalty, which deprived him of an essential tool of political action, drove him into self-imposed exile. People probably continued to comment for a long time in Athens on this memorable trial over the crown, the "battle of the orators" (Theophrastos, *Characters* 7.6). The speech of Aiskhines, *Against Ktesiphon,* and the speech of Demosthenes, *On the Crown,* as preserved, offer the rare opportunity— as does the case on the embassy—to read the two versions set side by side, the one for the prosecution, the other for the defense. The oration *On the Crown* offers additionally the interest of Demosthenes providing a retrospective synthesis of his own political action.

Alongside the political orations, the private court pleadings of Demosthenes contribute a great deal to the understanding of Athenian social customs and are rich sources for information on Attic law. They reveal a lawyer of great ability.

We do not possess any speeches of Demosthenes later than 330, although we know that he delivered some, notably to defend himself when he was indicted (and condemned) for corruption in the trial over the Harpalos affair (323). His death, finally, still belongs to the history of rhetoric, because it presents the emblematic figure of the orator pursued by soldiers and falling heroically, in conditions full of symbolism, for his ideas. Greece had revolted against Macedonia after the death of Alexander the Great, and the suppression was severe. Among the conditions imposed upon Athens was the surrender of the anti-Macedonian orators. Hypereides and Demosthenes fled. The former was captured, tortured (his tongue was cut out), and put to death. Demosthenes committed suicide by consuming a poison concealed, it is said, in the stylus he used for writing.

Juxtaposing Isokrates and Demosthenes highlights their clear differences as much of character as of political choice (vis-à-vis Philip) and rhetorical method. The one was a "closet" orator, who practiced and conceptualized an ideal of "leisure" (which P. Demont has shown amounts to staking out a new mode of political action away from the crowd). The other was a fully engaged orator, in the thick of every struggle. Isokrates was a stylist, while Demosthenes was an animal of the public forum who asserted that "delivery" is the most important part of the art of oratory. Thus Isokrates and Demosthenes became in the ancient tradition the symbols of two distinct and even opposing attitudes, one devoted to the beauty of the spoken word and ideas, the other to their effectiveness. Philip himself is said to have compared the orations of Demosthenes to soldiers, because of their bellicosity, and those of Isokrates to athletes, because of their spectator appeal (Pseudo-Plutarch, *Lives of the Ten Orators* 845D). If there is any truth in this opposition, it is still necessary not to forget the points the orators share in common, two especially that will be elaborated below. Isokrates like Demosthenes saw in rhetoric a means of political action; Demosthenes like Isokrates keenly felt how important for rhetoric were hard work, upbringing, and education.

The Republic of the Orators: Reality and Image

The preceding observations have shown the importance of rhetoric in Athenian political life. This importance, which is real, became a myth in addition, in the sense that both the ancients and the moderns have interpreted and set it up as a model.

Demosthenes notes the role of orations, which is an Athenian specialty: ". . . [your] political system is based upon speeches" (*On the Embassy* 184); and again, on the *epitaphios:* "You alone of all mankind publicly pronounce over your dead funeral orations, in which you extol the deeds of the brave" (*Against Leptines* 141). Likewise Isokrates: "It was the greatest and most illustrious orators who brought to the city most of her blessings"; "You have been educated as have been no other people in wisdom and in speech . . ." "Furthermore, everyone obtains here that practical experience which more than any other thing imparts ability to speak" (*Antidosis* 231, 294–296). On the basis of such clear statements, the Athenian authors gave top billing to "freedom of speech" *(parrhēsia),* that is, to the role of public discourse, in particular, of debate and deliberation, as well as to the figure of the orator as counselor of the people. Perikles, as early as Thucydides, shows this (2.40.2): "It is not debate that is a hindrance to action, but rather not to be instructed by debate before the time comes for action."

The works of the historians and orators are interspersed with reflections of this sort, which aim to emphasize the usefulness for Athens of speeches and deliberations. They carefully distinguished the true orator from the counterfeits, the for-hire perversions, such as the sophist, the logographer, the sycophant, and all the bad "watchdogs of the democracy" who devour the flock entrusted to their care (Demosthenes, *Against Aristogeiton* 1.40). The orator in the true sense of the term *(rhētōr)* appears as the counselor dedicated to the common good, who knows how to draw upon the lessons of history in order to propose the best course of action (e.g., Thucydides 3.42–43; Isokrates, *Panegyric* 1–10; Demosthenes, *On the Crown* 276–88). The people, for its part, receives praise for its deliberative capability: "It is beyond the power of mortal men to take away from you the right to determine and to approve the best policy" (Demosthenes, *Against Timokrates* 37). Aristotelian philosophy lends support to this conception by relating deliberation to the indeterminacy of future events, to the theory of contingency, and to the theory of action: the activity of deliberating, not only with oneself but with others, is a genuine part of man's essence and of his connection with time. It brings into play the virtue of "prudence" *(phronēsis)* and plays an essential role in human affairs (*Rhetoric* 1.4–5; *Nikomakhean Ethics* 3.5; 6). In a democratic regime, the multitude is able, within certain limits, to reach wise solutions and to show itself superior, as a collectivity, to the value of the separate individuals who constitute it (*Politics* 3.11). The orator is the antithesis of the tyrant, because he does not take power by force of arms. (*Politics* 5.1305a7–15).

In this way an image of Athenian political rhetoric was created, the city's own self-image. The moderns, in turn, took it up, and it has played a major role in thinking about democracy, where conceptions of speech, freedom of expression, and decision-making in common occupy an essential place. This reading of the history of Athenian rhetoric can be summed up in the famous formulation of Fénelon: "Among the Greeks everything depended on the people and the people depended on the spoken word" (*Lettre à l'Académie* 4). To cite present-day reflections, we can note, with Paul Ricœur, that in a democratic State "political speech is inherently implicated in the activities of public deliberation which unfold in a free space of public discussion" ("Langage politique et rhétorique," in *Lectures I* [Paris, 1991], p. 166). The recurrent issues of "public space" and "political space," discussed in contemporary philosophy by Jürgen Habermas and Hannah Arendt, involve debate on matters affecting the members of the city, persuasion, and argumentation. The space for political communication is a space for discourse. And all of that, in the final analysis, comes from Athens—from an image of Athens at once true and mythic.

This is why it is necessary, while emphasizing the capital importance of the practice of oratory at Athens, to mark its limits as well. First, the orators were not the only ones leading the policy of the State: there were also elected magistrates—generals *(stratēgoi)* and treasury officials—who played a decisive role without having necessarily to deliver speeches.

Moreover, although every citizen had in principle the right to speak in the Assembly, only a minority, in practice, had the talent or the necessary motivation. Thus it was often the very same people repeatedly on the podium, facing an audience given to disorderly conduct. "Orator," legally defined, was any citizen who spoke or proposed a decree; "orator," as commonly used, was anyone who spoke regularly and who guided civic policy. According to the calculations of M. H. Hansen, if those present were reckoned in the thousands in the Assembly, the citizens who were active from time to time were counted in the hundreds, and there were never more than twenty or so leading figures, who comprised a restricted elite. Finally, remember that citizenship was limited to free males and that women and slaves had no right to speak; many people were excluded from the deliberations. The sources stress the oratorical and public dimension of political action, to the detriment of other aspects. In this way they construct a fruitful, but partly skewed and theoretical, framework for interpretation, for the greater glory of rhetoric.

THIRD EXCURSUS

♣ The Canon of the Ten Attic Orators

The canon of the ten Attic orators traditionally includes: Andokides, Antiphon, Demosthenes, Deinarkhos, Aiskhines, Hypereides, Isaios, Isokrates, Lykourgos, and Lysias. The list was drawn up between the time of the Alexandrians and the Roman Empire at a date that cannot be determined precisely. The first time it is mentioned seems to be in the work of the critic Caecilius of Kale Akte (first century B.C.), who was the author of a treatise, now lost, *On the Character of the Ten Orators* (the *Souda,* K 1165). Quintilian (first century A.D.) speaks of the ten orators at Athens (*Institutio Oratoria* 10.1.76). Pseudo-Plutarch, of uncertain date, writes the *Lives of the Ten Orators*. In the second to third centuries A.D., "the Attic Ten," as Lucian calls them (*Scythian Oration* 10), are clearly attested. Hermogenes dedicates a vignette to each of the orators who make up the list (pp. 395–403, Rabe ed.; Kritias fills the vacancy left by Demosthenes, who is in a class by himself). The grammarians publish lexicons of the ten orators (that of Harpokration is preserved, while Photios in the *Library* 150, mentions those of Joulianos, Philostratos of Tyre, and Diodoros). The neo-sophist, Herodes Atticus, when his public cried out in praise, "You are one of the Ten," humorously replied, "I am certainly better than Andokides!" (Philostratos, *Lives of the Sophists* 564–65: Andokides, who was an amateur, was the least highly regarded of the Attic orators.) This list, after all, did not necessarily evolve in a straight line; it could not be established everywhere at the same time, and its composition could vary. As for the term "canon," there is no ancient usage in this sense (although there does exist a Greek word *kanōn,* "rule" or "norm"). David Ruhnken introduced it during the eighteenth century in his *Historia critica oratorum Graecorum,* borrowing the term from Christianity; this usage (a catachresis) inconveniently suggests a more binding character than was actually the case, since a list of orators clearly does not claim the same authority as a canon of sacred books.

The canon of orators is not an isolated phenomenon; on the contrary, antiquity established comparable lists for poets, historians, philosophers, artists, and so on. In each case, it was a matter of drawing up the list of recognized classics in a given genre, in order to establish a standard corpus for criticism, imitation, and instruction. In literature, the works held to be canonical were more often recopied, and it is these that have come down to us, while works left out have for the most part disappeared. According to one's preferred point of view, the canons can be said to have played a "destructive" role (I. Worthington), in the sense that they consigned to oblivion what they did not include, or, conversely, they can be said to have rendered a great service in ensuring the preservation of the works judged to be the best.

With the orators, the canon of authors stretches from the end of the fifth century to the end of the fourth. Those included were either Athenians (Andokides, Antiphon, Demosthenes, Aiskhines, Hypereides, Isokrates, Lykourgos) or foreigners who worked in Athens (Deinarkhos from Corinth; Lysias from a family of Syracusan origin; Isaios was either Athenian or from Khalkis on Euboia). Their preserved speeches, amounting to more than a hundred, are chiefly court pleadings and, to a smaller degree, political addresses. Added to these are a few examples of funeral orations *(epitaphioi)* by Demosthenes, Hypereides, and Lysias; panegyrics (Isokrates, Lysias); and fictional, pedagogical or literary speeches (Antiphon, Demosthenes, Isokrates). Thus, the selection reflects a definite bias; it elevates the Athenian moment, the Attic dialect, and the great genres of public eloquence.

This does not prevent a wide diversity of content, for the orations of the Attic orators deal just as well with mundane matters—pensions, verbal abuse, muggings—as they do with the very gravest crises of the State—the tyranny of the Thirty, the war against Philip. They depict as many shady characters as they do respectable citizens. The talents evident throughout this selection are remarkable (besides those of Isokrates and Demosthenes, there is the persuasive simplicity of Lysias, the elegance and verve of Aiskhines, etc.); and the language used—the Attic dialect in all its precision—lends itself admirably, as the situation demands, to the expression of facts, reasons, and emotions.

Among the authors of rhetorical works who have survived outside the canon, one can cite the following: Antisthenes (ca. 445–365), the founder of the Cynic school, who kept the company of the sophists and Socrates, and whose two opposing speeches by Ajax and Odysseus claiming the arms of Achilles are still preserved; Alkidamas (first half of the fourth century), author of *On the Authors of Written Speeches or On the Sophists* and of an accusation of Palamedes by Odysseus; as well as two contemporaries of Demosthenes—Apollodoros, several of whose court speeches appear in the Demosthenic corpus, and Hegesippos, one of whose public addresses is similarly preserved. Literature also offers imaginary or recomposed speeches, in the dialogues of Plato and in the historical works of Xenophon, most especially the apologies of Socrates by these two writers.

On the canon of the Attic orators, see two studies, one by I. Worthington, "The Canon of the Ten Attic Orators," in ibid., ed., *Persuasion: Greek Rhetoric in Action* (London and New York, 1994), pp. 244–63; and one by R. M. Smith, "A New Look at the Canon of the Ten Attic Orators," *Mnemosyne* 48 (1995): 66–79. These two authors differ on the origin of the canon (Caecilius according to Worthington, Alexandrian scholarship of the third or second century B.C. according to Smith). On the notion of canon in general, see Appendix One in B. M. Metzger, *The Canon of the New Testament* (Oxford, 1987); Part Three of R. Nicolai, *La storiografia nell'educazione antica* (Pisa, 1992). ✿

Teaching and Theory of Rhetoric

Oratorical practice rested upon a very active teaching program. The teachers of rhetoric at Athens were numerous, from the most renowned to the lesser known. Numerous, too, were the schools, and they differed from one another by level and objective. Someone could learn to speak, as Plato says (*Protagoras* 312B), either with a view to the "art" *(tekhnē)* or with a view to general cultural formation ("education," *paideia*), that is to say, either to make a career of rhetoric, or to improve himself culturally in a disinterested manner. The methods were certainly varied and in large part oral. One can easily imagine that they comprised lessons in theory, case studies, the learning of model orations set by the teacher, practical exercises in composition on real or fictional topics, as well as contests among the students, not to mention gesture and voice training.

Isokrates's is the best-known school, thanks chiefly to evidence found in the *Antidosis* (contrary to what was said in antiquity, Isokrates probably never composed a treatise on rhetoric). The term of study lasted up to three or four years. The students, who came not only from Attika but from all over the Greek world, paid high fees and offered gifts, in return for which two types of instruction were proposed to them. First, they would work on what the teacher called the *ideai,* a very broad word denoting all the "forms" of the speech, from the content (accusation, praise, etc.) to the stylistic figures, and the ideas, themes, and types of reasoning in between, in short, the entire spectrum of the art of the spoken word. Next the students would listen to speeches composed by the teacher, which they discussed and explicated in common, in a seminar-like atmosphere, as in the case of the *Philip* or the *Panathenaikos.* Beyond the technical rules, Isokrates meant to dispense a complete education, at once intellectual and moral, based upon the conviction that it is possible to speak well only if one thinks well and is a man of good will. A realist, after all, the teacher emphasized that education cannot be everything and that it can produce good fruit only from favorable soil: lessons and exercises must rest upon natural gifts. The numerous graduates of Isokrates's school illustrate the generalist character of an education that produced orators, writers (like the historians Theopompos and Ephoros), citizens active in public affairs, and important politicians, like the general Timotheos, Konon's son.

Athenian instruction used written texts: model speeches, collections of exordia and perorations, and especially those handbooks or treatises called *Tekhnai* ("Arts," with "of rhetoric" understood). The *Tekhnai,* for the most part, dealt with the judicial genre; utilitarian, they provided the means for composing a court speech with the least expense. But the two preserved examples are, it so happens, of a completely different order. They are complete courses in rhetoric, composed in the second half of the fourth century, which synthesize and deepen the inheritance of the Classical period.

The *Rhetoric to Alexander,* which dates from between 340 and 300 B.C., has been handed down among the manuscripts of Aristotle, although this attribution is certainly incorrect; the author could be the orator and historian Anaximenes of Lampsakos. The work in outline divides rhetorical discourse into seven categories ("species"): exhortation, dissuasion, praise, blame, accusation, defense, and investigation.

The author presents the topics and the arguments specific to each category (1–5; here there is an exhaustive inventory, notably of the chief criteria for the chosen course of action that constitute the internal structure of the deliberative speech). He then analyzes the means of persuasion common to all the categories, both at the level of argument and at the level of style (6–28). Finally, he shows what the structure and the sections of the speech ought to be in each of the categories considered (29–37).

He aims to provide as detailed a method as possible for allowing orators to produce rich, elegant, and persuasive speeches for every occasion, while avoiding the risks of disorganization, outlandishness, or failure of inspiration. To this end, he gives definitions, advice, and rules, which he deduces both from a systematic study of the subject and from an examination of the usages and norms current in his time. If it is impossible precisely to determine what his sources were, it is in any case clear that the *Rhetoric to Alexander* is inspired by earlier research, particularly that of the sophists and Isokrates on, for example, what pertains to oratorical categories, proofs, *topoi* of the encomium, the parts of the speech, and the stylistic figures. Moreover, some comments on minor points, what is written about exordia, for instance, seem to be based upon a practitioner's experience. One can therefore see in the *Rhetoric to Alexander* a sort of systemization of earlier and contemporary rhetoric. But at the same time this treatise shows similarities with the *Rhetoric* of Aristotle, in the way that it subsumes the seven categories or species under three genres or genera, or in the way it treats certain aspects of *topoi* and proofs. These similarities must derive partly from a shared background (for Aristotle bases himself too on contemporary theory and practice); they could have been reinforced by a reworking of the *Rhetoric to Alexander,* assuming that the text, during its transmission, underwent some modifications (tied up with the false attribution) that aimed to align it with Aristotle's treatise.

The *Rhetoric* of Aristotle

Aristotle's *Rhetoric,* then, is the crowning achievement of rhetorical theory in Classical Greece. This work is part of a series of studies Aristotle dedicated to rhetoric that featured two works now lost, the *Gryllos,* a dialogue from his youth, and the *Sunagōgē Tekhnōn* ("Collection of *Tekhnai*"), a compilation of the *Tekhnai* then in existence. The *Rhetoric* is generally dated to the second third or third quarter of the fourth century. Like the majority of Aristotle's work, it was not meant for publication, but was a working text, drawn up by the master for teaching purposes, and whose composition could have stretched over a long period of time. Hence the question, how to know if the present book 3 was part of the original project or whether it is a separate work added to the two preceding books by a later editor. The *Rhetoric* has many points of contact with the rest of Aristotle's work, particularly with the *Poetics, Topics, Refutations of the Sophists, Politics,* and *Ethics.*

Aristotle tackles the subject in a "scientific" spirit, that is, he treats it as a part of reality, requiring its own specific investigation, and he aims to establish a body of knowledge that will relate to other bodies of knowledge. The field considered is persuasive discourse; consequently, rhetoric will be not the art of persuading, as is usually said, but more objectively the faculty of "find[ing] out in each case the existing means of persuasion" (1.1355b25–26). The treatise of Aristotle provides the means for such a discovery by analyzing everything conducive to persuasion. Rhetoric so conceived is analogous to dialectic to the extent that both, each in its own way, "have to do with matters that are in a manner within the cognizance of all men and not confined to any special science" (1.1354a1–3). "The whole business of rhetoric is to influence opinion" (3.1404a1–2). In these terms, the study of rhetoric assumes both intellectual and practical utility. It permits truth and justice to prevail when judgment is called for, and it helps persuasion in circumstances where a didactic pronouncement is inappropriate and where it is necessary to be convincing through the use of commonly accepted opinions (before large audiences). It bestows the ability to maintain opposing points of view, which ensures "that the real state of the case may not escape us, and that we ourselves may be able to counteract false arguments, if another makes an unfair use of them." Rhetoric provides the means for self-defense through speech in dangerous circumstances (1.1355a21-b2).

Always with the universal in mind, Aristotle thinks like a man of his time, in and through the categories and oratorical forms of fourth-century Athens. This is why he gives priority to addresses to the people, in which he sees the most beautiful, most political, and most difficult of orations (1.1354b24–25; 3.1418a22), thus conforming to the Athenian institutional and ideological model.

Here is a brief outline of the *Rhetoric*'s structure:

Book 1:
— Chapters 1–2: Introduction. Definitions.
— Chapters 3–15: The three genres of oratory: deliberative (exhortation and dissuasion), judicial (prosecution and defense), epideictic (praise and blame). "Topics" and arguments (the so-called "specific *topoi*" or "places") proper to each genre.

Book 2:
After having set forth in book 1 the logical and objective proofs appropriate to each genre, Aristotle passes on to the means of persuasion useful for all the genres.

— Chapters 1–17. Subjective and moral proofs: how the orator presents himself (chap. 1); passions awakened in the audience (chaps. 2–11: anger, friendship, fear, shame, kindness, pity, indignation, envy, rivalry); adapting to the character of the audience (chaps. 12–17: character a function of age and social circumstance).

— Chapters 18–26. Logical proofs common to the three genres: "commonplaces," enthymemes, examples.

Book 3:

— Chapters 1–12. Style: its qualities, its methods.

— Chapters 13–19. The parts of the speech (exordium, narration, argumentation, peroration).

Many essential points are broached or formalized here for the first time, as far as we know: the definition of rhetoric and its place in the field of knowledge; the elaboration of the art into a system, with classifications and a technical language; the identification of three genres to which all possible rhetorical speeches must ultimately belong; the identification of two chief forms of persuasion, logical persuasion through demonstration, and moral persuasion through character *(ēthos)* and passion *(pathos)*, psychology thus entering into the arsenal of proofs; the systematizing of commonplaces *(topoi)*; the distinction between technical proofs (worked out through the speech) and non-technical proofs (brought in from outside, like physical evidence, for example); the distinction between deductive reasoning (enthymeme) and inductive reasoning (example), as well as the notion of "amplification"; the list of stylistic qualities; the analysis of the sentence (the period), metaphor, and prose rhythms.

Aristotle highlighted this fundamental idea: persuasion requires exploiting the forces already present in the listener. The good orator knows the cognitive competencies and pertinent mental associations of those listening to him. He builds on preexisting ideas and recognized values, and in this way he can effect the mystery of persuasion (mentioned above in the Introduction): to induce someone to think something he was not thinking before. The new thought is introduced into the mind of the listener from known and accepted premises. All the parts of the *Rhetoric* essentially come down to a vast inventory of these premises and of the means to persuade which rest upon them.

The paradox is that this treatise full of novel views was relatively little read in antiquity, because it belonged to the non-published works of Aristotle. These, while not totally inaccessible, did not enjoy a large public until the labors of the "editors" of the first century B.C., and by then it was too late for a big success, since other treatises had already established themselves. Besides, the *Rhetoric* is written in an elliptical and unadorned style whose difficulty deterred readers. The doctrine of the *Rhetoric,* however, spread widely, in the absence of the text itself, thanks to the teaching of the master and the writings of his disciples. So the ideas of Aristotle reverberated in the schools of philosophy and rhetoric; some almost achieved the status of dogmas (for example, the distinction among the three genres), while others provided material for discussion and further research.

The Philosophical and Moral Problem of Rhetoric

The Athenians did not only practice and think about rhetoric, they also criticized it. There is nothing surprising in this, if one recognizes it as a characteristic of contemporary Greek, and especially Athenian, thought never to be satisfied with the practice of things but to submit them to conceptual reflection and discussion. This is the Greek genius, perhaps. Whether in politics, philosophy, or mythology, at the same time as the Greeks advanced new conceptions, new systems, they subjected these conceptions and systems to discussion, analyzing their inherent problems. Rhetoric received the same treatment.

While the phenomenon of rhetoric developed and expanded greatly, the society of the time, in fact, displayed reservations and misgivings before a new art fraught with the possibilities of excessive subtlety, manipulation, and deceit. Outside of Athens, there were probably many who said with the Spartan Sthenelaidas "The long speeches of the Athenians I cannot understand" (Thucydides 1.86.1). In Athens itself, the critics expressed themselves openly. In the theater, characters both tragic and comic, as we saw, do not hesitate to question the art of speaking, and even in the courts, speakers found it a useful *topos* to win the judges' goodwill by introducing themselves as ignorant of quibbling, unaccustomed to public speaking, and incapable of fine words and twisted arguments. Such assertions attest to the existence of a widespread mistrust of rhetoric.

Plato and Rhetoric

This mistrust found a radical and more profound expression in the dialogues of Plato, which are a key chapter in the history of rhetoric. Plato dealt with rhetoric often; it is one of his work's important themes.

Socrates's criticism of the sophists is the starting point. One of the aims of the Socratic dialogue in Plato is to uncover false specialists and false values. From this perspective, the sophists offer a special target. They claim to possess a unique ability in the most important realms, precisely those which the philosopher claims for himself: upbringing, speech, politics, virtue. Thus numerous dialogues show Socrates vying with the most eminent representatives of the sophistic movement. The philosopher unmasks the sophists as dangerous charlatans and especially criticizes their pretension to be "speech experts" and to teach this expertise to others (notably in the *Protagoras, Gorgias,* the *Lesser* and the *Greater Hippias*). What is more, Socrates/Plato widens the gap as much as he can. Not satisfied with unmasking real persons, he constructs a conceptual image of the sophist in order to make of him the double, the evil double, of the philosopher (notably in the *Sophist*). The sophist, like the philosopher, lays a claim to "wisdom" and "knowledge," two ideas contained in the Greek word *sophia,* but the sophist supposes he possesses them, while the philosopher proposes to investigate them; the former calls himself "expert in *sophia*" *(sophistēs),* the latter the "lover of *sophia*" *(philosophos).* From rhetoric's point of view, this essential antagonism has as its consequence the establishment of a radical opposition between the sophistic art of speech and philosophy. It aims in passing to deny the conjoining of Socrates and the sophists—something Aristophanes, among others, did in the *Clouds*—by, on the contrary, marking out their total separation.

The Platonic criticism of rhetoric has, moreover, a political slant. As an adversary of the democracy, Plato can only denounce the art of oratory, one of the mainsprings of this type of government.

Finally, and this connects to the previous point, Plato had a personal reason for being fed up with rhetoric, because it was in the course of a trial that his master Socrates was condemned to death by a jury of the people. Socrates defended himself and failed to convince the jurors: for Plato, this outcome dishonored the jurors, not Socrates. The judicial system, based on the hearing of pleas, in this way proved its own perversity. So Plato was anxious to publish, after rewriting, the speech which Socrates had delivered on that occasion. The *Apology of Socrates* can be read as the model of the courtroom oration, which accords with the demands of philosophy and nevertheless (or rather, for that very reason) is ineffective in the scheme of persuasion present in Athens. It poses the serious problem of rhetoric, although still implicitly.

On these bases, both theoretical and personal, the thought of Plato develops in several dialogues, principally, the *Gorgias, Menexenos, Symposium,* and *Phaidros.*

The subtitle of the *Gorgias* is *On Rhetoric* (it goes back to later editors, not the author, but is appropriate nonetheless); from the start, the dialogue takes issue with the master of the discipline who gives his name to the title. Following his usual method, Socrates undertakes to undermine the pretensions of the self-styled specialist by demonstrating to him that he is completely ignorant of the subject he thinks he knows. The subject in question is the rhetoric practiced in meetings of the citizenry, that is, basically courts and assemblies. Since Gorgias professes to excel in this art, Socrates asks him to define it. This question is revealed to be more delicate than at first it appeared, and several fruitless attempts are necessary before arriving at the definition of rhetoric as the "producer of persuasion" (453A). It will still be incumbent on him to try and pin down what type of persuasion is at issue and to what it relates. This first discussion already gives the impression that rhetoric is a fugitive and poorly defined discipline, busied with speeches and persuasion for their own sake, without questioning itself sufficiently about their purpose. It is a matter of superficial knowledge, of an appearance of knowledge. Rhetoric, according to Socrates, is not an art, but an imitation of an art, in that it does not rest upon a true knowledge of its object.

This criticism, of an epistemological order, leads to a second, of a moral order. In looking to specify the end of rhetorical persuasion, Gorgias affirmed that this end must be in conformity with justice, but the continuation of the dialogue demonstrates that this assurance is a false pretense. Once Gorgias drops into the background, Polos and Kallikles, the characters who succeed him in conversing with Socrates, wind up, when pressed by the philosopher's questions, admitting that they have no concern for justice, of which, moreover, they have no knowledge. The art of persuading for them is nothing other than the means to dominate another and to impose upon him their own will. In a series of progressive revelations, the masks fall off, and Kallikles brutally unveils what lay hidden in embryo in the respectable speech of Gorgias: rhetoric is immoral, it is the way to succeed in the city, to save one's own skin, to wrest a liberty which is only license, and to take power at any cost. Behind the question of rhetoric, therefore, is the question of politics. Rhetoric is the expression of a perverted way of seeing politics, the way that prevailed in the Athenian democracy.

The height of skill is the way rhetoric makes itself all sweetness in order to achieve its ends. Far from sticking to bracing language to lead citizens to the good, which would be the property of the true political art, rhetoric tells its listeners what they expect and aims to please them. It permits persuasion all the more easily since it has minimized demands from the start. "For everybody [among the people and the friends of the people] is delighted with words that are designed for his special temper, but is annoyed by what is spoken to suit foreigners" (513C, Loeb modified). The excessively bruited power of the *logos* is a false power, because it is only used to further established values (success, material goods, etc.) and because it rests upon a false conception of the good and happiness.

In the last analysis, therefore, the problem of rhetoric encompasses the problem of the goal of life: "our debate is upon a question . . . what course of life is best" (500C). The answer, according to Socrates, is a dilemma. On one horn is the rhetorical life, which consists in looking for material success for oneself and for others. Miltiades, Themistokles, Kimon, and Perikles symbolized it, the great Athenian statesmen who developed the military and economic power of the city without concern for anything else. On the other horn is the philosophic life, which is directed toward the good and consists of taking care of one's soul and educating one's fellow citizens, whatever the cost. Its representative is the case history of Socrates himself, present everywhere beneath the surface, an example at once of moral success and, through his condemnation, of civic failure. (The antithesis between the orator and the philosopher is taken up again in the *Greater Hippias* 304A–B; *Theaitetos* 172C ff.).

Thus the *Gorgias* is a terrible indictment of rhetoric, in which Plato sees only intellectual and moral weakness, hunger for power, ignorance of the true good, a preference for committing rather than suffering injustice, and a perverted politics. It is diametrically opposed to philosophy. Telling images follow this denunciation, such as the doctor dragged before a tribunal of children by a cook and condemned because his medicines are bitter, while the cook's dishes are pleasant (521E): the doctor represents the philosopher, the cook the orator. The dialogue is studded with harsh expressions, fated to stick, stigmatizing rhetoric: "fawning" or "flattery" (*kolakeia:* 463B), "habit or knack" (463B), counterfeit politics (more precisely, "of a branch of politics," 463D), rule by the stronger "following the law of nature" (483E).

In several places, however, the dialogue entertains the possibility of a good rhetoric. Completely different from the preceding, this rhetoric would consist in "making the citizens' souls as good as possible and the persistent effort to say what is best," and it would be the property of an orator who was a "man of art and virtue" (*tekhnikos te kai agathos,* 503–4). It seems that there has never been an example of such an orator, unless one cares to mention Aristeides the Just (526A–B) and Socrates himself (521D), who are cited from a political rather than strictly rhetorical point of view. In the end, the *Gorgias* manages an opening by recognizing the at least theoretical existence of a rhetoric used in the service of justice (527C), "the genuine art of rhetoric" (517A).

The *Menexenos,* a dialogue contemporary with the *Gorgias* (ca. 385 B.C.), zeroes in, for its part, on the genre of the *epitaphios logos.* Athens, its rhetoric and politics, is still the issue (the young Menexenos is getting ready to debut in public life), but this time Socrates changes tactics, choosing banter and pastiche as his weapons. A conversation between Socrates and Menexenos introduces the dialogue, when Socrates praises the skill of speakers who give funeral orations. This entire section (an encomium of the encomium!) is ironic, and the admiring comments of Socrates in reality sound like so many criticisms: of the lie inherent in the genre, which praises the dead as a group, whatever their actual worth in life; of the flattery, which praises Athens to the Athenians; of the style, with its superficial allure; of the claims to improvisation, when in fact the speakers use prefabricated orations. Then Socrates takes it upon himself to recite a funeral oration, which he says he received from his mistress in rhetoric, Aspasia (a doubly sarcastic detail, since Aspasia was a woman and since she was the companion of Perikles, who thus turns out to be the target). The oration Socrates delivers is a pastiche illustrating the failings detailed in the introduction: insincerity, triteness, bombastic style, mechanical and artificial plan. In this way the *Menexenos* completes the criticism of the *Gorgias:* after eloquence in the courts and assemblies, the encomium; after the consideration of rhetoric in itself, the examination of a particular genre and the close study of its makeup; after vehemence and seriousness, irony and humor. But the attack of the *Menexenos* is no less grave, for all that; it targets the very patriotism of the Athenians and their celebration of national glories. It is piquant to observe that all antiquity was fooled (as well as some moderns): Greek and Roman readers took the *epitaphios* of the *Menexenos* seriously, without seeing the irony, because, we may suppose, the pastiche is relatively discreet and because it was difficult to imagine such a resolutely iconoclastic purpose.

The partygoers in the *Symposium* (ca. 380–375 B.C.) each deliver in turn speeches on Love. The fact that Plato refers to rhetoric in a dialogue as profound and important as the *Symposium* clearly signals his interest in it: the philosopher needs rhetorical speeches, as points of comparison and introduction, in order to conceive his philosophic discourse. As in the *Menexenos,* the genre envisaged is the encomium, with this difference, that the *Symposium* concerns contributions in a private setting, not public orations. Once again, practice and theory are skillfully brought together as each participant makes a speech and criticizes those that have preceded. The especially elaborate speech of Agathon is a pastiche in the style of Gorgias, which Socrates praises ironically. When all is said and done, a series of criticisms of the rhetorical encomium emerges, echoing themes already encountered in the *Menexenos.* Singled out are the poor choice of topics, the absence of truth, the predictable formats, the formalistic arguments, and the overly refined style. But the *Symposium* goes beyond the *Menexenos* by adding to the criticisms some positive considerations which amount to defining one sort of methodology for the good encomium. Socrates says (198– 99) that it is most important to know the subject intended for praise, to know it accurately for what it is, and to tell the truth; the plan of the oration will follow naturally from the subject itself and the words will take care of themselves spontaneously. The reader looking in the *Symposium* for illustrations of these principles will find them in the words of Diotima and Alkibiades, which occupy the last two sections of the dialogue. Diotima's speech is, in one sense, a praise of Love (212C), while Alkibiades' is a praise of Socrates (215A). The structure of the work thus suggests (Plato refrains from saying so directly) that these two sections, as philosophic speeches, are the corrected versions of the rhetorical speeches attempted earlier and therefore undertake, in some way, the "true rhetoric" adumbrated in the *Gorgias.* That is why these two sections outwardly resemble the rhetorical speeches in topic and stated intention but differ radically in their content and presentation. The *Symposium* thus takes a decisive step in the direction of a philosophic rhetoric.

The *Phaidros* (ca. 370 B.C.), another especially profound and complex dialogue, breaks through to the next stage. Still with Love as the topic, sample speeches and theoretical reflections recur, as well as criticisms of the *Tekhnai* and the orators. Lysias and Isokrates are mentioned by name. The innovation of the *Phaidros* is its development of a positive position dedicated to the conditions making a true art of oratory possible (269–74). A change in attitude toward Perikles marks this change of perspective. Where previously he had been attacked in the *Gorgias* and mocked in the *Menexenos,* he now appears, on the contrary, as a worthy speaker (assuming this passage is not ironic). With no limits to its choice of subject, the art of oratory—"if it exists"—must extend to all forms of speech. It will have producing persuasion as its end, since it is a "psychagogy" (*psukhagōgia,* that is, a leading of souls). Truth is its essential criterion: to speak well it is necessary to know the truth about the question under discussion and to say this truth, which can only be attained by the dialectic method of division and synthesis. On the other hand, since rhetoric is a "psychagogy," it is necessary to know the soul of the listeners (which implies knowing what the soul is in itself). In addition there are subsidiary, but not unimportant factors, like familiarity with the different types of speech, the combination of natural talents, of knowledge and practice, the ability to discern the opportune moment *(kairos),* the care for composing the speech as "a living being," so that it is a unified and organic whole. If all these conditions are met, then the speech will be valid. Thus the *Phaidros* completes the journey begun in the *Gorgias.*

To sum up this journey, we can use the terms doubling and "transposing" (A. Diès). There is a doubling in the sense that Plato makes the problem of rhetoric the problem of "the rhetorics," by drawing a distinction between common rhetoric and true rhetoric. This doubling is more than a distinction or an opposition. It is a transposition to the extent that true rhetoric goes beyond ordinary rhetoric and transports it to the realm of philosophy. True rhetoric has little in common with what people normally call rhetoric. It is really a science and a teaching, in short, it is the discourse of the philosopher. Ultimately, in its perfect state, it is not even made for men but for the gods: "But this ability he will not gain without much diligent toil, which a wise man ought not to undergo for the sake of speaking and acting before men, but that he may be able to speak and to do everything, so far as possible, in a manner pleasing to the gods" (*Phaidros* 273E). That explains why Plato totally leaves aside common rhetoric. In the ideal city described in the *Laws,* for example, ordinary speeches have no place: the State is not guided by addresses delivered before tumultuous assemblies. The art of courtroom pleading is forbidden and repressed by penalties that even go as far as capital punishment (937–38). As for encomia, only poetry is tolerated, in the carefully controlled form of hymns to the gods and anthems to worthy citizens, and then only after prior rigorous scrutiny (801E, 829C–E). Also permitted are funeral songs in honor of priests and epitaphs of no more than four lines (947C, 958E). If there is any kind of rhetoric admitted in the *Laws,* it is the rhetoric of the laws themselves, chiefly their preambles, which embody the just and regulated usage of speech. This is a far cry from oratory as practiced in Athens.

The Platonic texts have weighed on the entire history of rhetoric owing to the philosopher's authority, to the fundamental, thorough, and nuanced character of his critique, and to the literary and, yes, even oratorical genius with which he frames his criticism. At first glance, Plato can be thought to have done rhetoric a great deal of harm in so relentlessly denouncing its dangers and weaknesses. True enough, the *Gorgias* has never failed to provide weaponry for those contemptuous of the *tekhnē.* But from a historical point of view, it would be incorrect to adhere to this opinion. Taking into consideration the whole of ancient rhetoric, the fact that impresses much more is the fruitfulness of Platonic thought on the subject. The fruitfulness is twofold. For philosophers, Plato made them understand that rhetoric mattered, and that is why there is not a single school of philosophy in antiquity unconcerned with it. For rhetoricians, Plato made them understand that philosophy mattered, and that is why the ideas and problems of philosophy appear in the thought of numerous orators and in the stipulations of numerous treatises on rhetoric. The work of Plato establishes a dialogue between philosophy and rhetoric, and this dialogue is a major characteristic of ancient rhetoric's entire history.

Interchanges between Philosophy and Rhetoric

It is worth emphasizing the influence of philosophy on rhetoric, because it is sometimes misunderstood. Too often ancient rhetoric is thought of in terms of an opposition with philosophy, and that is not right. To be sure, all the representatives of rhetoric were not great philosophers. There certainly were many orators and theorists who hardly cared about ethics: cunning trial lawyers, cynical politicians, shifty sophists, cheap shysters retailing the tricks of the trade, fountains of learning without any conscience. But the large majority of orators recognized that if they were going to be persuasive they would have to build on values higher than those the given situation required in each case. They were not going to win the assent of the audience without referring to justice, the public interest, what transcended present expedience, the good itself. The figure of the people's counselor, mentioned above, embodies in itself this notion of an orator of necessity laying claim to higher ends. Accordingly, rhetorical theory integrated values and concepts borrowed from philosophy. This imported philosophy, more or less in harmony with the society's received opinions, and occasionally a façade, was not always to the liking of philosophers but nonetheless was still one of rhetoric's inspiring sources. Was it not said, rightly or wrongly, throughout antiquity that Demosthenes was the student of Plato?

To conclude, let us return to two authors who played a key role in the give-and-take between rhetoric and philosophy: Aristotle and Isokrates.

Aristotle, theorist of rhetoric, was a philosopher, indisputable evidence establishing the conjunction of the two disciplines. In accordance with his stance of objectivity, Aristotle chose to study the means of persuasion in themselves, abstracting from the scientific and moral worth of the statements with which persuasion deals. Hence he provides a series of analyses which can surprise and even shock. Aristotle inventories all the forms of proof, all the methods, including the most farfetched. He explains how someone can argue for two opposing views on the same topic. For example, if one wants to fault a team of mules, one will call them "daughters of asses," but if one wants to praise them, one will call them "daughters of storm-footed steeds" (*Rhetoric* 3.1405b). Aristotle also shows that the orator must adapt himself to the audience, even to its weaknesses and prejudices, and constantly see things from the viewpoint of public opinion. On all these points, Aristotle seems to accept the rules of the game fully and to multiply concessions to common rhetoric. But it is necessary to understand that only one stage of his thought about rhetoric is at issue here, a stage of methodological amorality, occasioned by the objective study of the *tekhnē*.

At the level of ends, the moral requirement remains intact, as some express statements emphasize: "The true and the just are naturally superior to their opposites"; "That which is true and better is naturally always easier to prove and more likely to persuade"; "One ought not to persuade people to do what is wrong" (*Rhetoric* 1.1355a). Besides, according to Aristotle, rhetoric does not constitute in itself a knowledge of the subjects with which it deals: to treat these subjects, it has to depend on the disciplines external to itself, like ethics, politics, and logic. Consequently, crucial philosophic notions are reintroduced into rhetoric, for example, the concept of happiness, which forms the topic of deliberations, the list of virtues, which dictates the program of the encomium, the study of the passions and characters, which is developed at length in book 2, or the theory of the enthymeme, which transposes into rhetoric the logic of the syllogism. Thus the *Rhetoric* of Aristotle creates a tight association between rhetoric and philosophy. It resembles in certain aspects the *tekhnai* criticized in the *Phaidros* (techniques of persuasion, parts of the speech), but in other aspects it is like the true rhetoric sketched in the same dialogue (connections with dialectic, typology of speeches, role of psychology). Aristotle clears a new path, which leads to the reconciliation of the technique's "value neutrality" (P. Aubenque, "L'Actualité de la *Rhétorique* d'Aristote," *Revue des Etudes Grecques,* 89 [1976]: xii) with the requirements of philosophy. Many will follow him in this direction.

Isokrates (who, according to tradition, was a companion of Socrates) shares the same concern for conciliation, but from a different approach. Where Aristotle is a philosopher who salvaged rhetoric, Isokrates is an orator and professor of rhetoric who will salvage philosophy. He will claim this term for himself, describing his own activity, throughout his life, by the word *philosophia,* and he was clearly aware of its conceptual and symbolic gravity. For him eloquence was inseparable from intelligence and virtue. "For the power to speak well is taken as the surest index of a sound understanding; and discourse which is true and lawful and just is the outward image of a good and faithful soul" (*Nikokles* 7, *Antidosis* 255).

In fact, a true philosophic system does not underpin the ideas of Isokrates; it is more a question of intuitions of a social morality. Among these intuitions, the conviction appears that the good is tied to success. This is because the man who is just and carries on just discourses is recognized and succeeds "most often." The feeling also appears that true knowledge is out of reach, opinion rules, and there is nothing absolute.

Basing himself upon such convictions, Isokrates engaged in a reflection on the concept of the *logos,* which he set forth in some celebrated pages (*Panegyric* 47–49; *Nikokles* 5–9, repeated in the *Antidosis* 253–57). *Logos* in Greek means both "word" and "reason," and for Isokrates this ambivalence is not an ambiguity. It shows that language engages thought. Proceeding from this postulate, Isokrates praises the *logos,* emphasizing that it is a gift of the gods, that it distinguishes man from the animals, and that it permits social life. Civilization and life in the *polis* (deliberations, laws, arts, inventions) rest on the *logos,* and so do justice and morality, cultural upbringing, knowledge and thought. Taking in some sense a realistic position toward rhetoric, Isokrates affirms that when all is said and done human society cannot transcend speech and that, on the contrary, it must make the most of this opportunity it possesses.

But "to make the most of" certainly does not mean to misuse. Quite the contrary, it is essential to make good use of *logos.* This is what brings Isokrates to advocate a rhetoric solicitous of truth and morality. All his teaching, as we saw, rested on this principle, and such an orientation was the hallmark of his entire career. The first stage consisted in repudiating the shifty speeches of judicial rhetoric to the benefit of orations of general interest (cf. *Praise of Helen* 1–13; *Against the Sophists* 19–20; *Panegyric* 188–89). The second stage was a growing thematic insistence on the utility of discourse, to the extent that at the end of his life he distanced himself somewhat from ceremonial eloquence, encomia, and stylistic inquiries, to prefer pure counsel (*Philip* 12–13, 27–28; *Panathenaikos* 1–4).

The Isokratean notion of a "philosophic" eloquence laid the foundation of humanism, of oratorical and literary culture, and has exercised a profound influence on the history of education in the West.

At the end of the fourth century B.C., rhetoric appears quite different from the way it looked a hundred years earlier. Athens, a huge city in comparison to most of the others of the time, was all the same a small world where ideas met and mingled, as in a crucible. Thus rhetoric developed there with great rapidity, through constant contacts and exchanges among individuals, institutions, doctrines, and problems. The elements established in Classical Athens, this circumscribed place and time, will never be forgotten. They form, in their force and complexity, a foundation for the further history of rhetoric.

Chapter Four

The Hellenistic Globalization

The period from the death of Alexander the Great until the emperor Augustus's consolidation of power (323–27 B.C.) radically differs from what preceded. After the relatively brief period of Classical Greece, an expanse of three centuries unfolds, rife with sudden shifts and witness to the creation of the great Hellenistic monarchies and to Rome's conquest of the entire Mediterranean region. After a phase of relative geographic concentration, Hellenism spreads completely throughout the ancient world and makes contact with other civilizations. States meet and confront one another, and in particular the Greek world meets Rome. All these upheavals had political, socio-economic, intellectual, and religious repercussions, which affected rhetoric among other things. Altering its temporal and spatial scale, rhetoric underwent the test of globalization. In the midst of crises, it had to adapt to an expanding and changing world.

The period was thus quite rich, contrary to a common and mistaken belief arising from gaps in information.[1] No speech of a Greek orator has been handed down directly between the fourth century B.C. and the first century A.D. Theoretic treatises prior to the first century B.C. have almost all been lost, eclipsed by the successors that used and replaced them. The investigation of Greek rhetoric must therefore have

---

1. A particularly regrettable gap, which has to be pointed out right away, concerns the teaching of rhetoric. It was during the Hellenistic Age that "preparatory exercises" and "declamation" became important parts of the standard curriculum. Yet we have practically no texts on the topic from the period. The manuals and works we do have date from the Roman Empire, and that is why this subject will be treated in chapter 6.

recourse, here more than elsewhere, to all the available sources, including those in Latin, fragments and indirect *testimonia,* inscriptions and papyri. Once this effort is made, the reconstruction reveals thrilling advances.

"Globalization," a word much in vogue today, sums up these advances. By it we understand the extension of rhetoric onto, if not a global, at least a Greco-Roman scale; the ongoing elaboration of a fuller or "global" system of rhetoric, integrating new technical aspects; and the definition of broader or "global" perspectives arising from the confrontation between rhetoric and philosophy.

Advances in Rhetorical Technique

In the realm of theory, it was a time for clearing new territories and expanding existing fields of knowledge. Technicians in the Hellenistic period, exploring sectors only glimpsed in the Classical Era, introduced and connected innovations bearing on style, argumentation, and oratorical delivery. Systematizing rhetoric is the great creative activity of the Hellenistic Age.

Style

"Style," "manner of expression" is called *lexis, phrasis,* or *hermēneia* in Greek, *dictio* or *elocutio* in Latin. One name associated with this topic is Theophrastos (ca. 370–285 B.C.), who was Aristotle's pupil and his successor as head of the Lyceum. It is said that, although he respected his master's authority, he was not afraid to differ with him (Quintilian, *Institutio Oratoria* 3.8.62). Of his numerous works, around twenty, now all lost, dealt with rhetoric, and one of the most often mentioned is the treatise *On Style (Peri lexeōs).*

According to Cicero (*Orator* 79), Theophrastos enumerated four qualities of style: correctness, clarity, appropriateness, and ornamentation. This four-part list elaborates on suggestions in the third book of Aristotle's *Rhetoric,* and subsequent theorists, including Cicero (*On the Orator* 3.37 ff.) and Quintilian (*Institutio Oratoria* 1.5.1; 8.1–3; 11.1), took it up, generally designating the list's four rubrics with the word "strengths" or "virtues" (in Greek *aretai,* in Latin *virtutes*). By establishing such a list, they sought to define objective criteria, a set of conditions to be met in order to achieve stylistic excellence. Examining the nature of these conditions reveals that they advocate above all a moderate and reasonable use of stylistic devices: ornamentation, while permitted and even required, must never do harm to the other qualities (correctness, clarity, appropriateness) fencing it in. The list of the stylistic virtues thus meant chiefly to draw a middle path between contempt for form and the abuse of over-refinement, in conformity with the Peripatetic concept of virtue as a "middle way" *(mesotēs),* that is, as the height of excellence equally removed from excess and lack. In this, Theophrastos opposed the sophists, and it is not surprising to learn that he criticized the constant use of antitheses and of either-or and parallel constructions (Dionysios of Halikarnassos, *Lysias* 14.2–4). Peripatetic stylistics also understood appropriateness, the third of the virtues, to consist in "using the relevant style, slight for slight themes, grand for grand themes" (Demetrios, *On Style* 120), exactly the opposite of the sophistic claim to make big what is small and small what is big.

Alongside the list of stylistic "virtues," an even more important list developed, the list of "genres" of style (in Greek, *kharaktēres tou logou,* in Latin, *genera dicendi*), which we glimpsed earlier apropos of Homeric rhetoric (chapter 1). It appeared for the first time in the *Rhetorica ad Herennium* (4.11 ff.), a Latin treatise of the first century B.C., which surely borrowed it from earlier Greek sources (there is debate whether Theophrastos was familiar with the list). Adopted by Cicero (*On the Orator* 3.177, 199, 212; *Orator* 20–21, 75 ff.), studied by Quintilian (*Institutio Oratoria* 12.10.58–72), the list enjoyed an immense influence during the Middle Ages in the West. It distinguishes three principal genres, each of which can be subdivided: the grand or serious style, the middle style, and the simple or restrained style. Its informing spirit therefore differs from that of the virtues list. It is not a matter of qualities that ought to be present together, but of options among which it is permissible to choose. Each of the three genres has its own merit, its own models, and its own recommended uses. So the Peripatetic interpretation, which would favor the middle style, is out of the question here, since the grand style and the simple style are not faults but possibilities just as valuable as the middle style. The theory of stylistic genres goes beyond a simple enumeration of normative principles and essentially recognizes that there are several ways to write well. That is why the theorists often advocate use of all three genres as the context requires, for the accomplished orator is someone who knows how to use the entire "gamut of styles" at will to obtain the desired effect (Dionysios of Halikarnassos, *Demosthenes* 2.4).

The treatise of Demetrios *On Style* presents a slightly different system. It has four genres, three roughly corresponding to the preceding trio (grand, "elegant" [*glaphuros*], simple), and a fourth, "forceful" *(deinos)*, characterized by the vigor, compactness, spontaneity, and abruptness demonstrated by Demosthenes and Demades. This original addition is not the only point of interest in a mysterious and important work—mysterious because its author and period remain unknown: the manuscripts attribute it to the Athenian philosopher and statesman Demetrios of Phaleron (ca. 350–283 B.C.), but it probably belongs to a later, conceivably Hellenistic Demetrios. The work is important because (assuming this dating is correct) it is the only Greek treatise, along with the works of Philodemos, preserved from the Hellenistic period and because it broaches numerous topics, not just the single issue of style.

The study of style involves a study of stylistic means: the different elements that, properly assembled, establish the total style, as each part contributes individually to the overall character. Theophrastos, according to Dionysios of Halikarnassos (*Isokrates* 3.1), distinguished on this point three means or levels: "the choice of words, their melodious arrangement and the figures of speech in which they are set." The first point implies a consideration of vocabulary within the confines of linguistics and literature. The second targets the disposition of words in the sentence, with the attendant effects of structure, sonority, and rhythm. As for the third (whatever the precision with which Dionysios here reports the thought and words of Theophrastos), it opens onto another important aspect of Hellenistic stylistics.

It was the Hellenistic Age that established the theory of tropes and figures. The actual practice was clearly quite old, and in the realm of oratory Gorgias had been its exemplar. Ever since the Classical period, individual procedures had been isolated and described, Aristotle's writings on metaphor providing the most celebrated illustration (*Rhetoric* 3.2–4, 10; *Poetics* 21). After these beginnings and under the influence of the Stoics's researches in grammar, the notions were clarified and lists composed. Fundamentally, the theory of figures rests on the ideas of difference and effect. The listed procedures are defined as changes or deviations from the "natural" usage of the language (which supposes a theory on the nature of language), and these deviations are accorded a special expressivity. Distinction is made between "trope" *(tropos)* and "figure" *(skhēma):* these two words, rather loose in the everyday language (*tropos* = "turn," "manner of speaking," *skhēma* = "dress," "demeanor," "pose"), became specialized terms to denote an effect bearing on a single word (trope) or an effect bearing on several words put together (figure). The concept of trope, moreover, was less widely used than figure, remaining absent from certain treatises or not explicitly singled out. Figures were subdivided into "figures of thought" *(skhēmata dianoias)* and "figures of diction" *(skhēmata lexeōs).* In the first case, the figure depends upon the content and remains if the same thing is said in different words; in the second case, the figure is bound up with the very words employed. For example (illustrations borrowed from the *Ad Herennium):*

— metonymy, which substitutes a word akin to the "normal" word, is a trope ("Ceres" for "harvest," "pikes" for "Macedonians");

— prosopopoeia, wherein an absent person or an abstraction speaks, is a figure of thought ("If our city, which has never known defeat, were to speak now, would she not express herself thus: 'I who am adorned with so many trophies'");

— anaphora, which repeats the same word or words at the beginning of successive phrases, is a figure of diction ("It is to you that we must attribute the merit of this action, it is to you that we owe recognition, it is to you that this action will bring glory").

In the time of Cicero, the doctrine was completely established and always presented as Greek:

The Greeks consider that language is embellished if such changes in the use of words are employed as they call tropes, and such forms of thought and diction as they call figures.

(Cicero, *Brutus* 69, Loeb modified)

The figures play an important role in Demetrios to the extent that for this theorist they serve to define the genres of style better. Other Greeks were interested in the topic, like Athenaios (second century B.C.) or Apollonios Molon (first century B.C.), who were authors of definitions of *skhēma*. Nowadays we know about the theory of tropes and figures from the treatise *On Tropes* attributed to the grammarian Tryphon (first century A.D., in Spengel, *Rhetores Graeci,* III, pp. 191–206) and from sources in Latin: book 4 of the *Rhetorica ad Herennium,* the works of Cicero *(On the Orator* 3 and *The Orator),* and the treatise of Rutilius Lupus (first century A.D.) *On the Figures of Thought and Diction.* The last is a partial translation of a Greek treatise by Gorgias the Younger, a rhetorician of the first century B.C., who was the teacher of Cicero's son at Athens. All these texts present lists that do not exhaust the subject, because the distinctions were incessantly discussed and refined, each theorist looking to enrich and stock better, as it were, his own book of specimens, like a Linnaeus before the fact. "There is an almost incalculable supply both of figures of speech and of figures of thought" (Cicero, *On the Orator* 3.201). This subject represented a considerable advance toward a better understanding of literature and language in general.

Numerous as well were the Hellenistic advances in the area of style. Mention should be made again of the research of Theophrastos on prose rhythms or those of Demetrios on the types of "sentences" (*sententiae* or periods) and "clauses" *(kōla).* Through lists and systems, which built upon one another, the very concept of style emerged, thanks to rhetoric. Among its original features, we should note how this concept accords pride of place to prose style, how it is closely bound up with reflections on grammar and linguistics, how it has aspects of literary criticism through its observations on authors' styles, and, finally, how it is based on standards: "virtues," recognized "genres," repertories of effects. This last characteristic surely reflects philosophy's influence on rhetoric. It follows that the act of writing is not prized as an idiosyncratic expression but is gauged against norms and models. Even if one looks for the personality of an author in his style, this personality is judged by the measure of values transcending the individual. Thus a rational and normative approach arose, and it remained the dominant approach throughout antiquity.

Argumentation

After style, argumentation was the second area where Greek rhetorical research developed in the Hellenistic Age. Hermagoras (second century B.C.), a native of Temnos in Asia Minor, is its chief illustration, for he thoroughly worked out a highly intelligent and useful system for the analysis of legal cases. According to Hermagoras, the majority of cases come down to a "rational inquiry" *(logikon zētēma),* that is, they depend on reasoned arguments. To guide the process of this inquiry, the following catalogue helps to ascertain just what is the "question at issue" *(stasis):*

1. Question of "conjecture" *(stokhasmos).* This *stasis* applies to cases where there is uncertainty about the actual facts. Example: a man is surprised next to a corpse and is accused of murder; the discussion centers on the point of knowing whether the accused killed the deceased.

2. Question of "definition" *(horos).* Once the facts are established, it remains to know how to define the situation from a legal point of view. Example: if it is admitted that the accused killed the deceased, is it involuntary homicide, second-degree murder, or premeditated murder?

3. Question of "attendant circumstances" *(kata sumbebēkos).* Once the act is defined, there is an interrogation as to how to qualify it, to understand the circumstances, the result, or the liabilities. Example: homicide can be called justified, advisable, or honorable (the case of tyrannicide, murder committed on the orders of a superior, etc.). This "question" is the most complex and is subdivided.

4. Question of "standing" *(metalēpsis).* The competence of the court is open to discussion and the question arises of transferring the matter to another jurisdiction.

Another form of inquiry was the "legal inquiry" *(nomikon zētēma)*, which occurs when the discussion centers on the texts of the laws applicable to the matter. It is not known whether Hermagoras used the notion of *stasis* with this topic (others will). The cases which can be introduced are "literal and extenuating" *(kata rhēton kai hupexairesin:* opposition between the letter and the spirit of the law), "conflict" between two laws *(antinomia),* "ambiguity" *(amphibolia)* of the law, and "inference" *(sullogismos:* application by analogy of a law that does not relate directly to the matter at hand, in the absence of a text precisely apposite).

The final category considered was cases "without question" *(asustata),* that is, cases in fact impossible to argue either because the facts are insufficient, one of the two sides clearly and completely overwhelms the other, the matter is too difficult or too obscure to clarify, or the two parties are exactly alike. Example: two men were neighbors and each had a beautiful wife; one night they met as each was coming out of the other's house; they accuse each other of adultery. Such a matter, according to Hermagoras, assuming it presented itself, offers no handle for reasoning, since the arguments one lawyer will employ against his opponent will immediately be turned back against him, the two sides hypothetically finding themselves in exactly the same situation.

Such in broad outline is the system of Hermagoras for "questions at issue," insofar as later sources permit its reconstruction (not without some uncertainty, made all the more so by the existence of other Hermagorases, who were also theorists of rhetoric). Although deliberative and epideictic orations could be included in the list (at the level of the third *stasis*), the overall system aimed principally at judicial speeches. In all probability, Hermagoras was not, properly speaking, the inventor of the *staseis* (nor of the technical term *stasis,* which could already have been used before him, nor of the idea, which grew in prominence as soon as Attic judicial eloquence recognized the need for every courtroom orator to choose a line of argument). No matter who were his predecessors, intellectual forefathers, and rivals (notably Athenaios, already mentioned, or Arkhedemos), Hermagoras had the eminent merit of constructing an epoch-making system that influenced both contemporaries and posterity. Thought about legal argument stayed within the confines of this system which was indefatigably taken up, discussed, and modified time and again to the extent that Quintilian, two and a half centuries after Hermagoras, will even go to the length of drawing up a comprehensive survey of received opinion on the subject (*Institutio Oratoria* 3.6). Students (doing declamation), litigants, and lawyers clearly had a definite use for the *staseis* system. With his pedagogically helpful presentation (it will be noticed, for example, how Hermagoras pushed the concern for symmetry to the point of insuring that there were four big subdivisions in each case), Hermagoras presented lists of preliminary questions that permitted the intelligent choice of the best line of argument.

Delivery and Memory

The third and last important area of theory was delivery and memorization of the speech. After Aristotle had observed that "delivery" is the part of rhetoric "which is of the greatest importance, but has not yet been treated of by anyone" (*Rhetoric* 3.1403b21–22), Theophrastos undertook to fill this gap by writing a treatise *On Delivery* (*Peri hupokriseōs:* it is probable, although debated, that this work dealt with rhetorical delivery). Athenaios likewise had handled the subject. It was a new field opening up for the craft. These research efforts came in the end to influence the treatments of the author of the *Rhetorica ad Herennium* (3.19–27) and Cicero (*On the Orator* 3.213–27; *Orator* 55–60), who study in detail the tones of voice, body movements, and plays of facial expression the orator uses to communicate his inner emotions.

As for memory, it was an important topic, since the most common and recommended method for delivering a speech was reciting it by heart. The poet Simonides (sixth to fifth century B.C.) is said to have invented memory technique, and the sophists to have studied it (Hippias, A 5 a11–12, Diels-Krantz; *Double Arguments* 9). The Greeks of the Hellenistic Age deepened the issue; names cited on this score are Kharmadas and Metrodoros of Skepsis (second to first century B.C.; cf. *Rhetorica ad Herennium* 3.38 and Cicero, *On the Orator* 2.360). Once more, we know of their theory from sources in Latin. The first actually preserved text on the art of memory is the *Rhetorica ad Herennium* (3.28–40).

There one finds a subtle system based on the ideas of "places" *(loci)* and "images" *(imagines)*. To memorize a speech, it was first necessary to imagine certain "places," different from one another and following in a determined order (for example, the rooms of a house, the regions of the signs of the Zodiac, or numbered locations). Then one formed mental images evoking, by direct or indirect association, the points one wanted to memorize. For example, in a case about poisoning, to recall the victim, one visualized him, either himself or someone able to suggest him, lying in bed; to recall the defendant, one imagined him standing over the bed, holding a cup; to recall the legacy, the motivation for the poisoning, one put writing tablets into the hand of the accused, and, to recall the witnesses, one put on the accused's ring finger a ram's testicles, the word *testiculus* (testicle) evoking the word *testis* (witness), while the scrotum itself, whose skin was used to make purses, alluded to the money by means of which the witnesses had been suborned. Each one of these images was arranged mentally in the "place" appropriate to its position in the speech. Finally, other images served to recall the very words to be used (for example, the image of Domitius for the expression *domum itionem,* "return home," pronounced *dom' itionem*); each image was located in its turn in its suitable "place."

At first glance, this system seems extremely complicated (the ancients themselves sometimes criticized in this regard the abuse of overcomplication). One could have the impression, as often happens with memory techniques, that the procedures were more difficult to memorize than what they were supposedly helping the speaker to recall. But the evidence remains: this system was used and it worked. Certainly, it was a matter of habit and training. Memory is cultivated and needs a method. When joined to a solid natural gift, the ancient method of artificial memory could give prodigious results. Some orators could memorize on the spot, as they went along, the speech they were in the process of writing and hold it in their memory indefinitely (Seneca the Elder, *Controversiae* 1, Preface, 17–18), or even restore word for word a speech they had prepared in their mind without having written anything down (Quintilian, *Institutio Oratoria* 10.6.4). In addition to its practical usefulness, the ancients' mnemonic system also supposes a reflection, both philosophical and poetic, on memory's very nature and highlights the role of images and spatialization in cognitive processes.

We must not leave Hellenistic theory without mentioning two other important insights, which we owe to Demetrios. The first concerns the theory of letter writing (or epistolography). Until the end of antiquity, this problem remained on the margins of rhetorical theory, properly so called; in the treatise of Demetrios, the first preserved text on the question, the subject comes up in a digression about the simple style (*On Style* 223–35). Demetrios is trying to define what is specific to the epistolary style, which he considers under the types of the personal letter. This, for him, supposes freedom, grace, absence of pomposity or didactic intent, moderate length, and friendliness above all. It must be suitable for the addressee, and the text must bear the writer's personal stamp, for "everyone writes a letter in the virtual image of his soul."

In contrast, the second insight differs radically, because it involves a method of dissimulation, coming as an appendix to the study of the forceful style (287–98). This method is called "figured speech" *(eskhē-matismenos logos),* that is, mannered or allusive discourse. The designation is formed off the word *skhēma,* which in this usage does not mean a "figure of style," but a "form" or "manner" given to a speech. This sense of the word *skhēma* goes back to Zoilos (fourth century B.C.), but Demetrios is the first to spell out for us how it functions. It involves manipulating words to hint at the intended meaning where a straightforward statement risks being inappropriate or dangerous for the speaker. What Demetrios chiefly had in mind was counsel or criticism where suggestion rather than bluntness was desirable, so as not to appear petty or—above all—insolent. For example, if it is necessary to criticize a sovereign for his faults, figured speech, instead of frankness, will take the tack of criticizing other individuals with similar faults or of praising those who have done the opposite. In front of the tyrant Dionysios, one will criticize the cruelty of Phalaris or praise the gentleness of Gelon. "The true nature of those in power . . . calls for that circumspection in speech which is called allusiveness" (Loeb modified).

Taking his examples from the Classical period, Demetrios summons the memory of the relations between Plato and Dionysios or between Demosthenes and the Athenian people. But there is no doubt that "figured speech" was just as important in the Hellenistic Age, before assemblies, monarchs, or provincial governors.

Philosophies Investigate Rhetoric

Many of the theorists cited above were philosophers or influenced by philosophy, and constant contacts between rhetoric and philosophy were a feature of the Hellenistic Age. They were complex: regarding rhetoric, it is impossible to reduce the attitude of every school of philosophy to a single stance, because the schools evolved and their heads in turn multiplied the nuances of the particular doctrine. Philosophers also generally responded to the question of rhetoric's worth with hedged answers like "yes, if . . ." and "no, except that . . ."

The principal bone of contention was whether rhetoric deserved to be called an "art," which many philosophers denied. Added to this were discussions on the usefulness of rhetoric for politics and on the risks of immorality and deceit inherent in the art of the spoken word. The memory of Plato's condemnation still lived. Moreover, the conflict within the realm of ideas was mirrored in a more down-to-earth rivalry between two disciplines competing to be the core of the curriculum, as well as among masters who were competing for Greek and, later, Roman students. Marcus Antonius (in Cicero, *On the Orator* 1.82–93) paints a striking sketch of such clashes when he reports a conversation in which he took part at Athens in 103 B.C. along with the Stoic Mnesarkhos, Kharmadas of the Academy, and the orator Menedemos. The first two denied rhetoric any value and insisted that it was necessary and sufficient that an orator be a philosopher, while Menedemos considered himself, on the contrary, the possessor of a special science distinct from philosophy.

Thus philosophy came to distance itself from rhetoric or to match itself against it; in any case, the debate left few philosophers indifferent.

That is why there existed in all the schools, along with the shifting game of antagonism and reconciliation, thinkers who reflected on rhetoric and sought to integrate it, in one way or another, into their philosophic vision of the world. Some Peripatetics, as we saw, did research following the adaptable and realistic lead of Aristotle. As for the Stoics, they approached the subject with less flexibility, considering eloquence as a virtue and therefore affirming that only the wise man could be the perfect orator. In their system, rhetoric is founded on truth, not probability. Along with dialectic, it belongs to "logic" (the science of human discourse), of which one part, the most important—dialectic—is the science of conversing by question and answer, while the other—rhetoric—is the science of continuous discourse. In order to define the difference and at the same time the kinship between dialectic and rhetoric, Zeno, the founder of Stoicism (fourth to third century B.C.), employed a famous image. He used to close his fist to symbolize dialectic and then open his palm and spread the fingers to symbolize rhetoric, showing in this way that the two sciences were different from one another in the degree of their tension and terseness. This, however, does not mean that the Stoics were fans of lengthy speeches; quite the contrary, they promoted and practiced a concise, pointed style, some might even say obscure and thorny, as Cicero, who did not like it, more than once remarked, and they added "succinctness" (suntomia) to the list of the four stylistic virtues. Kleanthos and Khrysippos, heads of the Stoa (fourth to third century B.C.), each wrote a treatise on rhetoric. The Middle Stoa, under Panaitios and his student Poseidonios (second to first century B.C.), represented a deepening and loosening up of the school's ideas. As for the Academy, its stance evolved toward a rehabilitation of rhetoric, during the time of Philon of Larissa (second to first century B.C.), who was Cicero's teacher and who taught at different times rhetoric and philosophy (Tusculan Disputations 2.9).

Philodemos (ca. 110–40 B.C.) is another important philosopher. Born at Gadara in Palestine, he studied at Athens, then settled in Italy where Julius Caesar's father-in-law, Lucius Calpurnius Piso, was his patron and Cicero and Vergil were his acquaintances. A magnificent dwelling at Herculaneum near Naples, probably belonging to Piso, was the meeting place of an Epicurean coterie formed around Philodemos. The place has been miraculously preserved thanks to the lava from the eruption of Vesuvius that buried Pompeii and Herculaneum in 79 A.D. Excavations, begun in the eighteenth century and still unfinished today, have drawn attention to this site, called the Villa of the Papyri, after the great number of carbonized papyri which it has been possible to unroll and decipher with great difficulty. The works of Philodemos, not transmitted elsewhere, are a particular feature of these rolls and reveal a mind of manifold interests. Philodemos wrote on various philosophical subjects, but he was also interested in politics (treatises *On the Good King According to Homer* and *On Freedom of Speech* [*parrhēsia*], not without contemporary implications in the era of Caesar), in poetry (he was himself a poet), in music and, finally, in rhetoric. We still have his *On Rhetoric (Peri rhētorikēs),* a long work, which an older, small treatise on the same subject *(Hupomnēmatikon)* preceded.

On Rhetoric is not a systematic treatise, but a polemical work directed against the pretensions of *rhetors* (specialists in rhetoric) and the erroneous ideas of philosophers belonging to various schools. True to Epicureanism, Philodemos is fundamentally hostile to rhetoric. He can only see in judicial and deliberative rhetoric a routine unworthy of the name of art, and in his estimation the true man of politics has no need for eloquence. He makes an exception, however, in book 2, for "sophistic" rhetoric, a large field, exemplified in his mind by Isokrates, which includes compositions written in a chastened style, that is, epideictic orations (of praise and blame) and school orations. To this type of rhetoric he grants the status of art, because it rests upon a science and rules, and he avers that Epicurus himself thought similarly, although other Epicureans disputed this (evidence like this shows that there were bitter debates over rhetoric among the school's disciples). Philodemos, this man "profoundly cultured" *(perpolitus)* in all areas of intellectual activity (Cicero, *Against Piso* 70), therefore recognized an aesthetic dimension to the art of the spoken word. But this welcoming stance remained carefully hedged, because sophistic rhetoric so defined was deprived of all political and practical usefulness (something Isokrates would never have accepted). Philodemos, moreover, expressed reservations in no uncertain terms about the moral validity of encomia bestowed by epi-deictic orators. It is otherwise worth noting that Philodemos knew a division of four types of style, similar to that of Demetrios, yet another indication of the multiplicity of research carried out on the system of the *genera dicendi* (Philodemos, *Rhetoric* I, p. 165, ed. Sudhaus).

Hellenistic philosophy by and large used forms of expression that were not without rhetorical interest, for example, protreptic (exhorta-tion, especially exhortation to philosophy), diatribe (a didactic text in lively style on moral subjects), *khreia* (an anecdote, a concise statement or response, striking and instructive), and consolation. The most rhetorical of all was the "thesis" *(thesis)*, which consisted in arguing on a given problem for purposes of instruction or classroom exercise. This form went back to the sophists: the commonplaces of Protagoras were *theseis* before the fact. Aristotle used the word "thesis" for such types of argument, and following him the "thesis" was practiced in all the lead-ing philosophical schools. There were collections of *theseis,* sometimes quite voluminous, published by the Peripatetics (Theophrastos), the Academy (Xenokrates, Polemon), and the Stoics (Herillos, Khrysip-pos). The intention was to develop and inculcate dialectic's procedures of demonstration and discussion, for often the exercise involved refut-ing an opposing position (argument *contra thesim*) or supporting in turn two contrary positions (argument *eis hekateron, in utramque partem*). In the second century B.C., Hermagoras introduced the *thesis* into the rhetorical system, when he divided oratorical material into two categories: general questions, or *theseis,* and individual questions, or *hupotheseis,* to be distinguished from the former in that they involve specific persons and circumstances. "Should one marry?" is a *thesis,* "Cato deliberates whether he should marry" is a *hupothesis.* Integrating *theseis* into rhetoric was tantamount to extending the domain of orato-ry to philosophy, a move which provoked lively protests from philoso-phers. The quarrel abated when a middle term was found, attested since the time of Cicero, which distinguished two sorts of *theseis*: the "practical," ending in action, the competence of orators; and the "theo-retical," purely conceptual and the perquisite of philosophers. For ex-ample, "Should one engage in the administration of public affairs?" belongs to the former; "Does a Providence rule the world?" to the latter.

A dazzling demonstration of philosophic eloquence took place in Rome in 155 B.C., when Athens was fined for having attacked Oropos. The Athenians sent as ambassadors the heads of three philosophic schools, Karneades from the Academy, Kritolaos from the Lyceum, and Diogenes of Babylon from the Stoa. They were to plead their city's cause before the Roman Senate and to sue for removal of the fine. During their stay in Rome, they lectured with so much talent that listeners admired in them the ideal of the three genres of style as distinguished by the rhetoric of the time. Karneades represented a model of the grand style, Kritolaos the elegant style, and Diogenes a more sober style (according to the contemporaries Rutilius Rufus and Polybios, cited by Aulus Gellius, *Attic Nights* 6.14.10). Karneades was especially impressive, because, speaking *"con brio"* and *in utramque partem,* he delivered an encomium on justice one day and spoke against it the next (Lactantius, *Divine Institutes* 5.14.3–5 = Cicero, *On the Republic* 3.9). The Elder Cato was scandalized and urged the Senate to respond as quickly as possible, so that Rome could be delivered from these dangerous emissaries. That is what happened, to the benefit of Athens, for the fine was reduced from five hundred talents to one hundred. This episode, which establishes an important moment when philosophy, or more precisely, philosophic doubting, took root at Rome, offers a revealing piece of evidence on philosophy's rhetorical dimension. Perhaps there is a parallel, *mutatis mutandis,* with the embassy of 427 B.C., which is thought to have introduced the Gorgianic style to the Athenians.

In addition to the development of the philosophic schools and connected with them (the ties between Aristotelianism and the Alexandrians are notably well attested), the Hellenistic Age witnessed the development of philology which had repercussions on the history of rhetoric. In some centers like Alexandria and Pergamon, scholars and intellectuals were employed in collecting, preserving, and interpreting the major literary works embodying the cultural identity of the Greeks. In this pursuit they published editions, commentaries, lives of writers, dictionaries, collections of proverbs, and so on, focusing research principally on the poets—Homer above all, but not forgetting the orators. Thus, the

Pinakes of Kallimakhos, a sort of "catalogue raisonné" of Greek literature (third century B.C.), contained a section "Rhetoric." The biogra-
pher Hermippos of Smyrna (third century B.C.) dealt with the Attic orators. Didymos of Alexandria (first century B.C.), a tireless compiler who
was nicknamed the "Book Forgetter" *(bibliolathas)* because he no longer
remembered his own works (and no wonder: they were said to number
over 3,500), wrote a commentary on Demosthenes, of which one part,
dealing with the *Philippics,* was found at the beginning of the twentieth
century on papyrus (Berlin papyrus 9780, ed. L. Pearson and S.
Stephens, *Didymi in Demosthenem commenta* [Stuttgart, 1983]). Moreover, advances in grammatical theory accompanied research bearing on
style, on tropes and figures, as we saw, and also on the parts of the
speech, on the norms of correct usage of the language *(hellēnismos),* or
on dialects (for example, the great Stoic critic and grammarian Krates of
Mallos in the second century B.C. wrote a treatise *On the Attic Dialect*).

The Life of Eloquence in the Greek World

On the Greek mainland, on Rhodes, and in Asia Minor, there were
schools for teaching rhetoric to young people through instruction in
the theoretical systems, through practical exercises, through the study
of the great works of the past, and through debate with the philosophers. This instruction had simultaneously a dimension of general literary culture, which developed what had been learned in earlier grades,
as well as technical aspects and a concern for ethical and civic formation. It prepared future notables for their ever more important role in
the functioning of cities as the Hellenistic Age went on and as an aristocracy of birth, wealth, and public benefaction progressively imposed
itself, in practice, on the framework of democratic institutions.

The chief context for the exercise of Greek oratory was the city-
state, where rhetoric was useful for all the actions of political life undertaken through public discourse: deliberations, elections, negotiations,
and relations with other cities, federal states, and superpowers. In view
of the general instability of the world at this time, as well as the impos-

sibility of any long-lived policy and the unceasing change of circumstances, debates were often ardent and unforeseeable. Rhetoric was likewise useful in the numerous situations which required handling legal files and making courtroom speeches: public and private suits, participation in the boards of defenders chosen by the city to represent its interests, or mission as "extern judge"—a typical institution of the time—summoned as an outside arbitrator when a torn city proved unable to manage its conflicts on its own. Then the knowledge of the precepts of Hermagoras or the ingrained habit of declamation was certainly considered valuable. In addition, different types of literary men gave lectures in the cities, chiefly in the gymnasia, those civic institutions, which, over and above their original athletic purpose, became places more and more devoted to matters of the mind.

The rhetoric of the period certainly did not present itself as a technique divorced from the world, but as a general education preparing elites for public activity. In addition, it contributed to the maintaining of Hellenic values and participated in the movement to reinvigorate local traditions and research into the historical and mythological past. The cities of the Hellenistic world thereby constituted or reconstituted their political and religious identity.

FOURTH EXCURSUS

❧ Greek Political Eloquence Did Not Die at Khaironeia

It used to be said that the battle of Khaironeia, when Philip of Macedon defeated the Athenians and the Thebans in 338 B.C., marked the end of Greek liberty and consequently the end of the city-state system. Historians today have renounced this interpretation. They find, depending principally on epigraphic evidence, that the city-state remained a lively and active mode of political organization in the Greek world during the Hellenistic Age. The works of Louis Robert (1904–85), a world-renowned French scholar, played a major role in this change of view. Robert, who was the "compleat" Hellenist and remarkably expert in all aspects of Greek civilization, recognized quite clearly a further implication of this new approach, as it affected rhetoric. If the city continued to exist, the oratorical

practices bound up with the functioning of the city likewise continued, and so the received notion that Greek eloquence disappeared or
lost all importance after Demosthenes also had to be revised. It is
worth the effort to cite passages in which Louis Robert, throughout
his life, forcefully stressed this point. Not everyone has understood
the lesson; it bears repeating.

"It is a big mistake to think that the life of the city-states no longer had
importance in the Hellenistic Age or that the citizen no longer had tight
and necessary ties with his fatherland. Just as in the Classical period, he was
required, several times during the course of his life, to participate in decisions directly affecting his fortune, his liberty, and his life. And under the
Roman Republic one should think of the situation of the Greek cities
caught between Mithridates and the Romans, and between Romans in the
civil wars. The eloquence of the 'rhetor' Hybreas of Mylasa, for example, no
less involved the fate of his fatherland, between Rome and the Parthians of
Labienus, than the eloquence of Demosthenes and Hypereides." (*Etudes de
numismatique grecque* [Paris, 1951], p. 36 n. 1)

"Let us, by the way, get rid of the poorly-founded myth agreed upon by
modern historians (in political, institutional, and religious history), namely,
that political eloquence after Alexander and Demosthenes no longer existed. The history of the siege of Abydos by Philip [Philip V, in 200 B.C.] in
Polybios 16.30 and 34, of the citizens' heroic resistance and their self-mas-
sacre when the city fell, all of which was decided in assemblies and on the
advice of politicians and orators, is a bloody refutation of this theory. . . . It
is a fact among all the other facts which define the history of the Greek
cities of Europe and Asia from Alexander up to the peace of Augustus after
Actium." (*Monnaies grecques* [Geneva-Paris, 1967], p. 25)

"When, in 41, the Parthians with Labienus spread over Asia Minor, it
was a rhetor Zeno who got his compatriots to resist, just as Hybreas did at
Mylasa. . . . These deeds clearly reveal the role of the orators in the political
life of the Greek cities in the Hellenistic Age, including the first century
B.C. . . . It is the spoken word and constant political entreaties and policies
that count. . . . Resisting the Parthians or capitulating in 41 B.C. was just as
serious a matter for the life of the city and all the citizens, for the orators
preeminently, as deciding to fight at Khaironeia." ("Les inscriptions," in
Laodicée du Lycos [Quebec-Paris, 1969], pp. 306–7)

"The Greek city did not die at Khaironeia, or under Alexander, or during the course of the entire Hellenistic Age. To be sure, Athens and Sparta
no longer play the role these cities used to play in the Mediterranean—or in
the Aegean. But this decline in active international power does not change

anything in the workings of civic life, its activity, its responsibilities, and its dangers. The few great cities of Greece simply revert to having practically the same life hundreds of Greek cities had in the Classical period: no importance in world history, but responsibility for their own fate in the midst of wars, dangers, and hostile powers. Indeed, one might say, to the contrary, that Rhodes, or even Byzantium, plays a role in world politics in no way inferior to the role Athens played previously. In the unleashing of wars and princely rivalries, which were added to conflicts among neighbors, the fate—life, liberty, fortune—of each citizen still depends on the policy the assembly of the people will follow, and politicians and orators still have the same importance. It is even more so, if possible, when Rome intervenes in the affairs of the Greek world and subdues it little by little. In the second and first centuries, the involvement of the Greek cities multiplies in the conflicts and wars of Rome in the Aegean and Asia Minor, not to mention in the wars of Mithridates and in the Roman civil wars: a life of danger and, often, martyrdom." ("Théophane de Mytilène à Constantinople," *Comptes rendus de l'Académie des Inscriptions et Belles-Lettres* [1969]: 42 = *Opera Minora Selecta,* V, p. 561)

"The decrees for Polemaios and Menippos show sufficiently that the magistrates and ambassadors of Kolophon cannot do anything without 'persuading' the Roman magistrates, *peithein.* And this was the case throughout the second and first centuries B.C. Previously as well, it was a matter of *persuading* the powers that be, and first of all one's own fellow citizens on the best path to take. . . . In the majority of cases, the city was still active and it took full responsibility for its own fate. One has had to say this, and say it repeatedly. . . ." (Louis and Jeanne Robert, *Claros I: décrets hellénistiques,* I [Paris, 1989], p. 39)

A related phenomenon, likewise raised by Louis Robert, is the evolution of style in public documents, which increasingly bear a rhetorical stamp. It is another aspect of the presence of rhetoric in Hellenistic cities:

"I have occasionally noted the evolution, as it appears to me, in administrative writing style. After the style properly called Hellenistic, . . . the 'late Hellenistic Age' introduced contemporary rhetoric. I believe that this is owing principally to a social phenomenon. More and more the society's evolution removes the affairs of the city from the sovereign action of the people's assembly and the democracy and puts them in the hands of a minority of notables, more or less hereditary, who underwrite numerous essential services of the state with their private wealth and receive in return honors increasingly numerous and striking. This new aristocracy of the cities has a very careful upbringing, and it honors and cultivates *paideia* ('culture'); rhetoric takes an increasingly greater place in the education of the youth and elites; also the 'secretary,' a high official who writes decrees and letters, writes them according to the rhetorical taste of the day. This evolution continues under the Empire." ("Recherches épigraphiques, VII," *Revue des études anciennes* 62 [1960]:325–26 = *Opera Minora Selecta,* II, pp. 841–42) ❧

In 1972, C. W. Wooten counted around forty Greek orators of the Hellenistic Age known through *testimonia* or quotations; this number is a minimum and ought to be increased today, especially in view of the new names found in inscriptions. These orators can be divided into three principal groups, according to their date and the sources where they appear:

1. At the end of the fourth century and during the third, politicians are attested at Athens who continue the tradition of the Attic orators. Examples: Demokhares, the nephew of Demosthenes; Kharisios, who was compared to Lysias; or Kleokhares.

2. For the end of the third century and for the second, we know through Polybios and Livy of numerous politicians, from Greece itself and from Asia Minor, who participated verbally in the conflicts and negotiations of the day, within the context of the Aitolian and Achaian Leagues, the Macedonian wars, the war against Antiochus of Syria, and relations with Rome. To this series Kineas must be added, a brilliant orator from Thessaly, mentioned by Plutarch, who was counselor to king Pyrrhos in the third century. Polybios rather frequently records speeches delivered throughout the period he discusses (orations before assemblies, generals' exhortations to their troops, speeches by ambassadors), and he takes as guiding principles in this matter moderation and utility. He refuses every gratuitous display of eloquence on the part of the historian and seeks above all to reconstitute the arguments that were used, putting them back into their context so as to make more comprehensible their sense and import (12.25–28; 36.1).

3. For the second and first century, Cicero and Strabo take up the tradition and make us aware of yet other Greeks who are almost always in contact with Rome, involved in the wars with Mithridates and in the

civil wars. Particularly celebrated at the time was Hybreas of Mylasa, who governed his city in the midst of the Parthian wars and the intrigues of Marc Antony and Labienus and who knew how to turn a striking phrase in his assembly speeches and declamations. From men such as these, a composite portrait emerges of the Hellenistic orator. Typically he was from an influential family, studied in an important center of learning, participated actively in politics and diplomacy, and practiced oratory informed by theoretical research and contemporary philosophic controversy. Often he was a professor and a man of letters.

A good example is one Potamon of Mytilene on Lesbos, who played a leading role in the political life of his city (ca. 75 B.C. to 15 A.D.; the evidence about him is collected in F. Jacoby, *Die Fragmente der griechischen Historiker*, Part II, B, no. 147, and by R. W. Parker in *Zeitschrift für Papyrologie und Epigraphik* 85 [1991]: 115–29). Numerous inscriptions in his own and other cities paid him homage. A monument to his glory, named the Potamoneion, was erected on the acropolis of Mytilene, and his entire family, particularly his son, shared in his power and renown. He successfully conducted three embassies dispatched by his fatherland to Julius Caesar and Augustus. He wrote an *Encomium of Brutus* and an *Encomium of Caesar,* a curious pair whose historical background is unfortunately unknown. Around 33 B.C., he took part, with Theodore of Gadara and Antipater, in a contest of eloquence at Rome whose purpose was to select the rhetoric teacher for the future emperor Tiberius, a child at the time. Theodore won. Besides his encomia, Potamon was the author of historical works and a treatise *On the Complete Orator (Peri teleiou rhētoros),* which can be compared, in any case for the title, with Cicero's *Orator.* He had a school and excelled, it is said, in declamation. Philanthropist and orator, moving between the Greek world and Rome, Potamon exemplifies the rhetoric of the era.

Inscriptions, of which there never cease to be new discoveries and publications, permit a close-up look at orations actually delivered. For instance, a decree, dating from 206/205 B.C., was found in 1965 by the excavators of the sanctuary of Leto at Xanthos in Lycia. It records the arrival in Xanthos of an embassy from Kytenion (a city of Doris in Greece, north of Delphi) and gives a synopsis of the ambassadors' speech (edited by J. Bousquet in *Revue des études grecques* 101 [1988]: 12–53]. They were seeking financial aid for the reconstruction of their ramparts, which an earthquake had destroyed. Here is an example of an oratorical format quite common in the Hellenistic period—the ambassador's speech, more precisely, the ambassador's speech of petition for help after an earthquake, a well-attested custom. The ambassadors from Kytenion had recourse to the usual arguments in such cases (appeal to pity, praise of the city being solicited, promises of recognition), adding as well a complicated demonstration aimed at establishing a tie of kinship between Xanthos and Kytenion. Leto, goddess patron of Xanthos, was Apollo's mother, while Doros, the eponymous hero of the Dorians and therefore ancestor of Kytenion, was the grandfather of Apollo's wife, Koronis. This mythological montage was an appeal to motivations people of the time would have thought important (foundation narratives and legendary ties associating Greek cities on both sides of the Aegean), and that is why the emissaries saw in this a weighty argument. Alas, the inhabitants of Xanthos contributed only five hundred drachmas, which was not so generous (less than ten years later they will pay four hundred just for his fee to the rhetor Themistokles of Ilion who had come to lecture among them). The ambassadors' subtle rhetoric was answered by the no less subtle rhetoric of the Xanthians, a rhetoric we will always have with us, that of begging off—of ever so politely hemming and hawing:

You may be sure that the Xanthians, whose philanthropy is second to none, would display their goodwill, if the finances of the city were not so weakened. Since, however, the public resources have run out while expenses have continued to rise, and since the citizens will brook no tax increase according to an economic policy decreed to last nine more years, and since the wealthiest of the citizens have already paid large contributions expressly for the current crisis, all of which we have detailed to the ambassadors, for all these reasons the city does not have the means to help. At the same time, however, it is aggrieved to have to turn down relations fallen into such distress. Be it resolved therefore that the archons float a bond and pay the ambassadors with the proceeds five hundred drachmas for the rebuilding of their city's walls and extend to them the customary gifts of guestfriendship.

(trans. WEH, after Bousquet)

A stele containing an encomium of the goddess Isis, inscribed around 100 B.C. (ed. by Y. Grandjean, *Une nouvelle arétalogie d'Isis à Maronée* [Leiden, 1975]), was discovered in 1969 at Maroneia on the northern coast of the Aegean Sea. The introduction explains the circumstances of its composition: Isis cured the anonymous author of an eye disease, and he erects this monument of grateful praise, engraved in marble, to celebrate the power and benefaction of the goddess. This text belongs to a genre called "aretology," which, strictly speaking, is the narrative of a miracle performed by a god. Inscriptions and papyri from the Hellenistic and Imperial Ages preserve numerous examples, honoring Asklepios, Isis, and Sarapis especially. What stands out about the Maroneia inscription in this context is its pronounced rhetorical character. The text is in prose, and the plan, themes, and style conform to the rules of the encomium. The treatment of the subject shows a passion for generalization, which prompts the author to be satisfied with quickly mentioning his cure in order to develop at much greater length the praise of Isis overall (this generalizing can be seen in other documents relating to Isis as well). His tone belongs more to hymn than to narrative. Thanks to this document, we can glimpse yet another facet of Greek rhetoric, namely, religious rhetoric. Although traditionally literature had recourse to poetry to celebrate the gods and to communicate with them, prose, notably rhetorical prose, begins to be used for this purpose. This important innovation doubtless reveals a double change, affecting relations with the gods to whom the faithful begin to address themselves in a more direct manner (to the extent that prose, even elaborate prose, is more direct than poetry), and affecting relations with the literary language at the heart of which rhetoric takes an ever more prominent place.

In the middle of the first century B.C., Antiochus I of Kommagene (one of Rome's small vassal kingdoms) had a grandiose mausoleum built on Nemrut Dağ, one of the heights in the Anti-Taurus of present-day eastern Turkey. The monument, excavated by German archeologists at the end of the nineteenth century, notably brought to light a long Greek inscription engraved in duplicate and containing the rules of a religious foundation created on the site in honor of the gods and the deified ruler (ed. W. Dittenberger, *Orientis Graeci Inscriptiones Selectae*, 383; H. Waldmann, *Die kommagenischen Kultreformen* [Leiden, 1973], pp. 59–79). Befitting the solemnity of the site and its purpose, the text, in which the king speaks in the first person, is written in a style that is extremely elaborate in its plan of figures, diction, and rhythms. Described by Eduard Norden as a "dithyramb in prose," the Nemrut Dağ inscription is an important document for our knowledge of Asianism, the stylistic current then very much in vogue.

The notion of the "Asiatic style" (in Latin, *asiatica dictio* [Cicero], in Greek, *asianos zēlos* [Strabo]) appears in the first century B.C., but the phenomenon it covers was much older and lasted throughout the entire Hellenistic period and beyond. This is a showy and recherché style, practiced by orators and writers from Rhodes and Asia Minor (whence its name) and also by authors from other places: the Athenian Amphikrates, for example, seems to have been an "Asianist." According to Cicero, there were two types of Asianism: one "sententious and studied," illustrated by the two brothers Hierokles and Menekles of Alabanda; the other "swift and impetuous" with "refined and ornate" diction, illustrated by Aiskhylos of Knidos and Aiskhines of Miletos (*Brutus* 325). The one used short and rhythmic sentences built on brief clauses *(kommata)*, aphorisms, wordplay, conceits; the other, ease of expression, ornamentation, richness, poeticisms, neologisms. All gradations between these two extremes and all combinations were possible. Unfortunately, we no longer have the texts that would allow us to judge on the basis of evidence. Hegesias of Magnesia was the reputed creator of Asianism (third century B.C.; the evidence for him is in F. Jacoby, *Die Fragmente der griechischen Historiker,* Part II, B, no. 142). Author of a history of Alexander, an encomium of Rhodes, and other speeches, he has passed into history for his jagged style, rich in grandiloquent exclamations and daring effects. We can credit him, when speaking on Alexander's destruction of Thebes, with expressions like "woe has left voiceless the place of clarion voice" (Jacoby, F 7); "Laid low by a king's madness, their city has become more tragic than a tragedy" (F 10); "What woe, that the city which sowed the sown men of Sparta is seedless" (F 14). Or, again, this sentence, which was startling for its unusual word order: "From Magnesia the Great, of Sipylos a citizen am I" (Jacoby, F 19; all trans. WEH). Hegesias did not invent this unusual style *ex nihilo*. In fact, he developed and exaggerated stylistic effects harking back to the sophists and the Gorgianic style. Glimpses of the clipped Asiatic style appear in the citations of different orators handed down by Rutilius Lupus and Seneca the Elder. As for the other form of Asianism, it is illustrated by the Nemrut Dağ inscription noted above and by official public documents from the third and second centuries B.C.

Most ancient authors have a qualified or pejorative opinion of the Asiatic style, reproaching it for its excesses and lapses of taste. Hegesias became the *bête noire* of criticism, vilified in the second century B.C. by Agatharkhides of Knidos and put down by Cicero in a single phrase: "anyone acquainted with him need seek no further for an example of ineptitude" (*Orator* 226). The stylistic theories which developed at the time, emphasizing moderation, appropriateness, and the limited use of effects, were probably directed in part against the exuberance of the Asiatic style: the theorists defined the virtues to counter the prevalent vice. Hegesias, however, did have his admirers, among them Gorgias the Younger, who quoted him often in the treatise preserved by Rutilius Lupus, and perhaps Varro, if we may believe a witticism of Cicero. Cicero himself did not fail to be interested, even seduced a little, by contemporary Asianists. For us moderns, without the wherewithal to judge, the idea of Asianism is interesting because it spotlights a certain type of virtuosic, theatrical, baroque, even rococo style that really seems to have been an innovation of the Hellenistic Age. This innovation may call to mind the "baroque" style in architecture, the expressive sculpture, the tendency toward the "pathetic," the theatricality and tragic dimension observable, for example, in the art of Pergamon. Thus, the Asiatic style harmonized with the artistic currents of its era.

Chapter Five

The Roman Way and Romanization

"Carthage must be obliterated!"

> [*delendam esse Carthaginem,* the advice the Elder Cato is said to have pro-
> claimed constantly in all his speeches, no matter their subject] (cf. Florus,
> *Roman History* 1.31 [2.15], 4–5; trans. WEH)

*"For just how long, Catiline, are you going to abuse our patience? . . . What
times, what customs!"*

> [*Quo usque tandem abutere, Catilina, patientia nostra? . . . O tempora! o mores!*]
> (Cicero, *First Oration Against Catiline* 1–2; trans. WEH)

"I came, I saw, I conquered."

> [*Veni, vidi, vici,* Caesar's words, summing up his campaign against king
> Pharnakes] (Suetonius, *Caesar* 37.2; trans. WEH)

These sentences have been famous since antiquity, and they abide in
the memory of all who have studied Latin even today. What is the
source of their power? First, it derives from the power of those speaking:
Cato the censor, Cicero the consul, Caesar the dictator, statesmen holding the highest magistracies. Next, it comes from the circumstances, in
which the fates of Rome and its enemies, indeed, the fate of the world,
were at stake. And it comes from their very content, where rigor rules.
Finally, it comes from the inherent energy of the Latin language, which
permits saying a lot with few words. Plutarch, who translated Caesar's
sentence into Greek, observes that the original is superior because "in
Latin . . . the words have the same inflectional ending, and so a brevity
which is most impressive" (*Life of Caesar* 50.4). Through these examples,
an image emerges of politicians who do not waste words and who de-

pend more on their actions, their convictions and their personal authority. Such is the ideal of the old Roman, "beautiful with the patina of
age." This ideal lies beneath all Roman rhetoric—even if it clearly does
not sum it up completely—and that is where one must begin. It results
from specific circumstances, as much ideological as linguistic, social, political, or institutional. Let us lay out this background, which so profoundly differs from what is observable in the Greek world, and which
constitutes in a way "Roman-ness" in rhetoric. This Roman-ness will be
enriched later on by a "Romanization" of Greek spoils.

The Background of Roman Rhetoric

Greece had at its very beginnings a literature which made varied and
supple use of the art of speaking, and which set forth as models heroes
who were clever orators. This does not exist in Rome: no Homer here,
no Odysseus. On the contrary, the ancient Roman model is an orator
who speaks with careful consideration and who counts on his status—
age, nobility, prestige—to guarantee the worth of his words. The
"weightiness" (gravitas) and "personal authority" (auctoritas) of the orator are essential elements of the discourse; he is listened to not so much
for his words in themselves but for his position in the city, which necessarily gives his words their value, as numerous anecdotes relate. Thus
Appius Claudius, summoned before the Popular Assembly in the year
following his consulate (470 B.C.), refused to argue in his own defense
and instead blasted his accusers with the firmness of his remarks whose
strength derived from his prestige as a former consul:

There was the same expression on his countenance, the same arrogance in his
glance, the same fire in his speech; so markedly, in fact, that a great part of the
plebs feared Appius no less when a defendant than they had feared him as consul.

(Livy 2.61.6)

In the second century, Scipio Nasica, having to confront popular
protests, let loose: "Be silent, citizens, if you please! I understand better
than you what is for the public good"; similarly, Scipio Aemilianus:

"Let people to whom Italy is a step-mother hold their tongues." M. Aemilius Scaurus, when accused, defended himself with the following line of reasoning: "Varius Severus, who was born in some dago backwater, says that Aemilius Scaurus, corrupted by royal hire, betrayed the empire of the Roman people. Aemilius Scaurus denies any connection with such guilt. Which of the two are you going to believe?" (Valerius Maximus, *Memorable Doings and Sayings,* 3.7.3; 6.2.3; 3.7.8, Loeb trans. modified). History records that success crowned these words, the audience in each case impressed with the authority of the speaker, and these anecdotes were handed down as illustrations of the Roman tradition.

The spoken word at Rome is a serious matter. Originally it is sacred and involves the order of the world. The two verbs meaning "to speak" in Latin, *fari* and *dicere,* belong to two strong roots, which contain, respectively, the idea of speech that has religious value and is powerful by its very existence (root **bhā-,* cf. *fatum* = "fate") and the idea of speech with the authority to show what must be, to proclaim, to establish (root **deik-,* cf. Greek *dikē* = "justice") (also attached to the root *bhā-* is the Greek verb *phanai* = "to speak," which shows that the difference between Rome and Greece on this point is not to be exaggerated). The spoken word is "performative," in the sense that it is, in and of itself, an action, that it has efficacy and brings about a new situation. It serves to decree, foretell, or promulgate rules rather than to effect exchanges of views or to debate. Often it brooks no response. When poorly used, it is dangerous, creating deadly innovations. That is why communication, especially that which takes place in the public space, must be regulated, controlled, and subordinated. In aristocratic Roman society, everyone has a place, occasionally public offices, and he expresses himself accordingly. The pronouncements of priests and magistrates have particular weight, amplified by the ritual and the visible signs of power investing them (fasces, distinctive dress, curule chair, etc.).

It is not a question, therefore, of delivering brilliant and subtle orations, but appropriate speeches of which one can be proud. The principal quality is "trustworthiness" *(fides).* Forcefulness and brevity are its partners.

The very nature of the Latin language tended this way. Among its chief characteristics the phonetic autonomy of words, the absence of the article, the abhorrence of the abstract, and pithiness stood out. Poetry exploited all these potentialities, beginning with the pre-literary *carmen,* which plays with rhythm and alliteration, and so did the legal and religious formulations, which are so important in archaic Latin. Archaic Latin prose, for its part, found achieving a periodic style difficult (Cicero, *On the Orator* 3.198). Instead, it demonstrates qualities of force, gravity, and richness chiefly by parataxis (Quintilian, *Institutio Oratoria* 12.10.36).

To teach this regulated use of speech there was only one school, the school of "ancestral custom" *(mos maiorum).* Since the importance of the extended family structure and the omnipotence of the *pater familias* were givens, the family was the first educational setting. The young boy, taken in hand by his father, learned to do as his father did, imitating his words and his manner. Oratorical education was therefore part of a larger process, which consisted in forming the social being through lessons and through example and in transmitting directly to him the values of his class and family, the sources of *auctoritas.* This is the way Cato the Elder educated his son, going so far as to make himself responsible for teaching him how to read. His contemporary, Aemilius Paulus, although of a more modern bent, and later, Cicero, likewise oversaw the cultural upbringing of their sons.

After that, when he had put off the *toga praetextata* and put on the toga of manhood, the young man graduated to "apprenticeship in public life" *(tirocinium fori).* Put in the charge of a leading citizen, he became a part of his retinue and was instructed by his example:

Well, then, in the good old days the young man who was destined for the oratory of the bar, after receiving the rudiments of a sound training at home, and storing his mind with liberal culture, was taken by his father, or his relations, and placed under the care of some orator who held a leading position at Rome. The youth had to get the habit of following his patron about, of escorting him in public, of supporting him at all his appearances as a speaker, whether in the law courts or on the platform, hearing also his word-combats at first hand, standing by him in his duellings, and learning, as it were, to fight in the fighting-line.

(Tacitus, *Dialogus* 34.1–2)

In this sort of upbringing, apprenticeship in the law had an important place. Cicero, for example, received his legal education from two great jurisprudents: his father took him to Q. Mucius Scaevola the Augur, and Cicero next moved on to Scaevola's homonym and cousin, Q. Mucius Scaevola the Pontiff. (Cf. J. A. Crook, *Law and Life of Rome*, on the place of law in Roman society.)

Such was the traditional background, as the ancient documents, as well as later historians' accounts present it. This ideological model of rhetoric harked back to old, pragmatic roots (peasant and military) of which the Romans were proud and which they deliberately cultivated. Thus it remained alive even in the face of innovations, especially in aristocratic and conservative families. It lasted through the evolutions of institutions and the vicissitudes of history.

In the first stages of Roman history, during the monarchy, oratory probably played a minor role. It was the Republican regime that developed the institutional use of the spoken word, before two principal types of audience, the Senate and the people, the two pillars of the state (following the formula SPQR: *Senatus populusque Romanus*).

The Senate had three hundred members (increased to six hundred by Sulla and nine hundred by Caesar), recruited for life from among the leaders of the great patrician families and plebeians who were former magistrates. It functioned as a council, called upon to deliberate and render decrees *(senatusconsulta)*. Although theoretically it had few decision-making powers, the Senate did, however, by reason of its prestige and the interplay of institutions, actually exercise some essential duties. It conducted foreign policy, had important responsibilities in religious and financial matters, and also intervened, by virtue of its powers of oversight and approval, in legislative and executive domains. Its sessions were not open to the public; they were held in the Curia, situated on the Forum (and sometimes in other enclosures, any place being acceptable as long as it was a "temple," that is, a consecrated space). The magistrate who summoned the meeting to order and presided read the day's agenda and then called upon the senators to express their views *(sententiae)*. Everyone spoke from his place, in an order determined by his rank of class and seniority, beginning with the "first of the senators" *(princeps senatus)*. Once someone had started to speak, he could not be interrupted even if he strayed from the issue. The lowest down on the list almost never got the chance to express themselves. Senators voted by physically moving to stand beside the speaker whose opinion they favored. The citadel of Roman eloquence during the Republic, the Senate represented a completely specialized situation for speech, where the discourse was framed by preexisting givens: highly experienced speakers and listeners, the weightiness of the social hierarchy, prearranged alliances among persons and groups, and *esprit de corps*. These factors did not destroy the power of discourse but did affect it, insofar as persuasion was preconditioned and not open-ended, though nonetheless real for all that.

The people, on its side, came together in the assembly settings called *comitia*: the Centuriate Assembly *(comitia centuriata)*, of a military character organized according to army ranks, and the Tribal Assembly *(comitia tributa)*, where the citizenry was divided by tribes. These assemblies had as their principal function the election of magistrates and the passage of laws. While the *comitia centuriata* met in the Campus Martius, the other assemblies took place in a spot designed for this purpose in the Forum, the Comitium, the political center of the city. It gave on to the Curia, and comprised a circular area, a tribunal (the Rostra, named after the prows [*rostra*] of ships hung there to commemorate the naval victory at Antium in 338 B.C.), and bleachers. Later on sessions were moved to the neighborhood of the temple of Castor and Pollux and to the Circus Flaminius, which all could accommodate thousands, indeed tens of thousands of people. In total, the popular assemblies convened numerous times, because elections came around frequently (most magistracies were elective and annual), and the legislative activity was considerable. The Roman citizen was summoned around twenty times at least during the year, for sessions that could last several days. "One scarcely exaggerates in saying that the citizen's job (at Rome) was a fulltime occupation" (C. Nicolet).

Voting was the assemblies' principal task. Speakers chosen in advance could voice their opinions there, under the authority of the session's chairman. In addition, some speeches were delivered in numerous, informal or preparatory assemblies, meetings, and deliberative (i.e., non-voting) gatherings. These speeches, in particular, declared candidacies and proposed laws. They were called *contiones* (the word *contio*, a syncopated form of *conventio*, originally denotes a gathering, then the speech pronounced in this gathering; it is also applied to the speeches generals deliver to their troops). The rhetorical difference between the oration before the Senate and the *contio* was quite marked:

And these ends can be achieved with less apparatus in the Senate, as that is a wise deliberative body, and one should leave room for many others to speak, besides avoiding any suspicion of a display of talent, whereas a public meeting *(contio)* permits of the full employment of powerful and weighty oratory, and requires variety. . . . But as the orator's chief stage seems to be the platform at a public meeting, it naturally results that we are stimulated to employ the more ornate kind of oratory.

(Cicero, On the Orator 2.333–34, 338)

The assemblies could be tumultuous, if we can believe Vergil, who, surely with the Roman reality in mind, compares Neptune's calming the waves to the orator's quieting the unruly crowd:

And just as often happens when in a great nation tumult has arisen, the base rabble furiously rage, and now torches and stones fly, madness supplying arms; then, if by chance they set eyes on a man honored for noble character and service, they are silent and stand by with attentive ears; with speech he sways their passion and soothes their breasts.

(Aeneid 1.148–53, Loeb modified)

As for judicial institutions, the praetor and the tribunals of the *centumviri* and the *decemviri* exercised civil jurisdiction. Criminal jurisdiction, exercised by the people (the *comitia* had judicial powers), was early on delegated to specialized juries, the *quaestiones,* either extraordinary *(quaestiones extra ordinem)* or—the most important—standing *(quaestiones perpetuae).* Instituted in the second century B.C., they were the chief venue for great legal eloquence. A magistrate, often a praetor, presided over these juries, which were composed of scores of jurors drawn by lot from preestablished lists, at first from among only the senatorial order and then from among members of the equestrian order[1]

---

1. During the Republic, these were essentially those members of the wealthy elite who did not belong to the Senate because they were too young to run for public office or because they chose not to pursue such a career. Also called "knights"—WEH.

and the tribunes of the Treasury as well, following an assignment varying case by case. The parties pleaded their own cases; it was common for
an accused to have several defenders. After the legal preliminaries, the
session was devoted to hearing the courtroom speeches and voting by
the jury. A rehearing was possible if the jury felt insufficiently informed,
with the result that the proceeding could last a long time. The purview
of the *quaestiones perpetuae* continued to increase throughout the second
and first centuries B.C., to include cases *de repetundis* (extorting funds
from Rome's subjects), *de peculatu* (embezzlement), *de ambitu* (election
fraud), *de maiestate* (any attack on the State, by abuse of power, among
other ways), *de sicariis et veneficiis* (armed insurrection and poisoning),
and so forth. Given the nature of these crimes, many of which implicated the higher levels of administration, the accused most often belonged
to the leading classes of the State. They were liable to capital punishment, exile, a fine or diminution of their civil rights; in any event, their
status and power were at risk, placed in the hands of their peers—
friends or adversaries. The members of the aristocracy settled their
scores and defined their spheres of influence through the expedient of
the courts. The *quaestiones perpetuae* actively participated in all phases of
the political combat of the last centuries of the Roman Republic.

The courts held session everywhere in Rome, and especially in the
Forum, which on certain days was "thick with tribunals" (Cicero, *Verrines* 2.5.143, WEH) all working at the same time. Sessions took place
in the open air or, in bad weather, in a nearby "basilica" (meeting hall).
The defense and the prosecution were seated on benches, the members
of the jury had seats a little higher, and the presiding magistrate was on
a dais. The first permanent courtroom (the Aurelium, on the Forum)
was built around 80 B.C. These settings, since they permitted the presence of a large public, often invested trials with an air of spectacle, owing to the solemnity of the oral proceeding, the impressive processions
(of lawyers, witnesses, relatives, clients, and friends) accompanying the
litigants, the theatricality (of litigants' wearing mourning clothes and
carrying images of the dead), and the eloquence of the patrons *(patroni)*.

The *patronus* was, in fact, the primary figure of eloquence in the law court. Patronage (here, again, a typically Roman concept) was a form of social bond, very old and deep, consisting in an exchange of mutual obligations between patron and clients. The latter had to show respect to their patron and to put themselves and their resources at his disposal, and in return the patron had to protect his clients, in the name of the values trustworthiness *(fides)*, care *(diligentia)*, and duty *(officium)*. This protection notably involved defending clients in legal straits. The patron was, therefore, by definition, of an elevated status, above the status of the client being defended. In contrast to the Athenian speechwriter, whose work was frequently considered infra dig, the Roman *patronus* possessed a personal authority and social influence that weighed heavily in the service of his client. After the lex Cincia (204 B.C.), a client was forbidden to pay his patron for a courtroom speech, according to a clause outlawing fees or gifts *ob causam orandam* (Tacitus, *Annals* 11.5.3); but the law did not rule out gifts given some time after the trial, or legacies, or numerous marks of recognition from those who had been defended. Originally intended to protect ordinary citizens from the greed of the powerful, the lex Cincia prevented the accused from being pressured in difficult circumstances and being extorted of large sums. But it aimed in no way to deprive patrons of the normal recompense for judicial aid, that is, the marks of gratitude lavished at leisure over the long term, the very sum and substance of *gratia*. This last is a rich concept, which encompasses at one and the same time the grace or "favor" of which one is the beneficiary and the "favor" returned, as grateful recognition. Within the context of judicial patronage, the members of the Roman aristocracy were therefore often led to speak in court to maintain their network of influence, which rested on complex bonds of kinship, solidarity, obligation, enmity, and vendetta. They absolutely had to be eloquent.

Thus all aspects of Roman political life required mastery of the spoken word, whether in the Senate, the assemblies, or the law courts. Eloquence was one of the necessary conditions of power, one of the essential "charisms" (J.-M. David).

Romans also practiced eloquence in the funeral eulogy *(laudatio funebris)* bestowed upon the dead of the nobility. At the time of the obsequies, after an impressive funeral cortege, the son or nearest relative of the deceased delivered an oration in honor of the latter and his family, on the Forum, before the assembled people. This practice lasted throughout Roman history, down to the Empire. After the fall of the Republic, the homage was no longer reserved to males but could be paid to women as well, and to the "private" panegyric *(laudatio privata)* was added a "public" speech *(laudatio publica),* that is, one delivered by a magistrate so charged, under the same conditions as the "private" eulogy. These orations, eminently political, played an important role in the self-affirming strategies of the great families. The *laudatio* tradition impressed the Greek historians of Rome, Polybios and Dionysios of Halikarnassos, who underline the peculiarity of the *laudatio* compared to the *epitaphios* at Athens (Polybios 6.53–54; Dionysios, *Antiquities of the Romans* 5.17). Whereas the Athenian speech was collective, dedicated to all of the city's dead, the Roman speech was private, dedicated to a family; whereas the Athenian speech praised soldiers fallen in war, the Roman speech praised great personages who had given the State a lifetime of service. The difference in rhetorical forms here reflects in a particularly striking fashion the differences in socio-political structures and ideological displays. At Rome, families preserved the text of the panegyrics, and these orations provided source material for historians as well as constituting the first monuments of Latin eloquence. Shakespeare has immortalized the *laudatio* by recreating, based upon ancient sources, Marc Antony's funeral oration for Caesar *(Julius Caesar,* 3.2).

All these forms of eloquence were practiced throughout the rest of Italy and in the provinces, where provincial senates, assemblies, trials, and funeral eulogies occurred. But at Rome itself, political communication had unique force and frequency, because the city was the center of power and the hub of all networks. There the game of influence and allegiances, of groups and factions founded on blood, interest, and conviction, gave to rhetoric an unparalleled intensity.

This intensity increased in the second and first centuries B.C., when social struggles brought the development of new forms of eloquence, associated with reform politicians depending on mass appeal (the so-called *populares*), with interventions by the tribunes of the plebs, or even with grandstanding by ambitious young men who launched their political careers in the "Public Arena" with a successful prosecution of a senator. The traditional rhetorical model of the senatorial aristocracy took a beating at the hands of orators with a preference for prosecution over the defense to which the ideal *patronus* more often inclined. Instead of maintaining a dignified and superior posture, they used violent forms of pathos, begged and pleaded for sympathy *(miseratio),* and gesticulated wildly. Hence rhetoric warred with rhetoric; rhetorical models with rhetorical models.

We should not forget, either, that the period from the third to the first century B.C. was the time of Rome's conquest of the entire Mediterranean region. The economic, political, and military interests at stake were huge, greater than they had ever been in any other city of the ancient world.

Finally, during the last days of the Republic, an atmosphere of permanent revolution prevailed, with all that that implies about acts of violence, corruption, and stress on institutions, assemblies, and courts.

All these elements combined to give an unprecedented ferocity to political struggles. The difference between Athens and Rome from this point of view is enormous. In comparison with the Athenians of the fifth and fourth centuries, the Romans of the Republic lived in a world more difficult to dominate morally and incorporate, a world, moreover, subject to external influences (money, Hellenism, etc.), a world mutating rapidly, where a single city, Rome, was in the process of becoming mistress of the world, a world of civil wars, dictatorships, and internal struggles. This was all part, as well, of the background of Roman rhetoric.

Stars of Roman Rhetoric before Cicero

Malcovati's collection of the remains of Republican Roman oratory numbers 176 names of orators, stretching from the start of the third century to the end of the first century B.C. Around half of these predate Cicero, while the rest are contemporary with him or slightly later.

These orators for the most part were prominent politicians, who exercised their eloquence in the institutional settings described above. Their orations, excepting Cicero's, have not been preserved, and are known only through rewritings, quotations, and *testimonia,* transmitted chiefly by Cicero in the *Brutus,* by the historians (Sallust, Livy, Dionysios of Halikarnassos, Plutarch, Appian), by those who collected *exempla* (Valerius Maximus), or by the scholars of the imperial era (Aulus Gellius). This transmission, of necessity, entailed selection and alteration. Nonetheless, it permits us to distinguish the key figures. We take a look here at those from the time before Cicero.

The first important speech of Roman history occurs with the fable of the dispute between the stomach and the other parts of the body, delivered in the opening years of the Republic, in 494 B.C., and reported by Livy (2.32) among others. The soldiers of the plebs had ceased obeying the consuls and had seceded to the Sacred Mount (or to the Aventine Hill). To negotiate with them, the Senate dispatched Menenius Agrippa, "an eloquent man and dear to the plebeians as being one of themselves by birth." Once introduced to the camp, he told a story: how the rest of the body seceded from the stomach, criticizing it for lazily nurturing itself at their expense, and how they began to waste away, so that they came to understand that the stomach, though nourished by them, nourished them no less in return. The speech had an immediate effect, and the wrath of the plebs subsided, so that it was possible to resolve the dispute (through the creation of the tribunes of the plebs). This famous anecdote has all the appearances of a legendary elaboration founded on an authentic base difficult to define. Rhetorically, it shows two important characteristics: political eloquence being deployed against a background of social conflict, and eloquence of an ancient, pre-technical type, resting on a simple narrative and not on reasoned demonstration. This is what interested Livy, who describes the fable as "in the quaint and uncouth style of that age" *(prisco illo dicendi et horrido modo)—* which does not mean that it might not be persuasive.

With Appius Claudius Caecus, we enter onto firmer historical footing, and this is why Malcovati begins her collection with him. He was a distant relative of the Appius Claudius mentioned at the start of this

chapter. Censor, then consul, at the turn of the fourth and third centuries B.C., responsible for measures having to do with religious cults,
alphabet reform, and publication of the law, builder of the Appian
Way, author, perhaps, of Pythagorean verses, Appius Claudius Caecus
was an enterprising and innovative statesman. He has a place in the history of rhetoric because of a speech he delivered to the Senate in 280
B.C., when he was already blind and elderly, in which he advocated the
rejection of peace overtures by king Pyrrhus, who had invaded Italy
(and rightly so, since Pyrrhus was to beat a retreat of his own accord in
the following years). It seems that a version of this speech circulated in
Cicero's day (besides the poetic version Ennius gave of it in the *Annales*), but it was probably not authentic.

Cato the Elder (Marcus Porcius Cato, called Cato the Censor, 234–
149 B.C.) was the first Roman orator to publish his speeches, not being
content to archive them privately (as was done, for example, with the
laudationes funebres). He circulated them, whether in separate form or
as part of his historical work entitled *Origins*. Cicero claims to have
read more than 150 (*Brutus* 65). We know of eighty, all nothing but titles or brief fragments.

The speeches of Cato go hand in hand with his brilliant military
and political career: addresses to the armies he commanded in Spain;
diplomatic dispatches at the time when he was an ambassador, at
Athens, for example; severe condemnations during his time as censor;
numerous courtroom pleadings; addresses to the Senate and to the
people. In 167, he delivered an oration before the Senate on behalf of
the Rhodians, against whom some wanted to declare war; in 149, the
last year of his life, he assailed before the people Servius Sulpicius Galba, himself a great orator, who only got off because of the pity he was
able to arouse in the judges. These two speeches show up among the
fragments of the *Origins* (books 5 and 7). Cicero praises Cato's oratorical talent highly, noting its effectiveness as well as its variety of tone and
form (Cato particularly excelled at invective); but at the same time he
expresses reservations about its still stiff, gnarled, and insufficiently
rhythmic style.

Two remarks drawn from a work of uncertain form addressed to his son Marcus show that Cato was also the earliest Roman theorist of rhetoric. The first asserts that "the orator, Marcus, my son, is a good man skilled in speaking" (frag. 14, ed. Jordan: *Orator est, Marce fili, vir bonus, dicendi peritus,* WEH). As profound as it is concise, this definition points up the necessary connection between two facets. One, oratorical competence, is the mastery of an art or technique *(dicendi peritus)*. The other is the moral and social quality of someone who belongs to the "good citizens," members of the upper classes and devoted to the traditional institutions and values of Rome (the sense of the notion *vir bonus,* which is found elsewhere in Cato's works). The second remark of Cato, "stick to the subject, the words will follow" (frag. 15: *Rem tene, verba sequentur,* WEH), opposes mastery of the case *(res),* in its factual and legal aspects, and mastery of the words *(verba)* used to plead it. More broadly, it is an opposition between substance and form, content and expression, practical stance and verbal stance, always with an accent on the first term of the antithesis. These two formulations agree, then, not in rejecting rhetoric outright but in rejecting a rhetoric that is all technique and language, a rhetoric of pure virtuosity. Cato condemns formalistic effects but recognizes as legitimate rhetoric based on values and facts.

Cato was as much a traditionalist in his practice as in his theory of rhetoric, but he was not a reactionary. Even as he was ostensibly laying claim to traditional values in his affirmation of the legitimacy of patronage, the role of the *bonus vir,* and the importance of *fides,* he was incorporating innovations, tirelessly speaking, publishing and theorizing. This tack suited his situation as a "new man" *(novus homo).* Since he did not belong, in other words, by birth to the Senatorial aristocracy and was not even a native of Rome, Cato built his career in large part thanks to his oratorical activity, but he was smart enough to deck out this non-traditional approach with constant references to Rome's core values. Other areas of his thought and action reveal the same marriage of traditional assertion and deep innovation, whereby he posed as the guardian of Roman values and the enemy of corrupting novelty, while all the time thinking about contemporary problems, whether imperialism or agriculture.

The Gracchi, Tiberius Claudius Gracchus (162–133 B.C.) and his brother Gaius (154–121 B.C.), represented an attitude quite the opposite of Cato's. Members of the highest nobility (their mother, Cornelia, was the daughter of Scipio Africanus), they attacked Senatorial privilege and during their tribunates succeeded in passing laws favoring the plebs and the equestrian order. They attempted reforms, especially agrarian reform, and wound up both being assassinated at the behest of senators. Because of the quality of their eloquence, Cicero deeply regretted their fate, although he in no way shared their political views: "Would that Tiberius Gracchus and Gaius Carbo [G. Papirius Carbo, Tiberius's contemporary and, like him, a reformer] had possessed minds as well disposed to the right conduct of affairs of state as they possessed genius for eloquence"; "in his [Gaius Gracchus's] untimely death the Roman state and Latin letters suffered irreparable loss" (*Brutus* 103, 125). To understand the rhetoric of the Gracchi, it is necessary to bear in mind the constant assemblies during which their laws were prepared and discussed, not only in Rome but in the countryside as well, when they were agitating for agrarian reform. It is necessary to picture the feverish meetings, the inflamed speeches, the brawls around the platform, an entire atmosphere of sedition and revolution. According to Plutarch, the eloquence of Tiberius was logical and poised, that of Gaius more stirring and passionate (*Life of Tiberius Gracchus* 2.2–3). The younger and better orator of the two, Gaius was noted especially for his vehement delivery, as he paced up and down the platform, waving about his toga for effect. Whenever he spoke in public, he used to position behind himself a flautist whom he charged with sounding the keynote (like a modern orchestra tuning to the oboe's A), so that he could place his voice comfortably (as reported by many authors, including Cicero, *On the Orator* 3.225).

The Gracchi's revolutionary rhetoric aroused in reaction a revival of the rhetoric of the *boni*. The two best representatives of this Senatorial rhetoric, from the turn of the second to the first century B.C., were Marcus Antonius (143–87 B.C.), grandfather of the triumvir Marc Antony, and Lucius Licinius Crassus (140–91 B.C.), two luminaries whom Cicero admired in his adolescence and whom he made the principal interlocutors of his dialogue *On the Orator*. Typical and eminent examples of Roman orators, with all the political dimension that this implies, they both went through the career of public offices up to the consulate and censorship, and were proconsuls in a province where Antonius succeeded in bringing back a triumph and Crassus did not. They delivered all sorts of speeches and were particularly great *patroni*. Marius had Marcus Antonius assassinated and had his head stuck on the rostra, while pleurisy, contracted during a speech in the Senate, carried off Crassus.

According to the witness of Cicero *(On the Orator* and *Brutus),* Antonius was especially good at judicial speeches, where he revealed an effectiveness to be reckoned with owing to the forcefulness of his demonstrations, his persuasive delivery, and his huge memory. On the other hand, he was not much of a stylist, nor did he publish his speeches, "so that, should he have occasion to regret anything he had said, he might be able to deny having said it" (Cicero, *For Cluentius* 140; Valerius Maximus, *Memorable Doings and Sayings* 7.3.5). There is no need to take this statement as a profession of shameless cynicism; it is, instead, a great lawyer's strategy to keep his hands free in order to defend with all the means possible each of his succeeding clients. He wrote a small treatise on rhetoric, which dealt especially with the "questions at issue."

Antonius relied above all on practical experience. Crassus, on the other hand, possessed a vast general culture and specialized knowledge of the law. Eminent for his style, sense of form, and skill in riposte, he put these qualities to good use in a difficult inheritance case, which won a lot of attention, the *causa Curiana,* where his solid legal arguments and his abundant rhetorical gifts carried the day.

The Conquest of Greek Rhetoric

From Appius Claudius Caecus, who opened Rome to southern Italy and its Greek influences, to Crassus, who spoke Greek perfectly, all the Roman orators came face to face with Greek and Greek rhetoric. This encounter had very important consequences.

The time has passed for thinking of the Romans as intellectually content to translate and imitate the Greeks. Contemporary scholarship has shown that matters unfolded in a rather more complex and interesting manner. The image that probably expresses the process best is conquest. Even as Rome took over the Mediterranean world by force of arms, similarly and simultaneously it took over the scientific and intellectual treasures of the Greek-speaking world, appropriated them, and put them to use for its own grandeur. From this flows in good part the culture of the Western world. Such was the Roman miracle, which took the handoff from the Greek miracle, and which constituted in effect the second birth of rhetoric. We would be completely mistaken were we to imagine the Romans as hicks slavishly translating Greek texts that were beyond their comprehension. It is necessary, rather, to imagine refined aristocrats, bilingual, by nature proud and cruel, taking possession of Greek rhetoric and rhetors and fashioning from them supplementary instruments of world domination. It is necessary to imagine thinkers giving a new life to Greek concepts.

Inevitably, while incorporating Greek culture after its fashion, Rome itself changed. That is what the celebrated verses of Horace mean: "Captive Greece took savage victor captive and introduced the arts to rustic Latium" (*Graecia capta ferum victorem cepit et artes / intulit agresti Latio: Epistles* 2.1.156–57, WEH). *Capta . . . cepit* is a highly rhetorical oxymoron, where Horace captures the complex phenomenon of the conquest and the resulting aftershock.

The Romans started with the principle that the art of the spoken word was a Greek specialty—a conviction that finds expression, even after Cicero, in the Augustan poets:

Others [than the Romans], I doubt not, shall with softer mold beat out the breathing bronze, coax from the marble features to the life, plead cases with greater eloquence [*orabunt causas melius*] . . .

(Vergil, *Aeneid* 6.847–49)

To the Greeks, the Muse gave native wit, to the Greeks she gave speech in well-rounded phrase.

(Horace, *Ars poetica* 323–24)

According to the national stereotypes, the Greeks were best as specialists in the arts and sciences and in philosophy, while the Romans were more disposed to agriculture, law, administration, or war. Indeed, as far as rhetoric is concerned, the gap was large. In the third century B.C., Greek rhetoric had achieved a very high degree of refinement, when Rome did not yet have any comparable knowledge. So the Romans went looking for the art of speaking right where it was, with the Greeks.

In the second and first centuries B.C., young Romans often spent periods of study in Athens, in Asia Minor, or on Rhodes, in order to obtain the instruction offered there by rhetoricians and philosophers. The itinerant magistrates in the Greek-speaking provinces happily attended lectures and debates. There is, for example, in Cicero's treatise *On the Orator,* the case of Marcus Antonius stopping over at Athens during his journey to Cilicia, or of Licinius Crassus, who as quaestor in Asia Minor often visited the rhetorician Metrodoros. The same Crassus, Cicero adds, was trained in his youth to do Latin translations of the greatest Greek orators. Exiled politicians put to good use their forced leisure time by listening to this rhetorical expert or that.

On the other side, Greek rhetoricians and philosophers used to spend time in Rome or Italy, sometimes as political exiles from their own country and drawn by the protection of powerful patrons. Such was the case of Panaitios, Philon of Larissa, and of Philodemos. The Gracchi had Greek rhetoricians for teachers, including the very eloquent Diophanes of Mytilene, who taught Tiberius Gracchus. Aemilius Paulus surrounded his sons with Greek instructors, in whose number were "grammarians and philosophers and rhetoricians" (Plutarch, *Life of Aemilius Paulus* 6.9). The Greek language was widely known at Rome by this time. Apollonios Molon, orator and theorist of rhetoric, teacher of many Romans on Rhodes and at Rome, came on an embassy to Rome in 81 B.C. to plead the case of the Rhodians, and he was the first ever to address the Senate in Greek without an interpreter.

The teaching of rhetoric in Greek was not enough. To meet a growing demand for this kind of education, instruction in Latin developed, transposing and adapting Greek models. Manuals of rhetoric were written in Latin, like that of Marcus Antonius or the *Rhetorica ad Herennium,* and orators practiced oratorical exercises with their students. Lucius Plotius Gallus, a "client" of Marius, opened the first Latin school of rhetoric at Rome in 93 B.C.

The importation of Greek rhetoric into Rome did not fail to arouse resistance. The very notion of an art of the spoken word, conceived of as a technical faculty to be used and transmitted at will, conflicted with the values of "trustworthiness" *(fides),* "personal authority" *(auctoritas)* or "apprenticeship in public life" *(tirocinium fori).* Since it also came from the Greek world, this art was, by definition, foreign to the national Roman tradition. Moreover, when the art was taught in Latin, it represented an extra danger in the eyes of the senatorial aristocracy, to the extent that this powerful weapon, rhetoric, was then put within reach of a greater number in a form easy to use again. All these reasons explain the distrust exhibited by certain Romans, who were still thoroughly familiar with Greek culture, like Cato, who wrote that it was necessary "to take a survey course" in Greek literature, "not to major in it" *(inspicere, non perdiscere: To His Son Marcus,* frag. 1, ed. Jordan, WEH), or like Crassus and Antonius, who pretended "the one, to hold a poor opinion of the Greeks, and the other . . . never even to have heard of them" (Cicero, *On the Orator* 2.4). In 161 B.C., a decree of the Senate expelled philosophers and rhetoricians from Rome. In 92 B.C., Crassus, as censor, issued an edict with his colleague forbidding schools of rhetoric where the masters taught in Latin *(rhetores Latini).* This measure, which might seem strange coming from a man who was himself a great orator, appears to have yielded to a complex web of political motives. These involved aristocratic reaction against a means of promoting *populares* and the intellectual desire to defend a liberal education, including the culture of Greece, philosophy, and history, against pragmatism and contemporary relevance. The reactions of distrust, however, and the occasional counter measures did not have any lasting effect against the irresistible movement of rhetoric's acclimatization in Rome in the last two centuries of the Republic.

This acclimatization entailed the creation of a vocabulary. Rhetoric encountered here a general problem, found in other areas as well, notably in philosophy, the sciences, architecture (Vitruvius), and so on: the problem of creating a specialized Latin in a field where there already existed a Greek terminology. The reasons for such a creation are self-evident. Even if many people understood Greek, the switch to Latin was indispensable to insure the intellectual autonomy and grandeur of Rome. The difficulty lay in knowing how to go about accomplishing it. While bemoaning the initial inferiority of Latin compared to Greek for expressing complex and subtle thoughts (see, for example, the declarations of Lucretius on "the poverty of our mother tongue," *De rerum natura* 1.832, 3.260), the Romans knew quite well how to remedy the situation. They thought, as Quintilian puts it, that "we have to take risks" (*Institutio Oratoria* 1.5.72, Loeb [Russell] trans.), even if the verbal creation seemed less easy in Greek than in Latin.

A first approach was simple transcription. Ennius (third to second century B.C.) wrote *rhetorica*, a transcription of the Greek *rhētorikē;* Lucilius (second century B.C.) wrote *schema,* a transcription of the Greek *skhēma.* A second approach, more complex and fruitful, consisted in translating and transposing, an operation that elicited new configurations and semantic fields. For example, Ennius rendered *peithō* ("persuasion") by *suada:* while its root connects the Greek word to the idea of "trust" (compare *peithō* with *fido, fides*), the Latin word evoked the idea of "pleasing" and "sweetness" (compare *suada* with *hēdus, suavis*). When applied, the one to Perikles, the other to Marcus Cornelius Cethegus (cf. Cicero, *Brutus* 57–59), these two words pointed up a difference, an unexpected difference given the role the men played, between the authority of the Greek, nicknamed the Olympian, and the ingratiating language of the Roman.

To denote "rhetoric," Latin used especially *eloquentia* ("eloquence") and *ars dicendi* ("art of speaking"). To denote "orator," it used several words: *rhetor* (transcription of the Greek *rhētōr*), which is applied to the master of rhetoric and is often pejorative; *orator,* the noblest term, which was originally applied to someone who speaks on behalf of another (ambassador, spokesman), and whose use was subsequently extended to any individual capable of speaking well, while often preserving the nuance of public person, faction leader, or representative of a group; *patronus,* which, as we have seen, refers to a specifically Roman reality and encompasses a social bond as much as rhetorical ability; *advocatus,* which properly denotes someone who aids a litigant; *causidicus,* a pejorative term.

To denote "stylistic figure" (Greek *skhēma*), Latin, from Quintilian on, mostly favored *figura* (in the sense of "form," "aspect"). But all sorts of other attempts had preceded this translation: *exornatio* ("ornamentation") in the *Rhetorica ad Herennium; ornamentum* ("ornament," "adornment") in Cicero, who also used *lumen* ("brilliant effect"), *conformatio* ("shaping"), *forma* ("form"), *gestus orationis* ("gesture of speech"). To denote "proof" (in Greek *pistis, eikos, sēmeion, tekmērion*), Latin employed *argumentum, probabile, signum* without precisely matching one Latin word to one Greek word, but bringing into play resources proper to the Latin language. *Evidentia,* an invention of Cicero's, rendered "vividness," "clarity" and was palpably more complex than its Greek equivalent *enargeia* from an epistemological point of view. The words *aptum* and *decorum (quid deceat)* rendered "appropriateness"; *decorum* was particularly rich, because the root of the verb *decet* summons up simultaneously *docere* ("to teach," in the sense "to get across well"), *dignitas* ("dignity," "ability to impose oneself"), and *decus/decor* ("beauty"). "Purity of language," *hellēnismos,* became *Latinitas* (not *Romanitas!*). As one examines the details of terminology, examples of this sort multiply with the names of the "questions at issue," of the "parts of the speech," of each of the "figures," and so forth (cf. the Thesaurus at the end of this volume). They all display conscious and productive research, not without occasional experimentation, working toward a proper transposition and adaptation of Greek terminology which was itself far from being unified.

It should be observed that Latin words, although showing at first a sense distinct from the Greek original, often took over the meanings of the Greek they were matching, following the process of semantic calque or transfer. The semantic content of Greek words was then assimilated—conquered, one might even say. Thus the word *ars,* which derived from a different root from *tekhnē* and always preserved its own character (the sense of "ability," "manner"), took on all the meanings of *tekhnē* and functioned as its exact equivalent. In this way the specialized lexicon of Latin rhetoric was formed, whose influence was to be considerable, because it was from Latin that the rhetorical terminology of modern Western languages mostly derived.

The *Rhetorica ad Herennium,* a major treatise that rests on Greek sources and adapts them to the Roman context, illustrates the creation of a rhetoric in Latin. This is the first preserved Latin treatise and is also the first systematic manual we have after Aristotle's *Rhetoric* and the *Rhetoric to Alexander.* What is more, it is the first complete treatise, in that it covers all aspects of the art and offers, in a remarkable synthesis, a veritable compendium: all of rhetoric in one volume of a little more than two hundred pages. Its plan is complicated by the fact that the treatise follows several organizing principles at once (parts of the speech, genres of orations, tasks of the orator, etc.). The first two books, which deal principally with the legal genre, study the parts of the speech and the "questions at issue." The third book brings together precepts on invention in the deliberative and demonstrative (epideictic) genres, on arrangement, delivery, and memorization. The fourth book, which alone occupies almost half the work, is devoted to style.

Composed probably in the years 86–83 B.C., its author is unknown (the attribution to Cicero, which appeared at the end of antiquity, must be rejected; certain modern writers have proposed attributing it to Cornificius). The author draws on Greek sources, which he knows both from direct reading and from the teaching of a "professor" *(doctor)* who also remains anonymous. This use of Greek sources explains why we have encountered the *Rhetorica ad Herennium* several times in the course of the preceding chapter, as evidence especially of the Hellenistic doctrine of genres of style, figures, or memorization.

The author synthesizes these Greek sources, freely mixing, combining, and choosing, according to a method recalling *contaminatio* in the theater (an important concept in Roman Hellenism, denoting the cobbling together of a Roman comedy out of several Greek originals). Moreover, he essentially aims to naturalize Greek *tekhnē* in a process similar to that of the *rhetores Latini* whose schools a censors' edict had shut a few years earlier. One supposes, reading between the lines, that the author of the treatise was either a member of the equestrian order or more probably a senator, but close to the *populares,* who admired the Gracchi, had held military and administrative posts and was a partisan of Marius. He addresses his treatise to a certain Gaius Herennius, who, he says, requested it, and he proclaims his intention not to get lost in abstractions like the Greeks but to produce a user-friendly manual for a young Roman (1.1). His treatment of examples follows this plan. Instead of borrowing from several authors, he calls upon his own resources (4.1–10), either making up examples or drawing from his own speeches, in such a way as to tie in precepts with the actual conditions of recent history and Roman politics. The *Rhetorica ad Herennium* thus offers a complete and finished witness to the acclimatization of Greek rhetoric in Rome at the beginning of the first century B.C.

Cicero

Cicero (106–43 B.C.), whose name has cropped up several times in this and the preceding chapter, completely dominates rhetoric in the Hellenistic and Roman era. He has often been compared to Demosthenes, notably by Plutarch in the *Parallel Lives,* and he himself suggested such a connection when he called his orations against Antony *Philippics,* alluding to the *Philippics* of the Greek orator. In fact, it is reasonable to compare the exceptional oratorical talents of Demosthenes and Cicero, whose two political careers depended on the power of speech as they both fought for liberty and both ended up proscribed. Even their failures parallel each other, so true is it that any speaker, no matter how great, is not safe from an occasional stumble. Such was Demosthenes's misfortune when, as ambassador, he lost his composure and fell mute in front of Philip (cf. Aiskhines, *On the Embassy* 34–35). Similarly, Cicero, as Milo's lawyer, was agitated in front of Pompey's armed men (cf. Plutarch, *Life of Cicero* 35.5). But the comparison between Demosthenes and Cicero does not go far enough, because Cicero did not limit himself to being an orator and politician, in the manner of his Greek predecessor, but was equally a theorist, historian, and philosopher of oratory. In the history of rhetoric, he occupies an unparalleled place, since he played several roles at the same time, corresponding to those played at Athens by Demosthenes, Plato, and Aristotle together.

Born at Arpinum, around 70 miles from Rome, into an "equestrian" family, Cicero was a "new man," the first in his family to achieve the highest level of a political career. Personal genius and especially his mastery of language and thought help to explain his rise. Rhetoric was critical, as his brother Quintus reminded him: "Whatever you are, you owe to this" (*quicquid es, ex hoc es, Commentariolum petitionis* [Handbook of electioneering] 2, where *"hoc"* refers to Cicero's skill as speaker and lawyer). From adolescence he was educated at Rome, where he had a very broad-based instruction in law, philosophy, poetry, and rhetoric. For the last, his father entrusted him to Marcus Pupius Piso, an already well-known orator. He practiced declamatory exercises in Latin and Greek, composed Latin translations of Greek works (notably Plato's *Protagoras*), listened to the greatest orators of the day (Antonius, Crassus), and attended the philosophical and rhetorical classes, as we saw, of Philon of Larissa from the Academy. Later, in 79–77, he completed his education with a grand tour to Athens, Asia Minor, and Rhodes, which allowed him to frequent numerous Greek philosophers and orators, including Apollonius Molon, whom he had already heard at Rome and who took his education in hand at Rhodes. He returned from this journey a "changed" man (*Brutus* 316), less exuberant, more assured.

Cicero's oratorical career extends over almost forty years, from his first legal pleading, *For Quinctius* (81 B.C.), until his death. He delivered around 150 known speeches, fifty-eight of which are preserved. They divide into legal speeches, spoken on behalf of either the prosecution or the defense before tribunals, and political orations addressed to the Senate or the people. It has been calculated that Cicero won 82 percent of his cases (J. E. Granrud, in *Classical Journal* 8 [1912–13]: 242); this figure, an approximation, should not be considered an absolute fact, but it still captures well the effectiveness of someone who was a successful lawyer *(patronus)* and political orator. Given that Cicero did not completely write out his speeches before delivering them, the texts that we read are revised and rewritten versions, sometimes augmented or sometimes shortened (cf. the *For Murena*) with a view to publication. The author himself oversaw the publication, aided by his freedman secretary Tiro (inventor of a shorthand system called "Tironian notes"); his good friend, Atticus, took charge of having copies made and selling the finished products. In the first century A.D., the grammarian Quintus Asconius Pedianus provided the orations with highly valuable historical commentaries. In this vast corpus, three sets stand out as particularly important: the *Verrines, Catilinarians,* and *Philippics.*

Cicero was thirty-six and already well known as a lawyer when the cities of Sicily asked him, in 70 B.C., to represent them in the Verres affair. It was a serious case. Verres was accused of having committed theft and abuse of power to the detriment of the governed when he was propraetor in Sicily (the crime *de repetundis*), but he had the support of the Senate, and the great orator Hortensius was defending him. The Sicilians decided to approach Cicero not only because of his fame, but also because he had been quaestor in Sicily and had left a good memory behind in the island. Cicero accepted, since *fides* bound him to the Sicilians, whose *patronus* of sorts he became in taking charge of their interests. But he also accepted because it was a prestigious case and on the side which doubtless suited him (defense of Greek-speaking interests, fight against the stranglehold imposed by the Senate on political life). In the preliminary hearing, Cicero succeeded in having himself sanctioned as Verres's accuser instead of the nonentity Caecilius, whom the other side wanted *(Oration against Q. Caecilius,* called *"the Scrutiny,"* [*divinatio*]).

According to the law, such a trial was supposed to be in two successive proceedings, with a verdict pronounced at the end of the second. Verres and his defenders hoped to defer this second proceeding until 69, when circumstances would be more favorable: Marcus Caecilius Metellus, who favored the accused, would be the court's president, and Verres's lawyer, Hortensius, would be consul. While the defense, therefore, counted on delaying tactics, Cicero skillfully recognized the necessity for quick action. Although another case had been brought before the same court so as to postpone Verres's trial, and despite the fact that Cicero himself was running for aedile that year (he was elected), the brief was handled on the double. Cicero conducted investigations at Rome, where he audited Verres's accounts and the customs records, and in Sicily, where he assembled all the possible proofs of the governor's exactions. Within fifty days, the discovery for the trial was completed, and when the first round of arguments took place, in August of 70, Cicero's objective was to carry off such a crushing victory right then and there that his adversaries would capitulate. And that is exactly what happened. Instead of a majestic overture, orchestrated by numerous assistants, Cicero satisfied himself with a rapid-fire indictment *(First Proceeding against G. Verres),* and he had witnesses to the charge parade in—around fifty individuals and around thirty delegations sent by the Sicilian cities. Their depositions, which lasted eight days, were so overwhelming that Verres forsook his defense and voluntarily went into exile at Marseilles.

The case stopped there, with only a guilty verdict to complete it and the estimation of the damages owed to the Sicilians. But Cicero had prepared his arguments with the second proceeding in view. Although this did not take place, he still published the indictments, which he would have been able to deliver at that time—the *Second Proceeding against G. Verres,* in the form of five orations, each detailing an aspect of the crimes committed by the accused: *The Urban Praetorship, The Praetorship of Sicily, The Grain, The Works of Art, The Tortures.* The ensemble, remarkable both for its argumentative force and its literary talent, employs pathos, indignation, irony, and local color, sketching unforgettable scenes. With this publication, Cicero wanted to justify the trial verdict by making known the evidence he had at his disposal and to influence public opinion over the longer term, by denouncing the excesses of some of the senatorial aristocracy. With the case already pled, and victoriously, the written text, through the devices of literature, prolonged its life and gave it a lasting and trustworthy effect. Incidentally, the oration *The Works of Art* made an important additional contribution to the Latin language of art criticism.

After this victory, Cicero became the first of orators and a politician to watch. He was aedile, praetor, and finally consul, and it was in the last capacity that he had to confront the conspiracy of Catiline, which he forcefully suppressed. The set of the four *Catilinarians,* delivered over the course of one month (November 8 to December 5, 63 B.C.), mark out the stages of the consul's action. The first oration, addressed to the Senate, aimed at convincing the senators that the plot was quite real and at driving Catiline to leave Rome. Catiline, who was present at the session, sought to reply but did not succeed and was forced to quit the city. The next day, in the second oration, Cicero spoke to the people in the Forum to reveal the conspiracy, to explain his conduct toward Catiline and to threaten the latter's partisans who were still in Rome. Three weeks passed, during which Cicero (along with Hortensius, who now was arguing on the same team) found the time to secure the defense of Murena, whose acquittal he won. In the midst of all this, after some written proofs of Catiline's plot had been seized, Cicero had the conspirators arrested. He delivered, again before the people, the *Third Catilinarian,* in order to relate the decisive session the Senate had just held and to announce that Rome was saved, thanks to the gods and to Cicero. Two days later, the Senate assembled to determine the fate of the conspirators. Silanus demanded the death penalty, Caesar life imprisonment. In the *Fourth Catilinarian,* Cicero sided with Silanus and carried the day when the Younger Cato supported him. The condemned were executed that very evening, and Cicero informed the people of their deaths with the celebrated comment *"Vixerunt"* ("They have lived"). Catiline, who was not among the apprehended plotters, died fighting a month later.

From the viewpoint of rhetorical strategy, the orations against Catiline are complex, because each targets several audiences at once and several different purposes. Cicero addresses himself at the same time to Catiline's enemies, whom he wants to reassure and encourage, to Catiline's supporters, whom he means to threaten, and to the undecided, whom he tries to mobilize. Except for the fourth oration, whose purpose is clearly stated, these speeches do not aim at a definite decision, but rather to explain and justify the consul's action. They touch upon multiple themes, just as multiple as the motivations of Roman politics, simultaneously putting into play self-interest, patriotism, practical arguments, moral notions, and religious convictions. In these terms, the power of the set derives from the fact that, despite its richness, despite the complexity of the rhetorical situations and lines of argument, the whole is clear and unified. Cicero undertakes action for the greater good of the State: that is the impression he gives and wanted to give. Moreover, these orations are studded with memorable excerpts, especially the first, which contains two celebrated prosopopoeias of the fatherland and a magnificent final prayer to Jupiter Stator (Jupiter "who stops," who symbolizes therefore the need to "stop" Catiline's intrigues). Even Sallust, who was no admirer of Cicero, recognized the grandeur of this oration, characterizing it "a brilliant speech of great service to the Republic" (*Catiline* 31.6, Loeb modified).

The consulate was the highpoint of Cicero's career, and on this occasion he received the title "Father of the Nation." Twenty years later, he found himself in quite a different situation at the time of the *Philippics*. In the intervening period, he had known exile and return, the increasing instability of the Republic and the evolution toward a regime based on personal power, first Pompey's, then Caesar's. He had tried to weigh in as much as he could on political life, arguing cases often and writing often. And now came the threat of Antony, who was en route to seizing power in Rome after Caesar's assassination. The fourteen *Philippics* (fourteen preserved, that is, out of a total of at least seventeen) stretch from September of 44 to April of 43, with a break during the autumn, which Cicero put to good use to write the three books of the treatise *On Duties (De officiis)*. With the exception of the first, which still has a moderate tone, the *Philippics* violently attack Antony, whom Cicero, a partisan of Octavius, presents as an aspirant to tyranny and whom he wishes to have declared a public enemy. This set of speeches is nothing less than a monument in the history of invective, with Antony depicted as a monster who transgresses the laws of society, of nature, of humanity itself. The *Philippics* also provide a synthesis of Ciceronian themes on law, history, politics, and liberty. Finally, as was already the case with the consular orations, the collection is interesting because it contains at the same time addresses to the Senate and to the people, delivered on the same day or after a few days' interval *(Phil.* 3 and 4; 5 and 6). This allows a comparison of these two forms of eloquence and an appreciation of the varieties of tone and argument Cicero employs depending on the audience.

These invectives won Cicero Antony's hatred. So, when the second triumvirate was formed, the tactical alliance among Antony, Octavius, and Lepidus, Cicero's name figured on the list of the seventeen leading opponents whom the triumvirs condemned to death (November, 43 B.C.). Caught near Gaeta, at the moment when he apparently decided to leave Italy, Cicero was assassinated by a centurion. His head and hands were brought to Antony, who had them displayed on the Rostra.

Clearly, the *Verrines, Catilinarians,* and *Philippics* hardly exhaust Cicero's oratorical oeuvre. There are many other masterpieces in the corpus. There are likewise orations that show Cicero in a less favorable, or in any case less heroic light, and sometimes as even fawning and opportunistic.

In addition, in the addresses and courtroom speeches, elements of the encomium sometimes appear. Cicero (like the other Romans of his time on this point) was not terribly interested in the third genre, the epideictic oration or encomium, which, as a separate type of speech, is confined, as far as he is concerned, to the *laudatio funebris.* He did keep a place for it, however, in his theoretical thought, and he inserted formal encomia here and there in his judicial and deliberative speeches: the praise of Sicily in the *Verrines* (2.2.2–9), the praise of Pompey in the oration *On the Command of Pompey* (*De imperio Cn. Pompei,* 27–49), the funeral oration for the soldiers of the Mars legion in the *Philippics* (14.31–35). In this way, the work of Cicero represents a start in the acclimatization of the rhetorical encomium, a Greek invention, at Rome.

Summing up Cicero's oratorical genius, one must cite at least an admirable language used to its full extent, a very great power of argumentation, extensive knowledge of all things legal, an alliance of rigor, pathos, and mordant verve, freedom of form, and the ability to break the rules. When Cicero shared a case with several lawyers, he used to reserve for himself the peroration, where he appealed to the emotions with marvelous talent.

In his orations, Cicero defended a political ideal which one could describe as conservative and republican and which intended to favor the "good" citizens *(boni, optimates),* that is, not only the senators but also, seeking a somewhat enlarged sociological base, the "equestrians," the wealthy property owners, and the leading men of the towns and cities outside Rome. He endeavored to defend traditional institutions based on the Senate's authority, respect for the law, "concord of the orders of society" *(concordia ordinum),* and "the agreement of gentlemen" *(consensus bonorum),* under the guidance, if possible, of an exceptional man who would be the guarantor. Rhetoric is one of the places where he formed his political ideas and put them to work.

Naturally, these ideas changed and varied over time and in response to circumstances. In the orations, there are adaptations to suit the audience, as noted above. For example, when he speaks before the Senate, Cicero (according to the calculations of G. Achard) devotes 16 percent of his argument to highlighting the nobility of the action he has in mind, and when he addresses the people, only 1 percent, while, inversely, the argument of practicality occupies a place twice as great in the orations to the people as in those to the Senate. In the courtroom speeches, there is adaptation to the client and the case, and on this topic Cicero set forth an entire list of the duties for a *patronus* to perform (echoing the reflections of Antonius cited above). According to Cicero, the lawyer must in no way seek to express his own personal point of view, but aim at what is useful for the case:

But it is the greatest possible mistake to suppose that the speeches we lawyers have made in court contain our considered and certified opinions; all those speeches reflect the demands of some particular case or emergency, not the individual personality of the advocate. For if a case could speak for itself no one would employ a pleader.

(For Cluentius 139, Loeb modified)

Cicero also considered the defense more noble than the prosecution, and he preferred defending a guilty person to accusing an innocent man:

It is always the business of the judge in a trial to find out the truth; it is sometimes the business of the advocate to maintain what is plausible, even if it be not strictly true.

(On Duties, 2.14.51)

Practitioner of eloquence, Cicero was also a teacher. In accordance with the norms of "apprenticeship in public life," any number of young men from the equestrian or senatorial aristocracy, brought by their fathers, attached themselves to him to learn at first hand the art of judicial patronage. His entourage also included admirers and friends, younger than himself, in whose company he engaged in oratorical exercises throughout his life. Even in 46 and 44, he was discussing topics like "the ways to bring about peace and civic concord" with Hirtius, Dolabella, and Pansa (*Letters to His Friends* 9.16.7; *Letters to Atticus* 14.12.2), and practicing oratorical technique as both a healthy diversion and a thinking through of the current state of politics. Some years earlier, in 49, Cicero argued political propositions *(theseis)* from both sides *(in utramque partem),* in Greek and Latin, in response to present circumstances and on the topic "What stance to take to a tyrant?" (*Letters to Atticus* 9.4).

Cicero was equally a theorist, a theorist of oratory in general and at the same time a theorist of his own practice. He began very early, since his first treatise, *On Invention (De inventione),* dates from the middle of the 80s (perhaps 84–83 B.C.). A contemporary of the *Rhetorica ad Herennium,* it shares with that work connections difficult to fix exactly, a situation not unlike in some ways the connection between the *Rhetoric* of Aristotle and the *Rhetoric to Alexander. On Invention* and the *Rhetorica ad Herennium* show many similarities; the two authors depend, if not on the teaching of the same master, at least on the same basic doctrine professed in Rome at that time. Cicero's treatise, however, is less thorough than its fraternal twin. As the title indicates, it deals only with argumentation, considered according to the different genres and the different parts of a speech, with special emphasis on the theory of "the questions at issue." A study of the other parts of rhetoric—style, memorization, delivery—is announced at the end of the work, but this project was apparently never realized. *On Invention,* moreover, also differs from the *Rhetorica* on individual points of doctrine and in its lesser sympathy for the *populares* and its greater openness to Hellenism and philosophy. The treatise testifies to the extensive research of an author scarcely more than twenty years old. More than just a fully accomplished work, it served Cicero as a useful manual for preparing the arguments of his courtroom speeches. Thirty years later, he will distance himself from *On Invention* as "the unfinished and crude essays, which slipped out of the notebooks of my boyhood, or rather of my youth" (*On the Orator* 1.5).

The fully developed Ciceronian theory is found in what the author described (*On Divination, De divinatione* 2.4) as his five oratorical books: *On the Orator (De oratore)* in three books, the *Brutus,* and the *Orator.*

On the Orator, composed in 55 B.C., is a dialogue that Cicero sets in the time of his adolescence (91 B.C.) and casts with men he knew and admired, especially Crassus, Antonius, and Mucius Scaevola the augur. Without restricting himself to reporting actual exchanges, Cicero does respect the character and broad outlines of his speakers' views, in order to have them bring forth problems dear to his own heart. It is not merely a question of indulging in a melancholy evocation of the departed, but of using the past to reflect on the present as well. In 55 as in 91, the stability of the Republic and the authority of the Senate were arguably being threatened, and Cicero, who deeply believed that rhetoric had a role to play in defending institutions, inserted into this dialogue implications for the Roman politics of his time. Setting forth the rules of rhetoric amounted to considering the conditions for the healthy functioning of the State.

The discussion principally unfolds between Crassus and Antonius. The first book has a debate between the two on the definition of rhetoric and on the qualities required of the orator. Book 2, given over almost entirely to Antonius, presents precepts relating to "invention," arrangement, and memorization. The third book, dedicated to Crassus, deals with style and delivery. So the whole contains the elements of a complete treatise, while avoiding the dryness of a Greek manual thanks to the literary charm of the dialogue format. Cicero was thoroughly versed in the research of his Latin and Greek predecessors (in a letter he says he has encompassed here "all the theories of rhetoric held by the ancients, including those of Aristotle and Isokrates," *Letters to His Friends* 1.9.23). He rethinks these sources in his own manner, incorporating them into his own conceptions and his own experience, and he does not hesitate to give detailed rules which occasionally involve technical innovations, for example about "questions at issue" and style. It is in this dialogue that the famous Ciceronian theory on the three tasks of the orator appears: "the proof of our allegations, the winning of our hearers' favor, and the rousing of their feelings to whatever impulse our case may require" (2.115, summed up elsewhere in the three words "teach, please, move," *docere, delectare, movere*).

But, more than in technical analyses, the principal contribution of *On the Orator* resides in the very way it conceives of eloquence. Cicero does not restrict himself to rules but wants to take everything back to basics, defining the studies and the thinking preliminary to eloquence's exercise, in other words, the theme of general culture essential to the orator. Crassus and Antonius face off on this issue in the first book. Crassus maintains that the orator has to possess competency in law, history, politics, natural science, and philosophy since rhetoric's domain is universal and all these subjects will come up in the cases one will have to handle. Antonius develops the opposite thesis, that it suffices if the orator possesses a large experience of life and has dabbled in many fields; for, being able to obtain expert advice on technical points, he can do without any specialist competency. But when the conversation resumes the next day, in book 2, Antonius admits that he has exaggerated merely for the fun of contradicting Crassus (2.40) and that at bottom his way of thinking is not averse to handling questions of general import. Rather than an opposition, there is a difference of accent between the exalted demands of Crassus and the qualifications of Antonius, which recall Crassus back to the real world. Cicero himself sides with Crassus, whose position he expressly approves (2.5–6) and to whom he provides in book 3 a new disquisition on the same subject.

If this debate takes on so much significance, it is because it hits upon a fundamental problem according to Cicero. The question is one of knowing whether rhetoric is a technique without content, a collection of recipes applicable at will to any topic, or if it is a complete art—putting into play all a person's qualities, supposing wisdom and knowledge in its expression and exercising its ability to persuade because of the values it rests upon. Cicero opts for the latter. Some Greeks had already perceived this dilemma, as well as Cicero's option, but the dialogue *On the Orator* is the first text of ancient rhetoric to develop this idea in all its ramifications. The principal ones are these:

— *Knowledge of law.* This is a profoundly Roman theme, going farther than mere legal competence. In maintaining that the orator must know the law, Crassus indicates that the problematic of truth is insufficient. The orator does not speak to communicate the truth, but to make political and social life function on solid legal and moral foundations.

— *General Questions (theseis).* Every individual case harks back to a general question that encompasses it. For example: Milo killed Clodius, who had laid an ambush for him. The case consists in knowing if Milo had a right to kill Clodius; but the *thesis* in the background asks whether someone has the right to kill an ambusher, in other words, to what extent is self-defense legitimate. Cicero, who had shown reservations about *theseis* in the treatise *On Invention,* here recommends them in the treatise *On the Orator,* and he insists on the need to broaden the issue and to pose the underlying problems which it raises (obviously such generalizing has to remain confined within sensible limits and subordinated to the case at hand). Following this line of reasoning, rhetoric is not just a routine but aspires to be a way of getting to the bottom of things.

— *Connections with philosophy.* Philosophy is the essential element in the orator's general culture. The art of persuading, as Cicero conceives it, rests completely on "philosophic foundations" (A. Michel). Whether it is a matter of the means of argument (reason, logic, commonplaces), proper use of the emotions, aesthetics and the search for beauty, jurisprudence, or political science, wisdom must be joined to eloquence (3.142: *sapientiam iunctam . . . eloquentiae*). The New Academy's doctrine, here influencing Cicero most profoundly, included elements of doubt and skepticism appropriate to the relativism and probability inherent in rhetorical discourse and to the realities of a situation where one says "now one thing, now another" (2.30: *alias aliud*). It is Karneades reconciled with Aristotle (3.71).

— *The image of the ideal orator.* This demanding conception of rhetoric delineates the image of an ideal orator, magnified, finding substance not only on the moral and intellectual plane (possessing wisdom, he is at once virtuous and able to embrace philosophic teaching, for these two aspects are bound together), but also on the political plane (he directs the State: 3.63, 76; his speech is "royal," 1.32) and on the religious plane (he is "divine" and seems "almost a god": 1.106, 202; 3.53). Hence the chosen titles, *On the Orator* and the *Orator,* which effectively bypass the art to embody it in the figure of the one exercising it. The question then arises of knowing whether such an orator exists. Antonius used to say that he had known "well-spoken" men *(diserti)* but never yet a single one who was truly "eloquent" *(eloquens)* (1.94). In the *Orator,* the "supreme orator" *(summus orator)* is an ideal like the Platonic forms. But surely Cicero, who could never be accused of excessive modesty, thought of himself as the embodiment of the orator, perfected, cultivated, philosophic, and capable of a great political future (it was still possible to believe this in 55).

On all these points (including the personal reference), Cicero will not change later. He remains faithful to these convictions and takes them up again in the two succeeding works, the *Brutus* and the *Orator.* Composed nine years after *On the Orator* (in 46 B.C.), however, these two treatises address a new situation: the development of Atticism (or neo-Atticism), whose chief representative was the orator and poet Gaius Licinius Calvus (82–47 B.C.). Calvus and his friends promoted a form of eloquence which they called "Attic," in imitation of the Attic orators, especially Lysias, and which was characterized by clarity and verbal exactitude, indeed a certain dry spareness. This aesthetic was not without connection to Stoic conceptions of rhetoric and the works of some grammarians (including Caesar in his treatise *On Analogy,* dedicated to Cicero). In the name of this conception, the neo-Atticists went so far as to criticize the style of Cicero, reproaching its want of simplicity, its excessive fulsomeness, its figures, repetitiveness, emotionalism, and its rhythms. The *Brutus* and the *Orator* were written in the context of this rhetorical polemic. They are dedicated to Marcus Iunius Brutus (85–42 B.C.), the future assassin of Caesar, a philosopher and orator, as well as Cicero's friend, to whom Cicero dedicated several other works. Cicero would have had in mind guiding Brutus's thoughts on oratory, if it is true that Brutus tended to favor the ideas of Calvus. He would also have wanted—since for Cicero aesthetics and politics are not separated when rhetoric is at issue—to have Brutus think on the example of Demosthenes and on the republican ideal rhetoric conveyed, at the time of Caesar's dominance in Rome.

The *Orator* has three principal parts: a definition of the ideal orator; a synthesizing statement of the rules of rhetoric, especially rules of style; and finally the study of a more limited and technical area, "word order" *(de verbis componendis),* the part of *elocutio* that consists in placing words in the sentence in such a way as to attain the best effects of euphony and rhythm. While reprising many of the themes of *On the Orator,* the *Orator* therefore adds a deeper treatment of stylistic questions. Cicero protests against a niggardly and monochrome conception of prose oratory. He defends, or better, develops a theory of a fuller understanding, rich and almost musical in certain ways, which he had always held on this issue (scholars of the nineteenth century were wont to speak of Cicero's "copious" and "cadenced" prose, that is, a prose founded on "abundance" [*copia*] and "rhythm" [*numerus*]). He also rises up against use of the word "Attic" by Calvus and his friends, making the point that Attic eloquence is not only Lysias. It includes Isokrates; it includes Demosthenes. So, according to Cicero, it is not justified to comandeer the epithet "Attic" to the sole advantage of the simple style. The right way to reclaim the Attic orators is to be eclectic, imitating the qualities of each of them, or else to take inspiration from the great model who sums up in his own person the qualities of all: Demosthenes.

Composed a few months before the *Orator,* the *Brutus* presents a new facet of Ciceronian thought on rhetoric, its historical dimension. Prompted by a manual on chronology Atticus had sent him, and relying on his own research, reading, and personal memories, Cicero traces here, in dialogue form, a history of Roman eloquence, the first of its kind. At the start, he paints a picture of Greek rhetoric, which is quite important in itself (notably because it uses the lost work of Aristotle, the *Collection of the "Arts"*). He then goes on to list in chronological order all the Roman orators, famous and less famous, from the beginning of the Republic up to his own day, analyzing in detail the characteristics of their eloquence, an exposition that is an invaluable source of information. It is also a hymn to the glory of rhetoric, whose difficulty and demands it demonstrates, while retracing rhetoric's slow perfecting, culminating in Hortensius and Cicero himself. While he is at it, the author does not forget, once more, to respond to the criticisms of the neo-Atticists.

Cicero wrote as well three small treatises on rhetoric: *On the Best Sort of Orators* (preface to his own translation, now lost, of the orations *Against Ktesiphon* of Aiskhines and *On the Crown* of Demosthenes); the *Branches of the Art of Oratory* (a manual for his son's use); and the *Topics* (a treatise on the commonplaces of argumentation).

Cicero's contribution to the history of rhetoric is not confined to his orations and treatises on the subject, important though they may be. Many significant innovations also appear in the rest of his work, looked at from a broader perspective.

Cicero "rhetoricized" philosophy, if one can put it so. Not content with introducing a philosophic dimension into rhetoric, he correspondingly introduced rhetoric into philosophy, following the idea that philosophy should be eloquent, and he developed an original philosophic language, where demonstration and persuasion come together. Cicero thought that "everything committed to writing should commend itself to the reading of all educated people," and that is why he appreciated, as a philosopher, the rhetorical exercises, the *dissertatio in utramque partem* (*Tusculan Disputations* 2.8–9, Loeb modified), all the means suitable for making a philosophic discourse just that, a discourse. When he was writing the *Tusculan Disputations,* Cicero used to declaim in the morning and give himself over to philosophy in the afternoon, a marriage of the two disciplines, even in the use of time, examples of which can be found throughout antiquity, from Aristotle to the Neoplatonists. Philosophy and rhetoric are thus complementary:

For there is a close alliance between the orator and the philosophical system of which I am a follower, since the orator borrows subtlety from the Academy and repays the loan by giving to it a copious and flowing style and rhetorical ornament.

(*On Fate* 1.2.3)

Cicero reflected on the connections between history and rhetoric and concluded that the writing of history obeys laws of composition and form no different from the laws of rhetoric (*On the Orator* 2.36, 62). Whence the famous dictum: history is a "branch of literature . . . closer than any other to oratory" *(On the Laws* 1.5: *opus oratorium maxime).* This theme has taken on a very contemporary relevance during these past years, among authors who emphasize that the writing of history cannot be neutral, that it conforms to rules and choices about writing, whether as narrative or as argument. In this light, history can be seen, at least partly, as itself a literary or rhetorical genre, and its epistemology includes not only documentary sources but also manners of exposition. (Cf. the works of Hayden White, especially *The Content of the Form. Narrative Discourse and Historical Representation* [Baltimore, 1987]; also R. Carpenter, *History as Rhetoric. Style, Narrative and Persuasion* [Columbia, 1995]. This problematic is one of the directions P. Ricœur envisaged in the three volumes of *Time and Narrative,* trans. K. McLaughlin and D. Pellauer [Chicago, 1984–88].)

Cicero likewise thought about the issue of conversation. In the treatise *On the Orator* (1.32), the art of engaged and civilized conversation is considered to be one of the strengths of the spoken word. Not judging it possible or even desirable to lay down rules on this topic as rigorous as those governing public discourse, Cicero did not elaborate a true rhetoric of conversation, but he did define an ethics of conversation (in *On Duties* 1.134–37). And he put his principles to work in a very rich literary endeavor, the dialogue. Beginning precisely with *On the Orator,* the form became more and more dear to him, because it allowed him to present varied opinions and to look for the truth without being dogmatic, and because it portrayed a conception of social relationships based on urbaneness, friendship, and educated leisure. Let us not forget, finally, letter writing—another form of conversation—for which Cicero has left a commanding model with his monumental correspondence.

Ciceronian rhetoric has exercised a capital influence on the history of Western culture in and through the notion of "eloquence." As Cicero exemplified it, and as it has been taken up after him, in antiquity, the Middle Ages, the Renaissance, and in modern times, this notion, based upon his works, was not reduced to just public discourse, but concentrated in itself the potentialities of literature, science, and humanism. It was a very broad and overwhelming conception of rhetoric, which opened to rhetoric a vast domain and to whose spread cultural institutions have contributed (for example, in nineteenth- and twentieth-century French secondary education, whose informing spirit was quite Ciceronian, the penultimate year was called "rhetoric" and the last year "philosophy").

One last Ciceronian topic is the relation between rhetoric and freedom. As he observed the ever-growing supremacy of military power, Cicero asserted the superiority, by right, of the philosopher-orator over the victorious captain and dictator. He made bold to write: "let armor yield to civilian dress" (poem *On His Consulate,* frag. 6, Soubiran ed.: *cedant arma togae,* WEH), and, again, "We are waging war with Antony . . . words against swords" *(contra arma verbis: Letters to His Friends* 12.22.1). He knew full well that at the time arms were winning, but he still advocated rhetoric as a model of civilization and as the means to make right prevail over might.

FIFTH EXCURSUS

♣ *Laughter as Weapon*

Laughter is probably not the first thing that comes to mind when we think about Roman rhetoric, or about Cicero in particular. And yet the orations of Cicero are strewn with humorous touches and irony meant to win the judges' good graces by making them laugh or smile, to deflect their attention from a weak point, or to discredit the opponent with ridicule or derision. Here are some examples.

Laughter to lighten up the atmosphere:

"Milo, on the other hand, . . . went home, changed his shoes and clothes, only to wait a while, as usual, for his wife to get ready" (*For Milo* 28,

Loeb modified). These words "as usual" *(ut fit),* in a narration whose slightest details are calculated, constitute an incidental aside meant to amuse the judges and to bestow an air of truthfulness on the rest of the recital.

Ironic praise:

"Rullus, a man who is, of course, neither avaricious nor grasping." (*On the Agrarian Law* 2.20, Loeb modified)

Play on the name of the opponent:

In the *Verrines,* Cicero plays repeatedly on the name Verres, which in Latin is identical to *verres* (pig, boar), and which also recalls the verbs *verro* and *everro* (to sweep up, to carry off):

(Concerning someone involved in the affair): "But suddenly, as though he had drunk of Circe's goblet, he turned in one flash from a man into a Verres [in the *Odyssey,* Circe turns the companions of Odysseus into pigs]; . . . as for this money, he sweeps *(verrit)* the better part of it into his own coffers." (*Oration against Quintus Caecilius* 57, Loeb modified)

(Concerning court decisions Verres made): "Some of them made the remark . . . that *ius verrinum* was of course poor stuff, pork *au verjus* rather than pork *au jus*" (*ius verrinum:* a double-entendre, signifying "justice of Verres" and "sauce for pork"). Cicero, after having gotten a laugh recounting this witticism, very ably continues in an extremely serious tone, asserting that he does not endorse the joke himself and that he only cites it as evidence of wrongdoing: "I should not recall these jokes, which are neither all that funny nor in keeping with the serious dignity of this Court, were it not that I would have you remember how Verres's offences against morality and justice became at the time the subject of common talk and popular catchwords." (*Verrines* 2.1.121, Loeb modified)

". . . Verres's full preparation to sweep the province clean" (*paratus . . . ad everrendam provinciam:* 2.2.19); "Gentlemen, was there ever a province swept by so veritable a broom *(everriculum)* as Verres?" (2.4.53)

(Concerning an alias used by Verres, "Verrucius," whose ending in a document had been erased): "Do you see that word 'Verrucius'? . . . Do you see the last part of the name, how the tail-end wallows in the erasure like a pig's tail *(caudam illam verrinam)* in mud?" (2.2.191, Loeb modified)

(Concerning Verres's failure to steal a statue of Hercules): The Sicilians "observed that this monstrous hog *(hunc immanissimum Verrem)* ought to be counted among the labors of Hercules quite as much as the celebrated Erymanthian boar." (2.4.95)

Play on words:

(Antony has made a gift of a piece of land to the rhetorician Sextus Clodius, who is giving Antony elocution lessons): "Mark the reason why his master has abandoned tirades for tillage *(ex oratore arator),* and possesses of public land two thousand acres of Leontine territory free from taxes." *(Philippics* 3.2.22)

Foreign locutions:

Cicero uses words of foreign origin, which stigmatize the opponent even more surely than insults, by playing upon the chauvinism and moral prejudices of the audience:

"Publius Clodius changed from his saffron *(crocota)* chiffon, his *turban de soie (mitra),* his high heels and purple garters, his bustiere, his maracas, and his monstrous debaucheries into—presto—an 'average guy'" (*On the Answers of the Soothsayers* 44, WEH).

Repartee, sometimes funny, sometimes biting, which breaks out during debates, for example, these instances reported by Quintilian:

Milo's accuser kept insisting on the time of the crime, in order to prove premeditation, and "repeatedly asked . . . when Clodius was killed. Cicero replied, 'Late.'!" (*Institutio Oratoria* 6.3.49, Loeb [Russell] trans.: the Latin word *sero,* meaning "late" and "too late," suggests that Clodius deserved to die sooner.)

". . . When a witness called Sextus Annalis had damaged his client, and the prosecutor kept pressing him, and saying, 'Marcus Tullius, can you say anything of Sextus Annalis?' he began to quote lines from Ennius, *Annales* Six, 'Who can the causes vast of war unfold?'" (6.3.86: Cicero pretends to understand "sixth" and "Annales" instead of the witness' name Sextus Annalis, tantamount to his denying the latter's very existence; the line of verse clearly is not chosen haphazardly but to fit the case.)

". . . Hortensius said to him [Cicero] as he was examining a witness in the trial of Verres, 'I don't understand these riddles'; 'You ought to, however,' said Cicero, 'because you've got a Sphinx in your house.' Hortensius had received a bronze sphinx of great value as a present from Verres." (6.3.98)

Banter:

"I waited for the man's expected law and speech . . . He orders an assembly to be summoned. A crowd gathers round on tiptoe of expectation. He unrolls a very long speech in very fine language. The only fault I had to find was that, among all the throng, not one could be found who was able to understand what he said. Whether he did this with some insidious purpose or takes pleasure in this type of eloquence, I cannot say; although the more intelligent persons standing in the assembly suspected that he meant to say something or other about an agrarian law." (*On the Agrarian Law* 2.13)

In the courtroom speech *For Murena (Pro Murena),* the entire oration is designed in a way to excite laughter. Servius Sulpicius Rufus and the Younger Cato had accused Murena of election fraud. Cicero's task as defense attorney was difficult because the prosecution's brief was strong and because the plaintiffs were respected individuals (Sulpicius an upright jurisprudent, Cato a Stoic well known for his strict morality) who were furthermore his own friends. Cicero chose therefore to undermine the accusation without attacking the accusers personally but by mocking their professed convictions and by implying that it was an excess of these convictions that prompted their attack on his client. With great verve he first poked fun at judicial science, its petty details and formalities, then he ridiculed Stoicism for its harsh intransigence. It seems that while he was speaking "loud laughter spread from the audience to the jurors" (Plutarch, *Life of Cicero* 50.5). And Murena was acquitted. Some modern critics are astonished that Cicero was in the mood for joking at the height of the Catilinarian conspiracy. They fail to see that in fact this joking (alternating with emotionally charged moments) was a rhetorical strategy calculated for the sake of the judges, to whom it was necessary to provide reasons for not agreeing with Sulpicius and Cato. Cato was not fooled, commenting after the trial: "We have a comedian for a consul" (Plutarch, op. cit., WEH). A venomous and spiteful remark, it was meant to criticize the inappropriateness of a consul making such use of humor, while recognizing at the same time that Cicero had won precisely because of it.

Laughter is therefore a rhetorical weapon that cooperates with persuasion by psychological means. Cicero, who was fully conscious of it, studied this weapon in his theoretical works, particularly in a long excursus in *On the Orator* (2.216–90).

Now the subject of laughter in rhetoric is more complicated than it at first appears, and upon examination a host of different problems arises:

— Laughter was a point of contact between Rome and Greece. There was a Greek tradition of laughter, in practice (comic plays, for example) and in theory (ever since Aristotle, analyst of "what produces laughter"—*to geloion*—in the *Rhetoric* 3.1419 b3–10, as well as in the *Poetics*—the lost section on comedy—and in the *Nikomakhean Ethics* 4.14). There also existed a Roman tradition of satire and comedy. Roman orators exploited these two traditions. And Cicero goes further than Demosthenes, really much further in the opinion of some: "Many think that Demosthenes had no capacity for it [laughter], and Cicero no discrimination in the use of it." (Quintilian, *Institutio Oratoria* 6.3.2)

— Laughter also poses a philosophical problem. It serves to criticize vices, to point out ugliness, but it raises the problem of appropriateness, moderation, and decorum.

— Laughter is bound up with the art of living, the conception of social life, as the words denoting humor and joking show, which are formed off the root meaning "city": in Greek *asteïsmos,* in Latin *urbanitas.* Cicero used to joke as well in his daily life (collections of his witticisms circulated) and in his correspondence.

— At the end of Cicero's life, the political problem arose: can one laugh in a dictatorship?

The rich problematic of laughter corresponds to what is characteristic of Cicero's method in general, as noted in the preceding pages: allied with a concrete use of speech in a given context, Cicero enlarges and deepens the topic in the direction of the intellectual, philosophic and political problems rhetoric poses.

Cf. A. Haury, *L'Ironie et l'humour chez Cicéron* (Leiden, 1955); M. S. Celentano, "Comicità, umorismo e arte oratoria nelle teoria antica," *Eikasmos* 6 (1995): 161–74; A. Corbeill, *Controlling Laughter. Political Humor in the Late Roman Republic* (Princeton, 1996); M. Trédé and P. Hoffmann, eds., *Le Rire des Anciens* (Paris, 1998). ❦

Cicero's Contemporaries

Cicero should not make us forget the numerous orators who were his contemporaries and who contributed to rhetoric's development at the end of the Republic. Just to recall the names: Hortensius (114–50 B.C.), Cicero's slightly older rival and friend, noteworthy for his Asiatic style; Pompey (106–48) and Caesar (100–44), who combined with their political and military abilities a true talent for oratory and so demonstrated how eloquence is one of the key attributes of the Roman statesman; Cato the Younger, also called Cato Uticensis (95–46), great-grandson of Cato the Censor, a Stoic, as we saw, lampooned in *For Murena,* heroic defender of freedom, about whom Cicero once wrote that he spoke "as though he were living in the Republic of Plato instead of Romulus's cesspool" (*Letters to Atticus* 2.1.8); Calvus and Brutus, mentioned above; or, yet another, Gaius Asinius Pollio (76 B.C.–4 A.D.), politician, orator, poet, and historian, who marks the transition from Republic to Empire.

One name deserves special attention, because it is a woman's, Hortensia, the daughter of Hortensius. In 42 B.C., when the triumvirs wanted to levy a special tax affecting 1400 noble Roman women, Hortensia, who was then the widow of Servilius Caepio, forced her way into the triumvirs' presence and successfully pleaded to have the measure withdrawn. Her speech has not been preserved, but according to Quintilian it was excellent (*Institutio Oratoria* 1.1.6). A Greek historian of the second century, Appian, gives a version of it which, while probably inauthentic, presents some interesting reflections on the interest of women in this affair and on the condition of women in general in the midst of the political conflicts and wars tearing Roman society apart (*Civil Wars* 4.32–33).

An oration by a woman is the exception in antiquity. If posterity has preserved and approved the memory of this one, it is because Hortensia was the daughter of her father and also because, for all the vigor of her intervention, essentially she did not depart from her assigned role as a noble Roman woman speaking on behalf of other noble Roman women (Valerius Maximus, *Memorable Sayings and Doings* 8.3, referring to two other orations delivered by women before magistrates, labels the speeches, on the contrary, freakish, "androgynous"). By its very rarity, the episode of Hortensia therefore sets off what is elsewhere the norm: the absence of women in the history of ancient rhetoric. This absence derives directly from the fact that women were largely excluded from the political, institutional, and intellectual activities of public life in general and were clearly left with very few occasions for delivering speeches or writing treatises. Philosophy, which was less directly tied to public life, was perhaps a little more welcoming to women than was rhetoric.

Anyone interested in feminine rhetoric in antiquity risks, therefore, being disappointed by the speeches women actually delivered because they were quite few in number and very poorly known. There still remain the tirades that different literary authors—almost all men—put into the mouths of female characters, for example, in plays, novels, historical works, and so on, compelling themselves to render, through these fictitious words, the idea that they themselves and their public had of the typical feminine speech. In short, it is a matter of character painting (ethopoeia), "in the manner of." A good example, among many others, of such a "feminine" rhetoric is found in book 8 of the *Antiquities of the Romans* by Dionysios of Halikarnassos. It presents long orations of Roman women, in particular Veturia, the mother of Coriolanus. Male imaginings of female discourse would undoubtedly be worth a probing rhetorical investigation.

To conclude the unit formed by chapters 4 and 5, if one draws up the balance sheet for the period which stretches from Alexander to Augustus, the innovations, as much Greek as Roman, appear numerous and important compared to the situation prevailing at the end of the period of Classical Greece. Rhetorical theory was enriched and systematized, the practice of eloquence underwent experimentation in varied and new political contexts, tastes evolved, Greece and Rome came face to face. Rhetoric became one of the pillars of Greco-Roman civilization, a status the Empire would confirm.

Chapter Six

The Empire

Innovation in the Tradition

Coming after a long period of civil war, the Empire meant the establishing of a strong and stable power under the authority of the *princeps* or "prince." This regime dominated the entire Mediterranean basin, both Latin-speaking provinces in the west and Greek-speaking provinces in the east. An immense and centralized structure, the Empire was built on strong foundations and accepted by the large majority of subjects. The reign of the famous *pax Romana* brought security and cohesion to the ancient world and in particular assured a cross-fertilizing of Greek and Latin regions.

The Greco-Roman world, however, came to know absolutism as the price for peaceful order. Called a principate or rule by a leading man, the imperial regime was an absolute monarchy, which diminished the initiative left to cities and citizens and changed the role of institutions inherited from earlier times. Hence the first question, one contemporaries themselves posed: what space was open to rhetoric in these new conditions?

Decline or Renaissance of Rhetoric?

The central text on this issue is the *Dialogus* of Tacitus. Before becoming a historian, Tacitus was a talented orator. In 100 A.D., along with his friend Pliny the Younger, he successfully prosecuted before the

Senate the case against the governor of the province of Africa, Marcus Priscus, for extortion and abuse of power. The emperor Trajan presided. Around the same time, he published the *Dialogus,* which reports, in the manner of Cicero's *On the Orator,* a conversation about rhetoric imagined to have taken place some years earlier (around 75 A.D.) between leading orators of the period. The participants raise as their principal topic the decline rhetoric has suffered between the Republic and their own day. By chapter 27, it seems established that the moderns are inferior to the ancients, despite Aper's efforts to argue to the contrary, and the discussion carries on with the causes of this decline. Two explanations are advanced. According to the first, the inferiority of present-day orators results from the defective character of their schooling (28–35). Whereas in the past future orators were brought up by inculcating in them a solid general culture and by giving them hands-on training through association with a great *patronus,* training today, the speaker Messala says, depends on learning by the "declamation" method, a narrow, artificial exercise using make-believe speeches that encourages only stylistic fussiness. According to the second explanation, political conditions account for present-day inferiority (36–41). As either Maternus, finally, or Secundus argues (the assignment of speakers is unclear because of a textual lacuna), during the Republic, the political stakes prompted important orations, while the current regime, by imposing order, deprived rhetoric of its greatest issues and left it with nothing more to say.

These two reasons are connected since, according to Tacitus, it is precisely the lack of real political stakes that has forced rhetoric under the emperors back upon declamation. The political explanation therefore precedes the pedagogical. This constitutes the principal lesson of the *Dialogus,* which thus erects a strikingly simple interpretative framework wherein the end of political liberty and the decline of rhetoric go hand in hand. Having come to this conclusion about Roman rhetoric, the author goes on to suggest that it could be extended to Greek rhetoric by comparing the periods after Demosthenes and Cicero (15.3; 37.6).

Analogous thoughts can be found in numerous authors of the first century A.D. Petronius (*Satyricon* 1–5, 88) denounces a decadence that would strike down rhetoric among other things, with declamation as a distinguishing mark. Seneca (*Epistles to Lucilius* 114) and Quintilian (*Institutio Oratoria,* e.g., 1.8.9; 2.10.3, and the lost treatise *On the Causes for the Corruption of Eloquence)* criticize the vogue for the "decadent" style. Pseudo-Longinus (*On the Sublime* 44) depicts a character professing a view similar to Tacitus's and who explains the disappearance of oratorical geniuses by the absence of liberty and "democracy." Seneca the Elder, for his part (*Controversiae,* book 1, Preface 6–10), turns to philosophical and ethical reasons. He blames natural adversity, the fact that everything that comes to be one day declines, and the depravity of contemporaries who, in thrall to vices, have lost the love for hard work and honor that animates great orators. This moral explanation, frequently reprised, was one that Pseudo-Longinus, notably, shared.

The accent is more or less pessimistic, according to the individual author. Some see in rhetoric's decline a profound social corruption or stifling of political life, while others think that it is merely the price to be paid for a much more momentous benefit, a stable and peaceful political order.

But confronting the assertions of decline, there is another current of a completely different strain. Dionysios of Halikarnassos, a Greek resident in Rome at the end of the first century B.C., in the preface to his treatise *On the Ancient Orators,* praises his own time because it represents, in his view, a renaissance of rhetoric. A decline set in previously, he writes, after the death of Alexander, when an uncouth and vulgar form of rhetoric spread (Dionysios is thinking of Asianism). But under Augustus, a classic rhetoric has come back, "philosophical" (in the Isokratean sense of the term) and sterling, owing to the power of Rome and the quality of its leaders, who promote culture. Contrary to Tacitus and Pseudo-Longinus, Dionysios sees in Roman domination—a process begun during the Republic and culminating in the Empire—the cause of rhetoric's renaissance, not its decline. In the second half of the first century A.D., in the *Dialogus* of Tacitus, Marcus Aper maintains the idea that oratory is still progressing and allows for great success in the present. A similar view appears in Quintilian (cf. *Institutio Oratoria*

2.16.18; 12.10.11) and in Pliny the Younger (cf. *Letters* 2.11.1; 6.11; 6.21.1; 6.23) who themselves strove in this direction.

These texts would merit separate investigation, because even though they deal with the same problem, they approach it from different angles. Each is located in a specific context, refers to its own way of conceiving its time and problems, uses its own criteria to define the "good" or "bad" state of rhetoric, and represents only a partial point of view on what was actually happening. Some look at Roman rhetoric chiefly, others Greek. Some behold a regeneration where others, judging by different criteria, see decline; one writer's renaissance is another writer's decadence. And those most driven to denounce stylistic corruption, like Seneca, are themselves the object of criticism for their corrupt style from others, like Quintilian.

To stay with the major issues, there are clearly two fundamentally opposing theses, decline and renaissance. Traditionally scholars, following Tacitus, have adhered to the decline thesis, as explained by the political situation. This is the source of the prevailing view in modern historiography that holds that rhetoric under the Empire no longer exists or is reduced to declamations, *recitationes,* and empty encomia (a view that carries forward and redoubles that examined above, about the decadence of Greek political eloquence in the Hellenistic era). Yet such an opinion caricatures the thesis by going further than its original proponents did, for they recognized that even in their own time good orators still existed (*On the Sublime* 44.1; Tacitus, *Dialogus* 36.2). The pessimistic assertions of the *Dialogus* did not in any way hinder Tacitus from delivering courtroom and funeral orations.

The truth in this analysis is that there was, in fact, a decline in certain forms of oratory during the Empire. Tacitus on this point lists sessions of the popular assemblies, the Senate, and the courts, which in earlier days used to call forth persuasive speeches and which have now been very much simplified or suppressed, since the will of the emperor has replaced oratorical persuasion. It does not follow, however, that the decline thesis can be accepted today just as the ancients propounded it. Not to mention the ethical considerations, for us passé, that often accompanied it, it has the drawback of being relative, in that it judges the rhetoric of the Imperial Age solely in relation to what went before. It fails to look for any originality in the new period underway. This is the reasoning of people caught in the past who did not have and still cannot have a synthesizing vision of the Empire. The Latin authors of the first century A.D. never stop wearing widow's weeds for Cicero. They take Republican Rome as an absolute point of reference, at the risk of judging the present too quickly and insufficiently distinguishing between the situation at Rome itself and the situation in the provinces.

The opposite thesis of rhetoric's renaissance is also partly true, insofar as it properly underscores a flowering which took place, not only in the time of Augustus but also in the following century with the "Second Sophistic," which we will treat later. This thesis, however, comes up against some objections, because it, like the preceding, belongs to a relativist construction, which judges the present according to the model of the past.

The ancient sources do not offer, therefore, a unified response that we today can adopt as is. The ancients' analyses contain interesting and just elements; the mistake has been to think that these analyses summed up the problem, which is, in fact, very complex, and to believe that Maternus had said it all. It is necessary, in fact, to take account of all the sources together, whereupon, getting beyond the false problems, a convergence does emerge. Whether they talk of decline or renaissance, all the texts actually agree that a change occurred in rhetoric, a "new order" so to speak. Contemporaries could not possibly see this phenomenon completely as it unfolded before their eyes. But they did notice it and try to interpret it with reference to the past they knew. It remains for us to define it more precisely.

To this end, we must supplement the dossier with another text. Plutarch's *Precepts of Statecraft,* written around 100 A.D., is a collection of pieces of advice addressed to the young man Menemakhos of Sardis, at the start of his career in public life. Sardis, as Plutarch underscores, is under Rome's authority. The types of political action consonant with independence, like declarations of war, changes of government, or alliances, are excluded. But there remain other forms of action by which a public man can be useful to his fellow citizens:

Nowadays, then, when the affairs of the cities no longer include leadership in wars, nor the overthrowing of tyrannies, nor acts of allegiance, what opening for a conspicuous and brilliant public career could a young man find? There remain the public lawsuits and embassies to the emperor, which demand a man of ardent temperament and one who possesses both courage and intellect. But there are many excellent lines of endeavor that are neglected in our cities which a man may take up, and also many practices resulting from evil custom, that have insinuated themselves to the shame or injury of the city, which a man may remove, and thus turn them to account for himself.

(*Moralia* 805A–B)

To be sure, this analysis remains retrospective. Just like the authors previously quoted, Plutarch examines the present in the light of the past, referring to the model of Classical Athens and Republican Rome. He looks for "what remains." He is concerned to mark out the difference between the conditions of the past and those of the present because Sardis had just gone through an insurrection, which Rome had harshly put down, and because he wants to encourage Menemakhos to be realistic and accept Roman sovereignty. That said, this passage, with its own agenda, presents a first catalogue of rhetorical forms then flourishing in the Greek cities of the Empire: courtroom speeches in public trials, diplomatic orations, addresses before the council and assembly seeking passage of all sorts of measures and reforms. Further on, Plutarch adds orations urging concord that are particularly useful for calming civil unrest (chap. 32).

Here in the *Precepts of Statecraft*, Plutarch is only interested in the political life of the local city. To round out the catalogue, it is necessary to add the speeches orators delivered in foreign cities, before provincial assemblies, and at Rome itself, in any of the three genres, judicial, deliberative, and epideictic, as well as the teaching and theoretical research that underpin actual practice. By taking into account all these aspects, which will be examined later in detail, we can recognize that the issue is not decline or renaissance, but redeployment. The Empire did not provoke a radical mutation, but a series of transformations, of changes of emphasis and innovation that make up a different landscape, even though the elements may not all be new.

Furthermore, the theme of eloquence's decline practically disappeared, apart from some late echoes, after the first century. The debate on this topic reflected the intellectual shock at the newness of the imperial regime. Once that was past, rhetoric evolved and prospered in a new setting with which contemporaries were comfortable.

General Characteristics of the Period

The present chapter encompasses the pagan period of the Empire, from the Augustan settlement to Diocletian's abdication (27 B.C. to 305 A.D.; the year 305 offers a breakpoint, because Constantine's reign began in 306 and he was eventually to establish Christianity officially and thereby inaugurate a new era). For the history of rhetoric, these three hundred years or so are distinguished by the unprecedented richness of the sources. Very many Greek and Latin texts have survived, and they allow us to assess, based on evidence, the scope of rhetoric in the society of the Imperial Age.

This profusion also contains a great diversity. From the political point of view, the Empire passed through phases that were very dissimilar: for example, the guise of republican forms under Augustus, tyranny at Rome under Domitian, a "golden age" under the Antonines, military anarchy in the third century, the administrative recovery with Diocletian's reform. When considering rhetoric during the Empire, it is necessary to keep in mind the very important differences that existed during the various periods, and likewise among the Empire's various locales, the difference between Greek-speaking and Latin-speaking, the uniqueness of each province, the gaps between small villages and large urban centers.

The third century poses a special problem. It used to be thought that this period, owing to its defining military insurrections and barbarian invasions, was a time of decline in most areas. Present-day scholarship prefers to speak in a more nuanced way of change through crisis. And in fact, in this chapter and in the Conclusion, we will observe factors showing that rhetoric continued to exist and transform itself during the course of the third century.

Literary Criticism

To return to the beginning of the Empire: it was an important moment in the history of literary criticism, and especially so for the ties between criticism and rhetoric.

Theoretically, literary criticism and rhetoric are not to be confused. While rhetoric is a precise technique aiming at oratorical analysis and production, criticism, which aims to make judgments about works ("criticism" comes from the Greek *krinein,* "to judge"), applies itself to all types of literary production and uses many different methods. Literary criticism is therefore, in principle, a broader concept than rhetoric. In antiquity, criticism started by dealing with poets, and it maintained them as objects of study thereafter, alongside or in preference to prose authors (Aristophanes, *Frogs;* Aristotle, *Poetics;* Horace, *Ars Poetica*). In order to study the works, it called upon different approaches: textual (establishing the text through internal investigation and comparing variant readings), biographical (lives of the authors), philological (learned linguistic, historical, and geographical commentary), and allegorical (the search for hidden truths in poetic narratives).

Poetics, in the sense Aristotle uses the term in his work of the same name, can be defined as a form of literary criticism that consists in the study of the basic elements of the work of poetry (plot structure, characteristic features, style, etc.). It, too, does not get confused with rhetoric.

There are, however, some places where the two disciplines meet, as Aristotle observes. Since he devoted two separate works to poetry and rhetoric, he clearly distinguished between these two arts according to their respective domains: imitation for poetry and persuasion for rhetoric. But he also pointed out important overlaps and common areas. He notes that everything in poetry concerning "thought" (demonstrating, refuting, moving, augmenting, diminishing) draws in fact on rhetoric (*Poetics* 1456a34–b2); conversely, he harks back to the analyses of the *Poetics* for the study of metaphor (*Rhetoric* 3.1405a3–6) or laughter (*Rhetoric* 1.1372a1–2; 3.1419b6–7) in rhetoric. The intellectual resemblance and the precise contact points between Aristotle's *Poetics* and

Rhetoric reveal the bridges existing in antiquity between rhetoric and poetics, and more broadly between rhetoric and literary criticism.

In short, these bridges are of two types, for literary criticism encounters rhetoric in two instances: when criticism deals with oratorical works, or when it uses concepts borrowed from rhetoric. The ancient commentaries on the Attic orators or Cicero illustrate the former, as do the *Controversiae* and *Suasoriae* of Seneca the Elder, whose work is a critique of declamations. Studies on the rhetoric of Homer (cf. chapter 1) or Servius's commentaries on the "questions at issue" *(statūs)* in the speeches of the *Aeneid* illustrate the latter. Similarly, Lucian's essay *How to Write History* criticizes contemporary historians and defines the virtues and faults of the work of history, basing itself among other things on categories drawn from rhetoric (invention, arrangement, diction, stylistic virtues, theory of the encomium, etc.). The two approaches merge when the subject is a study of an orator according to a rhetorical method, as in the essays dealing with Demosthenes (for example, *Rhetorical Figures in Demosthenes* of Tiberios): here literary criticism fully becomes rhetoric. During the Empire, such encounters between criticism and rhetoric were especially frequent because of the eminent place rhetoric held in the culture of the time. Two Greek authors at the beginning of the period played a key role in this regard: Dionysios of Halikarnassos and Pseudo-Longinus.

Dionysios of Halikarnassos

Dionysios of Halikarnassos, born around 60 B.C., settled in 30 B.C. at Rome where he lived for the second part of his life. Associated with the patrician family of the Aelii Tuberones, whose members were versed in the law and history, he died after 8–7 B.C. His work has two sides. *The Antiquities of the Romans* is a wide-ranging history of Rome from its origins to the first Punic War, but only the first half survives in its entirety. The *Critical Essays* is a collection of a dozen essays of criticism (there were more, but some have been lost) whose composition stretched over several lengthy periods coincident with that of the *Antiquities.* Some of the pieces were the finished products of his leisure, while others were epistolary *pièces d'occasion* in answer to a correspondent's request. Seven essays deal with the Attic orators *(Prologue to the Ancient Orators, Lysias, Isokrates, Isaios, Demosthenes, Letter to Ammaios* on Demosthenes and Aristotle, *Deinarkhos);* three deal with the historians (*Thucydides, Second Letter to Ammaios* on Thucydides, *Letter to Pompeios Geminos* on Plato and the historians); and two deal with problems of theory (*On Literary Composition* and *Imitation,* the latter surviving only in fragmentary form). The historical and critical sides of Dionysios's work, despite their different topics, are closely connected on two levels. In both groups, Dionysios espouses the same admiration and recognition of Rome, and in the *Critical Essays* he develops a theory of historical writing that echoes his own practice as a historian in the *Antiquities.*

The *Critical Essays* are the first body of criticism we have stressing imitation of the classical authors, an attitude that will prove fundamental throughout the Imperial Age. Dionysios meant to instruct. Subscribing to an Isokratean ideal of rhetoric as "political philosophy," that is, a moral discipline befitting the citizen, he wishes to propose models that will aid his readers in developing their eloquence and in particular their style. Detailed textual analysis and delineation of authors aim at highlighting "which characteristics of each of them we [should] imitate, and which . . . avoid" (*Prologue to the Ancient Orators* 4.2).

Towards this end, Dionysios established a reference standard composed entirely of ancient writers, in accord with the idea that the most brilliant era of Greek literature was the Archaic and Classical periods, especially fifth- and fourth-century Athens, and that this time should be the source of inspiration. Making literary criticism more precise and systematic than anyone before him, he applies to this corpus several refined methods: learned research on the authors (their biographies, influences they felt and exercised, questions of authenticity), long quotations and analyses of extracts, "comparison" *(sunkrisis)* of authors or passages, tasks of practical criticism like changing the word order in a given sentence or changing the meter used (switching from heroic hexameters to tetrameters, for example), all in order to display the inherent quality of the original better. Imitation will thus follow from familiarity with the authors and from being imbued with their style. But it will be critical and eclectic. Dionysios is not afraid to fault Plato and

Thucydides. He thinks that the great authors shone each for his different qualities and that it is necessary to take inspiration from the good each had to offer. Among the greats, the prize for oratorical virtuosity, in his opinion, goes to Demosthenes, an exemplar for whom Dionysios experienced a growing enthusiasm throughout his life "for both choice of words and beauty of composition" (*On Literary Composition* 18.15).

This concept of "stylistic composition" *(sunthesis onomatōn),* which he developed in *On Literary Composition* and in the *Demosthenes,* is the most interesting feature of Dionysios's thought, taking forward in an original way analyses such as those Cicero had given in the *Orator.* By "composition," Dionysios understands the placing of words and clauses so that the flow of sounds produces a striking auditory impression. Style is seen as a succession of phonetic and even musical effects, and that is what constitutes for him a very important aspect of literary works in general and rhetorical speeches in particular:

For the science of civil oratory is, after all, a kind of musical science, differing from vocal and instrumental music in degree, not in kind.

(*On Literary Composition* 11.13)

The factors bestowing beauty or harmony on a text's "composition" are melody, rhythm, variety, and appropriateness. He adds two other classifications to this arrangement, types of style (elevated, simple, middle) and "harmonies" (*harmoniai,* whether "austere" [*austēra*], "elegant" [*glaphura*] or middle). In all cases Dionysios prefers the middle or mixed type, which brings together (by alternating rather than mingling) the qualities belonging to the other two and which Demosthenes's style especially illustrates.

Dionysios's work is instructive in its attempt to take conceptual account of the impressions experienced intuitively in reading. He is proud of the fact that his work "is the product and the offspring of my learning and my mind" (*On Literary Composition* 1.3). His analyses exerted an important influence on later theorists, including Hermogenes, and they are precious for anyone today wishing to imagine the auditory dimension of Greek rhetoric. It is not surprising that Racine—a master of word music—reread the treatise *On Literary Composition* "with great pleasure," as he wrote to Boileau (Letter of 1693).

The Treatise *On the Sublime*

Boileau, however, preferred the treatise *On the Sublime,* which he translated in 1674 and which he made famous in France and all of Europe (cf. the "quarrel of the Ancients and the Moderns," Edmund Burke, Kant, Hugo, etc.). This strange little work is one of the summits of ancient literary criticism. Transmitted in the manuscripts under the name of Dionysios Longinus, with the variant "Dionysios or Longinus," the work's author is unknown. He is usually called "Pseudo-Longinus" to distinguish him from Cassius Longinus, a rhetorician and philosopher of the third century A.D. The work was written most probably in the first century A.D. Dedicated to the Roman Postumus Terentianus (also unknown), it aims at being useful to "political men" (*andres politikoi,* 1.2), since they need to know how to write and speak, but its program goes beyond practical utility. It aims to define literary excellence as well as the means of achieving it.

"The sublime" (*hupsos,* literally "height," "elevation") is the name for such excellence. In this, Pseudo-Longinus had a predecessor, Caecilius, who was himself the author of a treatise called *On the Sublime.* Caecilius of Kale Akte was the contemporary and friend of Dionysios of Halikarnassos and the author of numerous historical and rhetorical works, notably a treatise *On the Figures* and the study *On the Character of the Ten Orators.* Pseudo-Longinus criticizes Caecilius for not being up to his subject, and he undertakes the topic afresh, by elucidating what in his eyes constitutes the proper character of the sublime, namely, that it is of a different order from ordinary qualities:

The sublime consists in a consummate excellence and distinction of language, and . . . this alone gave to the greatest poets and historians their pre-eminence and clothed them with immortal fame.

(1.3)

The sublime is therefore superior to simple persuasion:

For the effect of genius is not to persuade the audience but rather to transport them out of themselves. Invariably what inspires wonder casts a spell upon us and is always superior to what is merely convincing and pleasing . . . [The sublime exercises] an irresistible power of mastery and [gets] the upper hand with every member of the audience.

(1.4)

The sublime cannot be bothered with exactitude and correctness:

Now I am well aware that the greatest natures are least immaculate. Perfect precision runs the risk of triviality, whereas in great writing as in great wealth there must needs be something overlooked . . . What then was in the mind of those demigods who aimed only at what is greatest in writing and scorned detailed accuracy?

(33.2; 35.2)

The sublime transcends the human condition:

With writers of genius . . . , while they are far from unerring, yet they are all more than human. Other qualities prove their possessors men, sublimity lifts them near the mighty mind of God.

(36.1)

To attain the sublime, or at least to attempt to do so, there exist technical precepts, since this is a matter of art and not only of natural gifts. First, one must not mistake the objective or take for the sublime what is only turgidity, affectation, coldness, or bad taste; the author draws up a list of faults to be avoided and criticizes the style of Gorgias as well as Asianism. Next, one must imitate the ancients, the principal models being Homer, Demosthenes, and Plato. In naming Plato, he takes aim at Caecilius, who had dared to rank Lysias above Plato: "for though he loves Lysias even better than himself, yet his hatred for Plato altogether outweighs his love for Lysias" (32.8). Pseudo-Longinus expresses his admiration for his paragons and quotes numerous passages, which he examines closely; his comparisons of the *Iliad* and the *Odyssey* (9), of Demosthenes and Cicero (12.4), or his analysis of Sappho's ode on the torments of passion (10) have remained famous. Finally, one must know and investigate the five wellsprings of the sublime, which the author enumerates and which form the outline of his treatise:

1. The ability to conceive elevated thoughts
2. The passions (there is no development of this point in the treatise; in the opinion of many scholars, this is probably because of a textual lacuna)
3. The figures
4. The tropes, especially metaphor
5. "Composition," that is, word placement

The division, normal in rhetoric, between content (1 and 2) and form (3, 4, and 5) is readily apparent in this arrangement, and all the list's concepts belong to rhetoric.

The sublime, as Pseudo-Longinus conceives it, does not result, therefore, from some invention out of nothing but is deeply anchored in the system of rhetoric. Essentially, it belongs to what the theorists of stylistic genres had defined as the "grand," "elevated," "forceful" style. Moreover, on numerous points, Pseudo-Longinus agrees with the concepts and critical methods of Dionysios of Halikarnassos such as denunciation of Asianism, admiration for the ancients, insistence on *sunthesis,* and so forth. This being so, whence, then, the originality of *On the Sublime,* so striking when it is compared to the other rhetorical and critical treatises of antiquity? It lies in the conception, at once philosophic and mystical, that the author has of literature. Characterized by Platonism and Stoicism (it is thought Poseidonios may have been an influence), Pseudo-Longinus builds on concepts from philosophy (for example: 7.1, true and false goods; 15.1–2, imagination [*phantasia*] and clarity [*enargeia*]); and, fundamentally, he thinks that it is impossible to be a great writer unless endowed with the highest morality, "Sublimity is the true ring of a noble mind" (9.2). Consequently, his conception of literature accords a large role to the individuality, the idiosyncrasy, of each author. In contrast to the purely rationalist approach then dominant, Pseudo-Longinus saves a place for spontaneity, enthusiasm, mystery. Even imitation is presented as an inspired and supernatural phenomenon:

For many are carried away by the inspiration of another, just as the story runs that the Pythian priestess on approaching the tripod where there is, they say, "a rift in the earth upbreathing stream divine," becomes thereby impregnated with the divine power and is at once inspired to utter the oracles; so, too, from the natural genius of those old writers there flowed into the hearts of their admirers as it were an emanation from the mouth of holiness. Inspired by this, even those who are not easily moved by the divine afflatus share the enthusiasm of these others' grandeur.

(13.2)

Pseudo-Longinus sought to pierce through the mystery of genius. He presents his teaching in an eloquent, imagistic, and powerful style reflecting its very subject, as Boileau observed (in the preface of his translation): "He himself often demonstrates what he teaches; and when he speaks of the Sublime, he is himself very sublime."

Archaism and Atticism

In their choice of models, Dionysios and Pseudo-Longinus attest to the Imperial Age's predilection for the "classics." The Empire was a period of great literary and intellectual culture, a culture nurtured, schooled, and anchored in respect for the past. Encyclopedias, compendia, and scholarly research of all sorts proliferated during this time. The book was an object of honor in countless public and private libraries, as well as in trade among bibliophiles, in bibliographic manuals, and in commentaries on authors. It was a time of reading lists, of "association with the ancients" (Lucian, *The Dance* 2), of the authority of the great books. All this created a climate beneficial to rhetoric, which rhetoric itself largely helped to create.

In the Roman world, the archaizing taste was all the rage in the second century A.D., most visibly in Fronto, whose correspondence reveals someone in love with the Latin language, constantly on the lookout for just the right way to say something, and especially susceptible to the charm of older words and the older writers who used them. No Vergil or Cicero for Fronto; give him Ennius, Plautus, Lucretius, and Cato the Elder. Another leading orator and writer of the period, Apuleius (of whom more anon), displays this same archaizing temperament. So does Aulus Gellius, who wrote the *Attic Nights* (mid-second century A.D.), a learned work that, while dealing chapter after chapter with the most diverse topics from all branches of knowledge, dotes on problems of Latin grammar and vocabulary and the explication of rare forms drawn from literature of the Archaic period. Without going so far in their archaizing, many modeled themselves on Cicero. One of the highest accolades one could bestow on a Roman orator was that he merited being numbered "among the ancients" (Quintilian, *Institutio Oratoria* 10.1.118), or that his vocabulary was "impressive and classical" (Pliny the Younger, *Letters* 1.16.2).

In the Greek-speaking world, admiration for the ancients took the form of "Atticism," a phenomenon even more widely dispersed than Roman archaizing. We have encountered the notion of Atticism above (chapter 5), in discussing Cicero's neo-Attic Roman contemporaries, and here it takes on additional meanings. Atticism for the Greeks of the Imperial Age meant speaking and writing in a language inspired by the Attic (Athenian) dialect of the fifth and fourth centuries B.C. and so quite different from the languages and dialects normally used in everyday life (that is, *koinē*, "common," Greek, which featured more or less literary formations, local parlance, and vernacular tongues). Courses, lectures, and published works thus made use of a linguistic medium peculiar to themselves, distinguishing them as objects of "culture." They achieved their end when all the elements of discourse—vocabulary, morphology, syntax—appeared as if they could have come from Plato or Demosthenes.

At first glance, Atticism can seem empty and artificial, but two considerations permit a better understanding. On the one hand, the phenomenon of a literary language, set apart from any living dialect, always existed in Greece, at least in poetry, from Homer and Pindar on. In our own time, Modern Greek has known a situation of "diglossia" (use of two types of one language) in the coexistence of a "purified" language and a "popular" (demotic) language. In the same way, Atticism represented the search for a language of culture based on a body of ancient texts and distinct from contemporary speech.

On the other hand, there were degrees of Atticism, from the rigor of the purists to the more pliable practice of those who were simply aiming for an elevated level of language or who were satisfied with a few words or elegant turns of phrase. Certain authors, like Lucian or Aelius Aristides, imitated Attic prose almost perfectly, while others, like Plutarch or the physician Galen (who was greatly interested in the subject), were less strict. Atticism affected, more or less, all the literary authors of the period. As a general rule, the closer to rhetoric and sophistic they were, the more pronounced their Atticism, since the rhetorical milieu acted as a conservatory of fine language and good usage.

Atticism supposed a sustained familiarity with the authors considered to be models, a fertilization through reading and philological and grammatical study to enable identification of their characteristic turns and phrases. So, during the Imperial Age, Atticizing dictionaries flourished like Phrynikhos's (second century A.D.). In 37 books, it was called *Sophistic Preparation* because knowledge of Attic usage was the first step in the rhetorical education of the sophists. *Paideia* ("cultural formation") rested on *mimēsis* ("imitation," "osmosis").[1]

In its linguistic dimension, Atticism is the symptom of a larger phenomenon, the attachment of the Greeks of the Empire to the great writers of the past (including the Archaic period and Ionian writers like Homer and Herodotos, enshrined in the same movement as the Attic writers). Their attachment went beyond literature, to include the ancient history of Greece, Athens in particular, and to the intellectual, artistic, political, and military glories of the eighth to fourth centuries B.C., the fifth and the fourth above all. By the same token, the Hellenistic Age is relatively neglected. This theme of Hellenic identity had already taken shape before (in the Classical period, and then during Hellenistic times, a great period for the writing of local history and all kinds of "roots" mania), but during the Empire it had an unprecedented development. In the field of rhetoric, the extraordinary importance attached to Demosthenes, who became during the Empire an absolute standard, *the* Orator par excellence, oratory's symbol and paradigm, was a hallmark of the fixation on Classical Athens.

Nostalgia had no part in this harking back to the past, because the Greeks under the Empire were perfectly aware of the advantages of the present. Rome was the guarantor of external and internal peace, of a privileged position for urban leaders and elites, and of status even for small cities, all characteristics that prevented the upper classes (to which cultivated men and orators belonged) from seriously regretting the time

---

1. Although it is fashionable to oppose Atticism and Asianism, the preceding evidence shows that the two notions did not exist on the same plane. Asianism is a form of style (cf. chapter 4). Atticism is a linguistic phenomenon and more broadly a collection of cultural standards. The two notions, therefore, are not antithetical: a speech may perfectly well be done in an Asianist style and in Atticizing language full of references to fifth and fourth century authors (e.g., Aelius Aristides, *Monody on Smyrna*). There is opposition only if Atticism is changed into a stylistic concept synonymous with sober simplicity (in the manner of the neo-Attic Romans, who made Lysias the paragon of Atticism, to Cicero's dismay).

of wars, empire builders, and democratic excesses. The memory of the Greece of yesteryear, as sustained as it occasionally was, was not some reverie of lovers of the past but something completely different, a nationalist myth, a showcasing of roots, an affirmation of Hellenic identity within the Roman Empire. The inhabitants of the Greek-speaking provinces yielded to Rome's political and military domination, while asking in return to be recognized and respected as Greeks. By affirming their culture, they staked a claim, not of independence (that was impossible), but of respect and privilege. The Romans, for their part, accepted this affirmation and claim because their empire was not in question and because the Roman elites were bilingual and open to Greek culture. In short, insisting on the values of Hellenism served the stability of the Roman Empire.

In Latin as in Greek, rhetoric confronted the tasks of the hour by building on a past not seen as a shackle but as a wellspring and vital power.

Rhetoric, Queen of the Curriculum

In outline, schooling had three levels in the Imperial Age: primary education, supervised by a tutor in the home or by a school teacher, in the course of which children basically learned to read and write; secondary education, given by the "grammarian" (in Greek, *grammatikos,* in Latin, *grammaticus*); and finally higher education, in which rhetoric, taught by the "rhetor" *(rhētōr, rhetor),* was the principal course of study, alongside more specialized subjects like philosophy or medicine. Rhetoric was the most popular by virtue of its generalist nature. It did not prepare for careers only in the law, but also in the civil service, administration, and politics. The vast majority of the Empire's movers and shakers "did" rhetoric.

The task of the grammarians was the teaching of language and the explication of the poets' texts. They laid the foundation of classical culture, so critical in the thought and society of the Empire. Sometimes, impinging on the domain of the rhetors, they anticipated the next stage of the curriculum by explicating prose authors and teaching the first preparatory exercises in rhetoric (the turf wars on this issue reverberate in Quintilian, *Institutio Oratoria* 1.9.6; 2.1).

The rhetors, present in very many cities, held private classes or occupied public chairs, either municipal or imperial, the most prestigious of which were at Rome and Athens. The professors, whose classes were often crowded, had "assistants" *(hupodidaskaloi, adiutores)*. They gave lessons on theory and oversaw assignments by listening to the students recite their compositions or declamations and then providing in turn their own "fair copy." More rare was the case of professors who limited themselves to their own declamations, refusing to listen to the students. Such a one was the Roman, Marcus Porcius Latro, who used to say that "he wasn't a schoolmaster but a paragon," and that he was paid "not for his patience, but for his eloquence" (Seneca the Elder, *Controversiae* 9.2.23, Loeb modified).

Leaving aside theory for the moment, the essential elements of rhetorical schooling were the "preparatory exercises" (in Greek, *progumnasmata,* in Latin, *praeexercitamenta*), then "declamation" (in Greek, *meletē,* literally "exercising," in Latin, *declamatio*).

Preparatory Exercises

The rhetorical exercises are an ancient practice, essentially going back to the Sophistic Movement of the Classical period. The word *progumnasmata* appears in the *Rhetoric to Alexander* (28.4), although the context does not permit us to know exactly what the term covers. Some isolated exercises, which eventually became part of the canonical series, are attested in the Hellenistic period and during the Roman Republic. Examples include the *thesis,* practiced by philosophers and rhetors, the encomium (on a papyrus of the third century B.C., *P. Mil. Vogliano* 3.123, ed. I. Cazzaniga and M. Vandoni, in *Studi italiani di filologia classica* 29 [1957]:133–73, and the paraphrase (Cicero, *On the Orator* 1.154). During the Empire, exercises of this sort were organized in a graduated series, which we know about for the first three centuries from Latin sources (Quintilian, *Institutio Oratoria* 1.9, 2.4; Suetonius, *On Grammarians and Rhetoricians* [part of the *Lives of Illustrious Men*] 4.7, 25.8) and from Greek sources (the *Preparatory Exercises* of Ailios

Theon and of Hermogenes or Pseudo-Hermogenes). Other, lost treatises are known by their titles, authors' names, and occasionally some
fragments. To these texts—teachers' manuals—rich papyrological doc-
umentation adds specimens of student compositions. We thereby catch
a glimpse of a pedagogical practice broadly spread throughout all the
Empire. Even if, as would only be natural, there were variations in
the number, order, and definition of the exercises, the agreement of the
sources remains striking, allowing us to speak of *one* doctrine of the
preparatory exercises during the Empire and testifying to the homo-
geneity of Greek and Roman education during the period.

Here is the series of preparatory exercises as presented in Ailios
Theon (generally dated from the first or second century A.D.), following the order of the edition by M. Patillon. We give the name and, if
necessary, the definition of the exercises, as well as an example of the
topics that the students, whether secondary or university, were asked to
treat (the manual adds detailed instructions on how to go about this).

— *Anecdote (khreia).* The anecdote is a saying or a deed, short and
meaningful, attributed to a famous person. The students are supposed
to explain and comment on it. For example, "When asked where his
treasure was, Alexander, king of Macedonia, replied, 'In them,' point-
ing to his friends." Other theorists mention the "maxim" *(gnōmē),* a
similar exercise.

— *Fable (muthos).* The exercise consists in telling a fable, to which a
moral is to be added (or inversely, given the moral, to think up an appropriate fable), to refute or confirm a given fable. An example is the
"Fable of the dog carrying meat." Note that refutation *(anaskeuē)* and
confirmation *(kataskeuē)* are sometimes presented (the case here) as
procedures applicable to the exercises, sometimes (with other theorists)
as independent exercises.

— *Narrative (diēgēma).* Composition of a narrative, especially on a
theme drawn from an ancient historian, or a reworking and commentary on an existing narrative (introduction, background, abridgment,
expansion, changing of order, refutation, confirmation). Example:
"Narrative of the Thebans' entry into Plataia in 431" (after Thucydides).

— *"Place" (topos)* or *"commonplace" (koinos topos)*. Line of argument directed against a criminal, in the manner of the perorations of prosecution speeches. Example: "Against a temple robber."

— *Description (ekphrasis)*. Descriptions of all sorts were possible, of people, actions, places, seasons, works of art, etc. Example: "Description of a war" (description, when of an action, becomes a little like narration but distinguishes itself from the latter by its quest for expressivity and the desire to summon the deeds, as it were, right before the eyes of the reader or listener).

— *Prosopopoeia (prosōpopoiia* or ethopoeia, *ēthopoiia)*. This exercise involved writing a speech, put in the mouth of a given character in a given situation, with words appropriate to the speaker and the subject. It includes the consolation, the exhortation, and the epistle. For example, "What would a husband say to his wife as he leaves on a journey?"

— *Encomium (enkōmion)* and invective *(psogos)*. Example: "Praise of Demosthenes."

— *Comparison (sunkrisis)*. Comparison deals with people or things, whether good (with the objective of finding which is the better by using the arguments of the encomium) or bad (finding which is worse, using the arguments from invective). Examples: "Compare Ajax and Odysseus"; "Compare stupidity and suffering."

— *Theme (thesis)*. Set questions like "Is the world governed by Divine Providence?" (theoretic thesis); "Should one marry?" (practical thesis).

— *Law Proposal (nomos)*. This involves writing a speech proposing a law, or, conversely, countering a proposed law. Example: "Argue against the following proposal: perpetrators of assault and battery will pay a fine of ten thousand drachmas, or else forfeit their rights as citizens."

The end of Theon's treatise, which has disappeared in the Greek manuscript tradition, but has been preserved in an Armenian translation, presents in addition five supplementary exercises:

— *Reading (anagnōsis)*. The master has the students read works of the orators and historians; he introduces and explicates the texts, and then asks the students to recite them from memory, with the appropriate gestures.

— *Listening (akroasis)*. The students listen to the recitation of a work, for example, a classic or contemporary oration, and then endeavor bit by bit to memorize the text, until they are able to produce it in writing.

— *Paraphrase (paraphrasis)*. This exercise can be oral or written. It proceeds by changing elements, adding, subtracting, and substituting. Example: Take an oration of Lysias and express its ideas in the style of Demosthenes.

— *Elaboration (exergasia)*. Redo a text so as to improve its thought and expression by presenting the same idea better or by supporting better the same thesis.

— *Contradiction (antirrhēsis)*. With reference to a given speech, compose its opposite.

Supplementary exercises existed which Theon does not take into account. Fronto, for example, had Marcus Aurelius practice the canonical exercises (narration, maxim, commonplace), but he also had him work on "image" (*eikōn* in Greek, *imago* in Latin), a topic Fronto held particularly dear, notably by assigning Marcus a series of ten images to develop. The exercise proposed an image to the student, whose task was to find a suitable application and elaborate it (cleverly reversing the orator's usual situation, which starts with facts and looks for an image as illustration). Marcus stumbled over the ninth proposal, which was worded as follows: "In the interior of the island of Ischia, there is a lake, and in the midst of this lake, again an island, which is also inhabited. Draw an image from that." Fronto offers his own version, according to which the interior island is Marcus himself, and Ischia his adoptive father, the reigning emperor Antoninus Pius. The interior island benefits from all the advantages of Ischia (climate, inhabitants), without experiencing any of the drawbacks (heavy surf, pirates, etc.). The image therefore signifies that Marcus enjoys all the advantages of a protected situation, in the bosom of the imperial palace, while Antoninus is charged with the conduct of empire. Marcus will be able to make good use of this image in the speech of thanks he would soon have to deliver on the occasion of his being given the title Caesar. The exercise will thus have a direct application, above and beyond its political and philosophic scope (Fronto, *Correspondence with Marcus Caesar* 3.7–8, Van den Hout, 2nd ed.).

While prose predominated, certain exercises could still be done in verse, like that ethopoieia, improvised in Greek, which the young Quintus Sulpicius Maximus, age eleven, recited at the Capitoline Games in 94 A.D. The text of forty-three hexameters dealt with the following topic, "What would Zeus say to criticize Helios for loaning his chariot to Phaeton?" When the boy died of an illness shortly after the contest, his parents had the composition inscribed on his tomb (cf. L. Moretti, *Inscriptiones Graecae Urbis Romae* no. 1336).

The canonical series, progressing from fable to legal proposal, to which all too often the preparatory exercises are reduced, does not, therefore, actually exhaust the subject. It forms the axis or spine of a still richer and more diversified pedagogical practice, which had several objectives simultaneously in view.

In their continuation of the education begun with the schoolteacher and grammarian, the preparatory exercises had a linguistic and literary purpose. They deepened familiarity with the classics, with an eye to perfecting language and imitating the great authors. They represented an apprenticeship in the structures of discourse, achieved through work in creative writing (albeit set within precise heuristic rules) and oral and written treatments of a variety of texts. Such training could not help but give students the feel for writing and for a supple virtuosity. After this education, the most gifted were equipped to compose writing of all sorts: administrative reports, letters, historical or philosophical works, memoirs, poems, and the like. The compositions and dissertations of modern teaching have preserved down to our own time an echo, sometimes faint and weakened unfortunately, of this type of pedagogy. The *Elements of Style* of W. Strunk and E. B. White in the United States and the *Exercices de style* of Raymond Queneau in France offer brilliant, if differing, examples of such a writing exercise.

A moral objective, especially in the first exercises, was not absent either. The anecdote, for example, was by nature edifying. This did not prevent ancient pedagogues from approaching subjects from real life and introducing murder cases, adultery, et cetera, so long as, for Theon, decent language was used and crude or vulgar words avoided.

Finally, the preparatory exercises, as their name indicates, were conceived of as a preparation for writing complete speeches. Following a carefully thought out progression, the students became familiar with the different parts of rhetoric: commonplaces, briefs for argument (both for proving and refuting), outlines and parts of the speech, style, memorization, and delivery. They touched upon each of the oratorical genres (encomiastic, deliberative, legal), and they learned how to write drafts capable of becoming the sections of a speech. By the time they got to the last exercises, thesis and legal proposal, they were on the threshold of the whole speech. They were ready for declamation.

Declamation

A declamation is a fictitious speech, that is, a composition meant for the training of orators and having the appearance of an oration actually delivered. It concerns mythological or historical deeds, or it may well be set in an indeterminate time and place. Following Latin usage, there is a distinction between *controversiae* and *suasoriae*. The former belong to the judicial genre and imitate a courtroom speech, either prosecution or defense, delivered before a tribunal, while the latter belong to the deliberative genre and imitate advice given before an assembly or council, supporting or opposing a measure or an action. Epideictic declamations, imitating an encomium or invective, are marginal and quite rare.

Fictitious speeches existed from the time of the sophists, the *Palamedes* of Gorgias being an example of an imaginary courtroom pleading, allegedly by Palamedes during the Trojan War. In the Hellenistic Greek world, declamation was practiced on historical themes, as papyrological remains attest; it became a feature in Rome during the first century B.C. It was then, toward the end of the Roman Republic, that declamation really took off, to the extent that it became one of the most popular forms of rhetoric during the Empire, and for us today one of the best known, thanks to numerous sources. Two authors give an idea of the phenomenon, in Latin, Seneca the Elder and in Greek, Aelius Aristides.

Seneca, called the Elder to distinguish him from his philosopher son of the same name, lived between the 50s B.C. and the 30s A.D. At the end of his life, he assembled a large compendium of the best declamation passages he had known during his lifetime, either through having heard them personally, or from oral or written sources. The work contains ten books of *controversiae* and one of *suasoriae*. Each subject of a declamation provides the material for a chapter, in which Seneca gathers extracts from numerous orations to show how each of the declaimers had treated the subject in question. He cites the "epigrams" or memorable sayings *(sententiae)* they severally pronounced, as well as some more extended samples; he analyzes the "divisions" *(divisiones)* they adopted, that is, the chief features of their arguments, the "points" to be examined *(quaestiones);* finally, he specifies the "colors" *(colores),* that is, the individual motivations ascribed to the persons and deeds of the case (this applies only to *controversiae*). That is why the manuscripts give the work the title *Epigrams, Divisions and Colors of the Orators and Rhetors.*

In sum, Seneca the Elder presents somewhat more than 70 subjects of *controversiae* and seven of *suasoriae*. He names 120 declaimers, of whom three-fourths are Roman and one-fourth Greek; furthermore, it happened that Romans declaimed in Greek and Greeks in Latin. On one and the same subject, he cites several declamations by different authors, sometimes ten or twenty or so; the topics were traditional and passed from one declaimer to another. Often, to demonstrate their virtuosity, declaimers used to treat the pro and con of the same issue.

Seneca's work thus constitutes evidence of the first order on Greek and Roman declamation at the beginning of the Christian era. The author, who is quite intelligent, sprinkles his collection with interesting personal reflections, not only on declamation, but also on rhetoric in general, on stylistic problems, and on connections with poetry.

A striking feature of Seneca's work is the excessive and violent, not to say outlandish, character of the situations brought up. They have only to do with raped women, disinherited sons, children kidnapped by pirates, poisonings, mutilations, stepmothers, tyrants, parricides, crimes and false accusations of every sort. The declaimers Seneca mentions, or perhaps Seneca himself in the selection he has made, gave pride of place to difficult cases and fantastic subjects, at the cost, sometimes, of truthfulness and historical accuracy. Here are some examples:

— "Law: A girl who has been raped may choose either marriage to her ravisher without a dowry or his death. Case: On a single night a man raped two girls. One demands his death, the other marriage" (*Controversiae* 1.5). It does not seem that such a law ever actually existed anywhere; the declaimers will, rather, have combined two separate stipulations, in such a way as to pose a dramatic alternative. But it matters little. The interest of this famous subject, found in other authors, lies in its difficulty, because the demands of both parties are well founded and yet irreconcilable. Hence the thorny discussions to determine which of the two rights ought to prevail. Among the epigrams, Seneca cites Latro's, who argued the first woman's case: "He [the rapist] was just getting ready for a third—but the night was too short for him" (Ibid.).

— "Antony Promises to Spare Cicero's Life if He Burns His Writings: Cicero Deliberates Whether to Do So" (*Suasoriae* 7). The declaimer here takes the role of counselor, addressing Cicero to enlighten him on which choice to make. The situation is imaginary: Antony never actually made this offer. After he has quoted examples of arguments aimed at dissuading Cicero from accepting, Seneca comments wryly: "I know of no-one who declaimed the other side in this *suasoria,* everybody worrying about Cicero's books, no-one about Cicero: though in fact that side is not so bad that Cicero would have been unready to consider it if he had really been faced with these terms" (7.10).

Turning now to the Greek orator of the second century A.D., Aelius Aristides, one finds declamations of a different tone, aiming above all at precise historical reconstruction, based on the best sources, as well as at forceful and subtle argument. Of the twelve preserved speeches (what is left of a much more voluminous output), eleven are situated in fifth- and fourth-century B.C. Greece. The use of strictly Atticizing language contributes to the pastiche effect, to the extent that in reading these declamations, one might almost make the mistake of believing himself in the presence of an actual speech of the Classical period (cf. the case of the oration *On the Constitution,* handed down under the name of Herodes Atticus, about which some puzzled philologues wonder whether it is a declamation of the second century A.D. or an oration of the fifth century B.C.). Exercises in classical culture, argument, and style, the declamations of Aristides verge on being tours de force, and all the more so because the author argues both pro and con *(in utramque partem)*, composes two distinct speeches tending in the same direction *(retractatio)*, or stretches dialectical virtuosity (in the *Leuktran Orations*) by combining these two methods. The subjects (all *suasoriae*) are the following:

— *Sicilian Orations:* for and against sending reinforcements to the Sicilian expedition in 414–413 B.C. (after Thucydides).

— *Orations on Peace:* one, spoken by an Athenian for peace with the Spartans in 425 B.C.; the other, spoken by a Spartan in favor of peace with the Athenians in 404.

— *To the Thebans Concerning the Alliance:* two speeches arguing for the same end, taken from an episode in the career of Demosthenes, in 338 B.C.

— *Leuktran Orations:* on a debate that occurred in Athens after the battle of Leuktra (371 B.C.) to determine what the city's diplomatic policy should be. Aristides orchestrated an ensemble of five speeches, one for alliance with Sparta, one for alliance with Thebes, followed again by one in favor of Sparta, one in favor of Thebes, and a fifth and final speech favoring neutrality.

— *Speech of the Embassy to Achilles:* inspired by the three speeches on this theme in the ninth book of the *Iliad,* Aristides composes a fourth of his own invention.

In Latin, we still possess declamatory collections ascribed to Quintilian and Calpurnius Flaccus and, in Greek, texts of Lucian *(Phalaris* 1 and 2, *The Tyrannicide, The Disinherited Son),* Lesbonax, Polemon, and Hadrian of Tyre, as well as numerous *testimonia* in Philostratos's *Lives of the Sophists* and the treatise of Pseudo-Dionysios of Halikarnassos, *On the Mistakes Made in Declamations* (chapter 10 of the *Rhetoric).* The importance of declamation as a phenomenon during the Empire is self-evident. It was so prized that it burst the bounds of the classroom to become a literary genre and a social pastime. Not only students practiced it, but also professors, including the most famous, established orators in pursuit of professional enrichment, celebrities, and even emperors. When a star declaimer performed, in a school or in one of a city's public spaces (Odeon, Council, theater), the crowds were big and the audience included leading individuals from society at large, as well as students and their colleagues. In such a situation, the performance was anything but dull and boring. On the contrary, it was a spectacle, where the resources of intelligence and fine language were on display, combined sometimes with demonstrations of virtuosity, like improvisation on a theme submitted by the audience, or "figured" declamation, an entire oration with a double meaning. The Asianist style was often required, with its flashes of wit, its pathetic passages, its histrionic delivery, and its lilting diction. In order to keep alive the memory of such sessions, the orators regularly used to publish their declamations.

The declamation phenomenon, however, did provoke criticism and admonitions. Authors who believed in the decline of eloquence (Tacitus, Petronius; cf. above) saw in declamation one of the principal symptoms of decline and did not have harsh enough words for an exercise they considered artificial and harmful. Students protested occasionally, like Marcus Aurelius, who complained that Fronto had given him an "implausible" subject (*apithanos:* Fronto, *Correspondence with Marcus Caesar* 5.38, Van den Hout, 2nd ed.), or like the future poet Persius, who made himself sick:

I used often, I remember, as a boy to smear my eyes with oil if I did not want to recite the noble speech of the dying Cato—a speech which would be much applauded by my idiot of a master, and to which my father, sweating with delight, would have to listen with his invited friends.

(*Satires* 3.44–47)

More seriously, professors and specialists themselves used to decry the dangers inherent in the unreal and old-fashioned character of the subjects. In declamation there is no audience to convince, no vote to win. So the orator who only does declamations risks forgetting the requirements of true persuasion and losing sight of the realities of the Forum, the courts, the Council, and the Assembly by composing works of art whose only end is themselves and by amusing himself with subtleties and the quest for originality to the detriment of persuasion's simple means. This risk was real; there are numerous anecdotes portraying brilliant declaimers whose actual speeches in court proved disappointing or ineffective. To deter this risk, declamation had to remain an exercise. It was a good thing only if it did not become an end in itself, as Seneca the Elder, Quintilian, and Aelius Aristides (*Orations to the Cities on Concord*, 1, 4) unanimously affirm. It must not take precedence over real eloquence.

But then, how explain the enormous success of declamation throughout antiquity?

First, no doubt, by its educational value. Declamation allowed for learning speech in all its facets: argument, style, delivery. Over and above this straightforward rhetorical utility, it had a cultural and intellectual content. It engaged classic culture (linguistic, literary, historical) as well as bodies of legal knowledge. It developed the aptitude for reasoning and taught how to synthesize complex and delicate cases.

Like the preparatory exercises, declamation was an active pedagogical method. It appealed to the creativity of students by inviting them to write their own orations, instead of sticking to the analysis of classic texts. It presented them with the possibility of inventing the details of the case that were not spelled out by the topic and of playing a quasi-theatrical role by getting inside a historical or fictional character.

It is essential not to exaggerate declamation's fantastic aspect, even if the subjects sometimes surprise us. Tyrants and pirates were actual features of the ancient world, not just in the Hellenistic Age, when declamation started to develop, but also during the Empire. Crimes, acts of violence, tortures all existed, in fact as well as in speeches. Tribunals even dealt with adultery (cf. the *lex Iulia de adulteriis*). Although liberties were taken with the law, with history, and with simple truthfulness, to spice up the exercises, not everything was fabricated, far from it.

Declamations could even harbor allusions to current events. For example, Latro declaimed before Augustus and Agrippa about an adoption case, just at the time when Augustus was about to adopt Agrippa's sons, Lucius and Gaius. Every one of Latro's words then had a charged meaning, and he ran the risk of displeasing the emperor (Seneca the Elder, *Controversiae* 2.4.12–13). Instances of this sort must have occurred frequently in the course of declamation's history, the veil of fiction permitting the broaching of contemporary problems.

Beyond carefully chosen allusions, declamation was the bearer of an ideology that it instilled in students and that reinforced adult allegiance. Through the stereotypes it presented, it conveyed social and moral values and prejudices concerning the ties between rich and poor, parents and children, husbands and wives, on politics, war, human relations, the characteristics of the tyrant, the valiant man, the misanthrope, and so forth. The imaginary city of the declaimers, "Sophistopolis," as D. A. Russell has called it, was the theater of a human comedy that featured real problems, with suggestions on how to interpret or to solve them. The historical reconstruction of the past in Greek declamation, moreover, characterized by its focus on the golden age of Classical Athens, was part of the movement affirming Hellenic identity.

Declamation, as spectacle, in addition offered educated people a literary entertainment of high quality, in some ways comparable to drama (as much to comedies of manners as to history plays or mythological plays), and this fact contributed to its success beyond the classroom.

Treatises On Theory

The Imperial Age produced a very large quantity of rhetorical treatises. First of all, there was the response to instructional needs, which called for manuals and comprehensive works aimed at students' and their professors' education in theory (which explains why many treatises supplement the preparatory exercises and declamation). Once graduated, the former students continued to repair to the treatises to gather inspiration for their oratorical offerings, whether occasional or professional. Secondly, research in the field of rhetoric also developed for its own sake, in a scientific and speculative fashion, prompting analyses ever more complex and refined.

The treatises preserved for the period under consideration divide into four large categories, presenting a rich variety of subjects (all dates are approximate and A.D.):

1. Manuals of preparatory exercises: Theon (1st to 2nd century), Hermogenes or Pseudo-Hermogenes (2nd to 3rd century)

2. Complete courses of rhetoric, covering the art's different areas, in more or less extended format, from simple epitome to multi-volume work: Quintilian (1st century), Rufus (2nd century), Anonymous Seguerianus (2nd to 3rd century), Apsines (3rd century), Cassius Longinus (3rd century)

3. Specialized treatises on any number of aspects: (a) on argumentation: Hermogenes (2nd to 3rd century) on the "questions at issue," Minucianus the Younger (3rd century) on ways of proof or "epicheiremes" *(epikheirēmata)*, Pseudo-Dionysios of Halikarnassos (3rd century) and Apsines (3rd century) on figured speeches; (b) on style: Pseudo-Aelius Aristides (2nd century) and Hermogenes (2nd to 3rd century) on the *ideai;* Rutilius Lupus (1st century), Alexander son of Noumenios (2nd century), Aquila Romanus (3rd century), and Tiberios (3rd to 4th century) on the figures

4. Treatises on the epideictic genre: fragment of Alexander son of Noumenios (2nd century), Pseudo-Dionysios of Halikarnassos (3rd century), Menander Rhetor (3rd century).

The works of Dionysios of Halikarnassos and Pseudo-Longinus studied above belong on this list. In addition, other treatises, case studies (conducted based on declamation subjects), and often lengthy commentaries have been lost to us, their authors nothing more than names cited by Quintilian, Suetonius, Philostratos, later Greek commentators or even by the Byzantine dictionary called the *Souda*. The period experienced an explosion of interest, which, it must be emphasized, did not occur without affecting the textual transmission. Technical treatises were meant for use and were not protected by the status of great literature. By virtue of being copied, commented on, and employed in all sorts of ways, some of them lost their integrity or their author's name. This explains the rather high proportion of texts, among the period's production of theoretical works, which are mutilated, anonymous, or of doubtful attribution.

Before examining the two major bodies of work, those of Quintilian and Hermogenes, we should flag the names of Apollodoros of Pergamon and Theodore of Gadara, active at Rome in the second half of the first century B.C., who were famous in their day and teachers of oratory for the future emperors Augustus and Tiberius respectively. They headed two competing schools, about which we are poorly informed. Scholars of the nineteenth and twentieth centuries have for long overestimated their rivalry, talking about "Apollodorians," as the holders of a rigid, quasi-scientific conception of rhetoric, and "Theodorians," in contrast, as devotees of freedom and variety. Today, in fact, we recognize that this opposition has to be cut back to more just proportions. The schools principally diverged, as we now understand it, apparently over the shape and sections of the oration. The Apollodorians recommended use of a set, prefabricated structure, while the Theodorians accepted a certain flexibility. But otherwise it is rather unlikely that there was any fundamental disagreement over the conception of rhetoric itself. Theodore was a rhetorician and the author of a *Tekhnē;* he believed just as much as Apollodoros in the usefulness of rules, and it would be a mistake to make him a paragon of free thinking when it came to rhetoric. The radical attitude of repudiating the very principle of rules and systems does not exist among the rhetoricians of antiquity; it appears only outside rhetoric proper, for example in the external denunciations made by certain extremist philosophers (Cynics, Skeptics).

The *Institutio Oratoria* of Quintilian

Quintilian's *Institutio* provides the best overview we have of ancient rhetoric and is the major work best to read when seeking to understand this discipline in depth. The Latin title literally means "the education of the orator," and as that indicates, the work covers the complete education, from childhood to adulthood. It is divided into twelve books, the author's own arrangement. Book 1 deals with the training given to children at the primary and secondary levels, before their entry into the rhetor's class. Book 2 devotes itself to the basics, to the preparatory exercises and the problem of how to define rhetoric. There then follows the body of the work, composed of two sets: five books (3 through 7) on the ways to find ideas (*inventio* or "invention") and to set them forth (*dispositio* or "arrangement," "speech plan"), and four books (8 through 11) on formulating them (*elocutio* or "expression," i.e., "diction," "style"), memorization *(memoria),* and delivery *(pronuntiatio).* The *Institutio Oratoria,* therefore, is organized in accordance with the five parts of rhetoric (invention, arrangement, style, memorization, and delivery), the traditional list of the time, going back to the Hellenistic Age, even as it regroups these elements into two blocks that basically correspond to content and form respectively.

Going deeper into the detail of these two sets, one finds first, in book 3, historical considerations and definitions, then the distinction among the three oratorical genres (deliberative, epideictic, judicial), with a rather elaborate analysis of the "commonplaces" of invention in the first two of the genres mentioned. There is no discussion here of invention in the judicial genre, because it will be dealt with abundantly in what follows. Book 4 examines the first parts of the oration (exordium or introduction, narration, different ways of presenting the outline). Book 5 gets to the heart of the matter, the proofs (confirmation and refutation, that is, a positive demonstration of the point of view being upheld and response to the arguments of the opposing side). Book 6 deals with the final part of the speech (peroration) and the feelings the orator excites in the listeners (pity, indignation, etc.), the latter topic appearing where it does because the peroration is a privileged (but not unique) spot for appealing to the emotions. This book also contains an important exposition on laughter. Book 7 is devoted to the theory of the "questions at issue."

The simple description of this first unit shows the extremely precise and thorough character of the theoretic divisions, but also displays some flexibility in the way they interconnect. One of the first elements of flexibility derives from the handling of the three oratorical genres. While in principle each of the genres constitutes a third of rhetoric, meriting equal treatment, in fact, the judicial genre takes pride of place, and the study of invention and disposition focuses mostly on courtroom speeches (prosecution and defense). This is not peculiar to the *Institutio Oratoria,* but can be found at all periods in any number of theoretical texts. It recognizes the guiding role the judicial genre had always played in thinking about rhetoric and qualifies the apparent symmetry of the tripartite structure.

A second degree of flexibility results from the way invention and arrangement intertwine. In principle, these two activities, the one consisting in finding ideas, the other in ordering them, represent two distinct phases of oratorical creation. But as soon as one totes up the "commonplaces" (types of argument) that the orator will be able to call upon, the order of the list, originally thought of as a heuristic order, tends to become effectively the order of exposition the speech itself will follow. This is what happens with the commonplaces of the encomium, for example, which offer not only a repertory of arguments but also an actual schema. Quintilian is aware of this problem. Without being able totally to avoid it, he stresses that disposition, properly understood, is not the same thing as mechanically applying lists and that it brings into play special supplementary principles.

Turning to the second set, book 8 deals with qualities of style and tropes, book 9 with the figures and word arrangement, book 11 with memorization and delivery. Book 10, coming between style and memorization and performance, is devoted to advice on essential readings, on the authors to be imitated, and on the ways to practice writing. Here, too, the rhetorical system is thought of as flexible. Quintilian noticed a certain inadequacy in the traditional teaching about style, and as a remedy he thought it necessary to add with book 10 some discussion of literary criticism and method, which has proved to be of the highest interest for readers today as a way for getting to know the intellectual horizon of orators and the material conditions of their art of writing.

Finally, book 12, in Quintilian's mind the capstone of the work, elucidates two requirements without which great eloquence is impossible—moral value and general culture. The orator, once educated by Quintilian, is then ready to confront the reality of the courtroom, and the work concludes with practical advice on what is the best age to start practicing law and on how to approach cases. Two final chapters return, not without some passion, to issues of style and the ideal of beauty and dignity.

The *Institutio Oratoria* was written in a little over two years (around 93–95 A.D.), its rapid production possible only because it synthesizes a whole career's worth of experience. Quintilian (ca. 30–after 95 A.D.) was a Spaniard who worked as a lawyer and professor of rhetoric in his home province and then at Rome. He became famous, pleaded important cases such as Queen Berenice's, and was appointed by the emperor Vespasian to the first public chair of rhetoric, numbering the Younger Pliny most notably among his students. He published only one of his own orations, as well as the treatise *On the Causes for the Corruption of Eloquence;* other speeches and a theoretic treatise circulated under his name, published against his will from stenographic transcriptions. It was only after he had retired and was still in charge of the instruction of Domitian's grandnephews, and in response to friends' requests, that he wrote the *Institutio Oratoria* and gave definitive shape to his own thought on rhetoric.

Quintilian read a great deal. He knew and discusses many Greek and Latin theoretic texts, which makes his treatment extremely valuable as a source for others' views. He surveys the practical history of problems, catalogues proposed divisions, tackles the issue of terminology (especially about the problems of translating from Greek into Latin) and tries to choose among the different systems. He adopts a reasonable position by pruning excessive subtleties and by occasionally proposing his own solutions. Besides the theorists, he also read the Greek and Roman orators, as well as numerous literary authors, and he had a remarkable knowledge of Cicero.

Building on this trove of mastered information, Quintilian wrote a "summa" in which he treats with care, honesty, and detail all the aspects of rhetoric. This is where the usefulness of the *Institutio Oratoria* lies, and this is what explains its success. What is more, the work is well written and personal (it even contains confidences about family losses that befell the author). Quintilian is precise and concrete (for example, in the important third chapter of book 11, on delivery). He does not hesitate to give his own personal view on problems or to take a stand on the controversial issues of his day. Never letting himself get stifled by his sources, he wants to set off what is special about Roman vis-à-vis Greek theory and practice and to define the contemporary conditions for eloquence (which are simultaneously a function of the evolution of custom, governance, and the vicissitudes of fashion) with reference to the inheritance of the past.

At the level of principle, Quintilian conceives a high idea of the art of oratory, which is indissolubly linked in his mind to culture and morality, and he sees in rhetoric the fullest realization of man and citizen. These conceptions are directly descended from the Ciceronian ideal to which Quintilian adheres and which he carries forward in his own manner, that is, in the manner of a learned and serene professor of rhetoric, untouched by Cicero's power and tension. Quintilian is a balanced writer, full of good sense and hostile to the excesses of Asianism and declamation. Classic, he looks for just the right proportion between reason and passion. Highly educated, he respects the great writers, whom he studies sympathetically but not complacently. Highly attentive to pedagogical issues, he develops the formative side of rhetoric. Seen in this light, perhaps he can be considered as one of the inspirations for the teaching of the humanities in the West (he was, it should be noted, one of the reference points for Jesuit education).

The Corpus Attributed to Hermogenes

Hermogenes is completely different. A Greek rhetorician, his personality eludes us, while his works, cold and austere, are purely theoretical. They are stingy with information on sources used, and they are devoid of any extra practical or moral dimension.

Philostratos's *Lives of the Sophists* (2.7) contains a short biography of Hermogenes of Tarsus (a city in Cilicia), in which we learn that this individual was a greatly talented youth, who at the age of fifteen declaimed before Marcus Aurelius but who lost his mind when he reached adulthood and sank into obscurity. It is not easy to reconcile this information with the impressive activity as a technical writer that the body of work under the name Hermogenes represents. This has sometimes prompted the supposition that there must be two men named Hermogenes, the one Philostratos talks about, and another contemporary who wrote the rhetorical treatises. A second, and more economical, interpretation posits one and the same man, all the while recognizing that Philostratos's information is insufficient to allow reconstruction of a satisfactory biography. No matter the hypothesis, the date of Hermogenes's works falls somewhere at the end of the second, or the beginning of the third century A.D.

There are five works handed down under this name:

1. The *Preparatory Exercises* (*Progumnasmata* or "warm-ups"), a manual in the tradition of Theon's but shorter

2. The *Questions at Issue* (*Peri tōn staseōn*), an important treatise, recasting the *stasis* system

3. *On Invention* (*Peri heureseōs*) in four books, the first three of which, as the title suggests, provide a method for discovering ideas for the different parts of the speech, while the fourth deals with style

4. The *On Forms of Style* (*Peri ideōn logou*), a monument of stylistic theory, of which more anon

5. *How to be Forceful* (*Peri methodou deinotētos*), a collection of brief chapters devoted to particular problems and to different "tricks of the trade."

The ensemble of these five treatises forms a complete *Tekhnē*, covering in detail all the aspects of rhetoric except memorization and delivery. This corpus, nevertheless, looks like an artificial creation, because the five treatises are probably not all by the same author. If the attribution to Hermogenes of the *Questions at Issue* and *Forms of Style* seems secure, doubts weigh on the authenticity of the other works (especially *On Invention* and *How to be Forceful*), which could be the work of one or more different authors added subsequently to the first two pieces.

The treatise *On Forms of Style* is the most interesting of the lot. The author says its usefulness is twofold: it should permit the ability both "to evaluate the style of others, either of the older writers or of those who have lived more recently," and "[to become] the craftsman of fine and noble speeches himself, speeches such as the ancients produced" (1.1, Wooten trans.). He affirms here rhetoric's two vocations, of critical theory and of productive art, each inextricably bound to the other within the framework of the classical standard.

By "form" *(idea)*, Hermogenes understands a stylistic key signature, a category or type that constitutes the tone of what is said. These forms are seven in number (counting only the principal forms, not their subdivisions), and each is obtained by virtue of "means" distributed over eight levels. Hermogenes presents his system, therefore, as a kind of matrix or double entry table, where the stylistic qualities to be attained are found across the top ("forms") and the "means" or constitutive elements of these qualities are found along the left side:

FORMS / MEANS	"clarity" (saphēneia)	"grandeur" (megethos)	"beauty" (kallos)	"liveliness" (gorgotēs)	"character" (ēthos)	"truthfulness" (alētheia)	"forcefulness" (deinotēs)
"thought" (ennoia)							
"approach" to the thought (methodos)							
"diction" (lexis)							
"figure" (skhēma)							
"clause" (kōlon)							
"arrangement" of words (sunthesis or sunthēkē)							
"cadence" (anapausis)							
"rhythm" (rhuthmos)*							

*Rhythm in fact is not a separate level, but results from the interaction of the two preceding levels, arrangement and cadences.

In order of importance among the means, thought and expression come first, rhythmic means playing a secondary role. If one wants, for example, to produce "clarity," and more precisely that kind of clarity called "purity" (katharotēs), one will have to use "thoughts" common to all and easily understandable, an "approach" consisting in an uncomplicated narration of events without any digressions, current, non-metaphorical "diction," the "figure" of uncomplicated grammatical structure, short "clauses" each containing a complete thought, an "arrangement" permitting hiatus, and iambic and trochaic "cadences"

(1.3). If one is looking for "grandeur," and more precisely "solemnity" *(semnotēs),* one will use "thoughts" dealing with the gods, divine things, or great human deeds, an "approach" both self-confident and authoritative, or else mysterious, "diction" sonorous and full owing to the presence of long vowels, straightforward "figures," brief "clauses," akin to aphorisms, an "arrangement" admitting of hiatus and particularly fond of spondees, and "cadences" long and open (1.6).

Putting this system to practical use involves nuance and subtlety. Some partial overlapping exists, among the different forms, at the level of certain components. Some figures of "solemnity," for example, are identical to those of "purity" (1.6, p. 250, 6, Rabe ed.: which all goes to say that grandeur ought to include a share of simplicity, a quite just and interesting observation). In some instances the matrix has gaps, as with "indignation" or "severity" *(barutēs),* a sub-species of "truthfulness," which only exists in "thought" and "approach" and which presents nothing specific at the level of the other components (2.8, p. 368, 17–18). Finally, and above all, the forms are not mutually exclusive but, on the contrary, often coexist, one and the same work being able to contain several elements each of which is characteristic of a different form, for example, the elements of both "clarity" and "grandeur," of "truthfulness" and "sweetness," and so on. In this case there is a mélange *(mixis)* of forms, and this mélange is highly advisable for giving a speech richness and variety.

"Forcefulness" is particularly important, since it is defined as the appropriate use of all the other forms, in accordance with the topic and circumstances. Hermogenes on this score distinguishes (2.9) among the forceful oration that looks it (e.g., the *Philippics* of Demosthenes), the forceful oration that does not seem so (e.g., numerous other Demosthenic orations, as well as the speeches of Lysias), and the oration that appears forceful but is not in fact (e.g., the precious and showy orations of the sophists). This discussion poses the problem, important in ancient rhetoric, of knowing just how much it is necessary "to conceal art" (on this problem, cf., among others, Aristotle, *Rhetoric* 3.1404b18; *Rhetorica ad Herennium* 1.17; Quintilian, *Institutio Oratoria* 1.11.3; 9.3.102).

The system of "forms" descends from the lists of "virtues" and stylistic "genres" developed in the Hellenistic Age (cf. above, chapter 4). Compared to them, it represents a notable enrichment, since in place of three virtues and three or four genres, Hermogenes's list comprises seven forms, and as many as twenty if the sub-species are included, a numerical increase that allows for a much more sharp and precise analysis. As for his list of means, it is based on research dealing with the constitutive elements of style, on the theories of tropes and figures, and on the works of a Dionysios of Halikarnassos in the field of harmonies and rhythms, and it proposes a classification of all these aspects. Thus the system of Hermogenes represents a synthesis and deepening of centuries of research in the area of stylistic analysis. In the second century A.D., other treatises on the "forms" existed before that of Hermogenes; they are all lost, save for the *Rhetoric* of Pseudo-Aelius Aristides, in two books, which presents a doctrine rather similar to that of Hermogenes. The topic of the "forms" was clearly a critical field for Greek rhetoric during the Empire. The treatise of Hermogenes seems to have outclassed its contemporaries by virtue of its systematizing bent.

In fact, Hermogenes intends to provide a matrix accounting for all the textual effects possible. Textual analysis is not for him a matter of intuition or feeling but an almost scientific description and classification using systematically arranged notions. From this point of view, the *Forms*'s endeavor parallels that of the *Questions at Issue,* and is just as, or even more, ambitious. These two works draw up a definitive taxonomy, the *Questions* for invention, the *Forms* for style. The study of style according to Hermogenes can be compared to a kind of chemical analysis, which isolates the principal elements (these are the *ideai*), defines the laws and proportions of their combinations, and classifies the resulting compounds (the texts).

For all that, Hermogenes's classification is still not abstract, and this for two reasons. First, the stylistics of the *ideai* is a total system, wherein the "form" is not torn from its context, but is in fact tightly bound up with it by the notions of "thought" and the "approach" to the thought. The thoughts are the subjects treated, the "referents" of the speech. The approach to the thought, that is, the manner of presenting the thought, is akin to the figures of thought (the distinction "approach" to the thought versus "diction" recalls the distinction "figures of thought" versus "figures of diction"), but it is not exactly the same and has a broader meaning. By introducing these two "means" in a prominent position in his table, Hermogenes indicates that the task of style cannot be understood independently of the subjects under discussion and that stylistic qualities are only operative with reference to the speech's content.

Secondly, Hermogenes relies constantly on close study of the great orators, especially Demosthenes. He had written commentaries on certain of the latter's orations, and Demosthenes in his eyes is the master of the mixing of forms and the unsurpassable model of the political speech (in conformity with the principles in vogue during his time, the theorist prefers archaic and classical literature, and has little to do with the moderns). At the end of the treatise (2.12), Hermogenes even widens his perspective, to envisage no longer just the orators, but all writers, including historians, philosophers, and poets, suggesting that, at least potentially, the theory of the forms of discourse applies to the whole of literature and contains a theory of literary criticism based on rhetorical concepts.

The Emperor as Orator

Within the confines of theory and practice, nothing better conveys the prestige of rhetoric during the Empire than this refrain: the emperor must be an orator.

It corresponded to a historical reality. The emperors, by their very role, had to deliver numerous speeches: addresses to the Senate or the Praetorian Guard, eulogies, diverse speeches before the citizenry of Rome, armies on campaign, the courts, provincial agencies and bodies, and so forth. Writing them down in carefully edited letters and imperial edicts gave added life to these spoken interventions. To prepare for their task, the emperors received training and practiced exercises. Augustus, for example, was the student of Apollodoros and delivered declamations daily during the War of Mutina; Fronto trained Marcus

Aurelius. It would be easy to multiply such instances. The Tabula Claudiana, an inscription that reproduces a Senatorial address of the emperor Claudius in 48 A.D., in which he sought to have leading men of Gaul admitted to Senate membership, preserves a famous sample of imperial speech. The text was engraved in bronze and displayed in Lyons, where it was discovered in the sixteenth century (*Corpus Inscriptionum Latinarum* 13.1668) and where it is now preserved; Tacitus gives his own version of the same speech in the *Annals* (11.24).

The emperors often used to seek assistance, whether because they had insufficient time themselves, or because it was easier, or because they were well aware of the importance attached to their slightest utterance and did not want to risk leaving anything to chance. Augustus wrote out in advance and read all his personal comments; whenever he had to deliver a speech in Greek, he wrote out his text in Latin and had it translated (Suetonius, *Augustus* 84, 89). Nero had recourse to Seneca's help, Trajan to Lucius Licinius Sura's. Sometimes there could even be doubt and questionings about the identity of the actual author. Some thought they recognized in Otho's speeches the oratorical style of the famous lawyer Galerius Trachalus (Tacitus, *Histories* 1.90.2), and people wondered whether Aelius Caesar had written by himself the "very pretty speech" of thanks to his father Hadrian or whether he had had the concerted help of his bureau chiefs and teachers of oratory (*Historia Augusta, Life of Aelius* 4.7).

Concerning Nero, Tacitus makes a telling observation:

The elderly observers, who made a pastime of comparing old days and new, remarked that Nero was the first master of the empire to stand in need of borrowed eloquence.

(Annals 13.3.2)

In other words, Nero was criticized for having proved to be an inadequate speaker. His subjects had expectations: in their eyes, imperial majesty required, among other things, an imperial command of rhetoric. This was an important theme during the Empire for numerous authors. Josephus recognized that Caligula had outstanding oratorical abilities, in both Greek and Latin (*Antiquities of the Jews* 19.208), while the Younger Pliny praises Trajan's eloquence (*Panegyric* 67.1) and Menander Rhetor that of any accomplished emperor (*On Epideictic Orations* 374.25).

As Seneca saw it, the emperor (Claudius, in this case) was, as such, "the universal consolation of all mankind," not only by his benefactions, thanks to which humanity forgets its ills, but also by his words, which have a special, almost oracular effectiveness since they bear the "weight" of his "divine authority" (*Consolation to Polybius* 14.1–2 [part of the *Moral Essays*]). Properly to appreciate this passage, which is not just empty flattery, it is necessary to recall that consolation was truly one of the emperor's missions, which meant, in the ancient view, taking care of his subjects, individually and collectively. When natural catastrophes (earthquakes, volcanic eruptions, etc.) occurred, for example, he exercised his generosity with disaster relief, speeches before the Senate on behalf of the suffering populations, and official declarations of condolence. Aelius Aristides thus asserts that Marcus Aurelius and Commodus, at the time of an earthquake in Smyrna, "employed the most divine and glorious instruments, when they consoled us with their words and proved . . . how great a thing is culture joined with kingship" (*Palinode for Smyrna* 8, Behr trans.).

Fronto particularly stressed this theme, almost to the point of hyperbole:

[The emperor's eloquence] strikes fear, wins love, arouses energy, extinguishes impudence, encourages virtue, destroys vices; it persuades, it coaxes, it teaches, it consoles. . . . Other generals before you [Lucius Verus, to whom the letter is addressed, and his brother Marcus Aurelius] have subjugated Armenia, but, by Hercules, a single letter of yours, a single oration of your brother about you and your virtues will redound more to your glory and make you more famous in the eyes of posterity than princely triumphs, no matter how numerous.

(*Letters to Verus* 2.1.9, Van den Hout, 2nd ed., WEH)

For it is the task of the Caesars to sway the Senate for the common weal, to address the assembled people on matters varied and multiple, to right justice gone awry, to write letters to the world, to rebuke the lords of the nations, to check with edicts the misdeeds of allies, to praise deeds well done, to suppress the seditious and affright the fierce. Verily, all these things must your words and letters accomplish.

(*Letters to Marcus Aurelius on Eloquence* 2.6, Van den Hout, 2nd ed., WEH)

Beyond the factual reality, we are dealing with an ideological model that sees in the emperor *the* orator *par excellence,* the greatest public speaker, eulogizer, and consoler. At a distance of several centuries, this model took up from the Athenian democratic model and substituted the latter's conception of an orator of the people and for the people with the conception of an orator who effects from on high the good of his subjects. It was, then, a matter of a higher rhetoric, authoritative and sealed with the majesty and divinity, or quasi-divinity, that characterized the Roman emperors. This ideal rhetoric accorded at the time with the importance of the art of the spoken word, of which it represented the superlative version. It is self-evident that it went far beyond normal practice, to which we now turn.

The Practice of Oratory and the Irresistible Rise of the Epideictic Genre

The Judicial and Deliberative Genres

The letters of Pliny the Younger are chock full of hard evidence about the practice of Roman judicial eloquence at the turn of the first to second century A.D. The court of the centumvirs heard numerous cases. Pliny called it his "arena" (6.12.2), where he practiced law daily, lamenting the bad days when the cases appeared trivial and the listeners vulgar and inattentive (2.14), but glad when he carried off victories (4.16), as in the notorious affair of Attia Viriola. She was a lady of high society, a senator's wife, and she brought a suit to reclaim her share in an inheritance of which her eighty-year-old father had deprived her when he rewrote his will in favor of his new wife, after only eleven days of marriage. The four relevant panels heard the case at the same time, 180 jurors, in a Basilica Julia besieged by the curious, amidst a crowd of lawyers representing the litigants. Pliny made a brilliant plea for the plaintiff (6.33).

The Senate sat as a high court of justice for those of senatorial rank; it regularly heard trials of governors charged with theft or other crimes committed in the exercise of their office, like Marius Priscus or Julius

Bassus (2.11; 4.9). In these two cases, Pliny spoke for five hours (in one go for the former, with a recess for the night in the latter).

Last, the emperor surrounded by his counselors had judicial power outranking all others in both civil and criminal cases, in the first instance as a court of appeal. Pliny was invited as a lawyer to join Trajan's council when the emperor was holding a court session of several days' duration in a villa near Rome. The seriousness of the work in which he participated impressed him, as did the beauty of the setting and the emperor's friendly welcome (6.31).

In the Greek sources, such as the *Lives of the Sophists* by Philostratos or inscriptions, it is clear that the Greek orators of the Imperial Age enjoyed an important, and often lucrative legal practice, whether speaking before local jurisdictions, before the emperor's representatives (governors, legates, etc.) who were delegated to render justice in his name, or before the imperial court itself, where they were present to defend their own interests or those of their native land (city or province).

Real court speeches, therefore, gave them ample material on which to exercise the skills acquired in declamation and classroom theory. The majority of the great orators of the time were trial lawyers who built brilliant political careers on their courtroom success. They delivered orations, necessarily very numerous, dealing with an array of subjects, including civil and criminal affairs and all sorts of political, administrative, and fiscal questions. They often published and circulated copies, even though the majority of them have not come down to us (the major preserved example is the *Apology* of Apuleius). The importance of judicial rhetoric was self-explanatory in a litigious and bureaucratic society like that of the Empire, where judicial discourse belonged to the most firmly anchored Greek and Latin traditions.

The reality of the emperor, nevertheless, distinguishes the period. Many cases were political, and he and his freedmen[2] controlled them. Anxious to preserve their authority and to snuff out any hint of opposition, some emperors multiplied charges of treason, aiding and abetting the enemy, and black magic, accompanying them by extraordinary

2. Freedmen, in this case, of the emperor's household, staffed and sometimes headed imperial bureaus—WEH.

forms of procedure which denied the accused his customary rights and subjected him to terrible punishments. Informants *(delatores)* made the system work. Professional accusers, they denounced crimes, real or imagined, and brought prosecutions before the courts to win personal favor and financial gain. Moreover, by the second century, it seems, the leading role given to the emperor and his representatives provoked a retreat from the use of juries, as the importance of councils and bureaucrats grew. This ultimately brought a more administrative treatment to judicial matters and gave greater weight to the law and jurisprudents. One observes a sort of bureaucratization of justice and an increased importance of briefs, to the detriment of the live word. It was not, perhaps, that there was less rhetoric, only a different kind of rhetoric. Thus, courtroom speeches often took the form of appeals, petitions, embassies, or requests brought before a court of last resort.

The emperor's weight was more palpable still in the deliberative genre. Since the *comitia* had ceased to assemble, the sole central deliberative body was the Senate, where the debates rolled on under the emperor's authority, an authority never questioned, always felt, and during some reigns crushing. In comparison to the emperor's power, the Senate had only subordinate competence which progressively diminished over the course of time. The chief decision-making went on in the imperial council *(consilium principis),* whose membership varied and numbered scores of specially chosen senators, bureau chiefs, praetorian prefects, and jurisprudents. Their responsibilities (beyond the judicial competence discussed above) covered legislation, finances, military affairs, foreign policy, and so on.

The Senate and, even more, the imperial council formed closed groups, limited in number, ruled by the power of their imperial chairman and charged to assist him with their advice. Between the two types or poles of the ancient deliberative genre—the address delivered before a sovereign assembly and the advice expressed in the leader's or monarch's council—imperial Rome gravitated toward the latter. Contributions in such circumstances were not meant to win popular assent but to carry weight in a restricted and strictly controlled decision-making process.

Deliberative eloquence had more latitude in the provinces, before the cities' local bodies, the provincial assemblies, and of course the army legions when generals addressed them. Certain exceptional cases were able to affect the fate of the Empire. It was with an address that the military tribune Antonius Honoratus convinced the soldiers to remain loyal to Galba and not to listen to the speech that the usurper Nymphidius had prepared to win them over to his own cause, even as Nymphidius drew near, a copy of his speech in hand, written for him by an advisor. Nymphidius declined to deliver it (Plutarch, *Life of Galba* 14). Other similar cases presented themselves during the usurpations and anarchy of the second and third centuries. More often, debates dealt with everyday issues, in conformity with the limited ability granted to the local authorities. If the central power made the big administrative, political, and military decisions, the provincial assemblies, consisting of representatives from the cities of the province, had to oversee certain issuings of coinage, the celebration of the imperial cult, intercity accord, and relations with the Roman authorities. The assemblies and city councils looked out for the status of their city in the Empire, for the magistracies, local finances, relations with the governor and other imperial officials, and for all sorts of not unimportant questions which they preferred to regulate at the local level, avoiding as much as possible the intrusion of Roman authority.

The *Bithynian Orations* of Dio of Prusa, which date for the most part from the end of the first and the beginning of the second century A.D., document this point exceptionally well. They comprise:

— Four speeches "on concord" (nos. 38–41), delivered, respectively, at Nicomedia, Nicaea, Prusa, and Apamea (four cities in Bithynia), before the Assembly of the people or, in one instance perhaps, before an enlarged Council. They try to smooth over the differences that set these cities against one another on the matter of honorific titles and regional questions, and to emphasize the risks of discord and the advantages of a good neighbor policy.

— Ten speeches delivered to the civic bodies of Prusa (Assembly or Council) on divers matters (nos. 42–51). In one, earlier than the rest of the series, Dio defends himself against the charge of starving the citizenry, after an uprising over grain in the course of which the rioters tried without success to stone him and to burn down his house with his wife and child inside. In others, he expends rich persuasive powers to promote a costly program of civic renewal and beautification for Prusa, which met with community resistance. It involved major construction, notably of a monumental portico, requiring demolition and relocations. Yet other speeches deal with civic troubles and disorderly sessions of the Assembly, financial management, relations with the successive governors of the province, elections of magistrates, privileges won for the good of Prusa, honors decreed to Dio himself, or criticisms and accusations leveled against him.

These orations, which represent only a fraction of Dio's public involvement during the period, demonstrate rhetoric's role in municipal life. The weighty influence of leading citizens, of whom Dio was one, stamped the cities' social and political structure. At Prusa, Dio occupied an eminent position as the scion of a rich and illustrious family. Proud of his ancestors and aided by his son, he also enjoyed imperial favor, in addition to the personal prestige as a philosopher and former exile he wore as a badge of honor. In this situation as a "Prime Nabob," he sought incessantly to have his programs adopted and to rebut his numerous opponents. Rhetoric was essential to this activity. His orations dealt with concrete and specific issues, and persuading the listener was their goal. Their style was more or less ornate, as the occasion demanded. The *Bithynian Orations,* taken as a whole, impress with their variety, culture, and often ironic or biting wit.

The Epideictic Genre

Alongside the judicial and deliberative genres, the Imperial Age witnessed the rise of the epideictic genre, a very ancient form which then underwent a rebirth. Its name means "display, ceremony" (*epideixis* = "exhibition," "public lecture," "oratorical display"), and since Aristotle, its content has traditionally been defined by "praise" (in Greek, *enkōmion,* in Latin, *laus*) and "invective" (Greek *psogos,* Latin *vituperatio*). Although Isokrates was a noteworthy practitioner, it huddled in the background in Classical and Hellenistic Greece and in Republican Rome, a poor relation to the more popular judicial and deliberative genres. But during the Empire this situation changed, and the third genre enjoyed an unprecedented development. The treatises handed down under the name of Menander Rhetor provide the best guide for describing this phenomenon.

Entitled *Division of Epideictic Orations* and *On Epideictic Orations,* respectively, these Greek treatises are the work of two different authors, of whom one (which one it is difficult to say with certainty) is Menander of Laodicaea in Asia Minor, a sophist who wrote a commentary on the work of Hermogenes and the *Preparatory Exercises* of Minucianus the Elder. Each of the authors (conventionally called Menander I and Menander II) dates from the second half of the third century A.D. Building on the reading of classic models, observation of contemporary practice, and earlier theoretical works, they strive to stake out the whole field, to classify matters in an intellectually satisfying way, and to assemble as well practical tips then in use, while providing helpful advice for would-be orators. Hence, the panoramic aspect of their approach.

The first treatise divides epideictic material according to the subjects to be praised. First comes the praise of the gods, or "hymn" *(humnos).* Through the different subdivisions envisaged, the model structure of a complete hymn emerges, composed of the following sections: initial invocation; praise of the god's nature, then of his birth (genealogy); next his mythic deeds, which reveal his powers; concluding prayer. The author then moves on to the second category, praise of countries and cities, and here as well he provides a model structure, which for a city comprises the site and geographic setting; its foundation and settling; the political system, scientific, artistic, and athletic activities, the public order; finally, and most important, virtuous deeds, whether of the inhabitants taken as a whole or of individual citizens. The rest of Menander I's treatise is lost. It meant, according to the outline announced at the beginning, to deal with the praise of human beings and animals, and to conclude with the praise of inanimate objects and abstractions.

The loss of the chapter on human beings is particularly regrettable because people were one of the most frequent topics of the encomium and the relevant paradigm was a central issue in epideictic theory (and functioned as a model for the paradigms of the other topics). According to different sources (Quintilian, Theon, Hermogenes, Pseudo-Dionysios of Halikarnassos, Menander II, et al.) we know that the encomium of a human contained, in broad outline, the following rubrics: family background and birth; upbringing; physical attributes; accomplishments throughout his life, manifesting moral qualities (virtues); death (if a eulogy).

The paradigms laid down by Menander I and his like are menus of commonplaces *(topoi)* meant to guide invention and arrangement simultaneously. The theorist's task is to set forth, for each type of topic, a list of rubrics inventorying the different points to be treated. The orator who wants to write an encomium has only to follow this guide—which does not mean that he will have nothing else to do. It is incumbent on him to adapt the treatment of each rubric to the specific nature of his topic, to shorten, select, specify, and flesh out the skeleton of theory and then to advance to the stylistic effort of giving voice to his ideas. Lists of *topoi* direct and provide a framework for oratorical creation; they are not its substitute.

Looked at from a different angle, the commonplaces of the encomium are important for the history of *mentalités*. Since most authors present more or less similar lists, it is right to conclude that there was general agreement during the Empire on the repertory of points to be examined for praising either a god, a city, or a human being. The theoretical treatises and orators' speeches in both Greek and Latin conveyed and adapted this teaching on the encomium that the schools had instilled (since an elementary form of the encomium was part of the preparatory exercises). The menus of commonplaces suppose a definition of each object considered and a reflection on why it is valuable. For instance, the *topoi* for the praise of a person essentially imply that a man's worth is to be judged principally according to his background and his deeds; if a city's grandeur is the topic, the commonplaces underline the importance of geography and history; when it comes to the gods, they ally theology and mythology. These lists are just as much images of the world, and their detailed study offers a very interesting insight into the mental universe of the ancients.

A point particularly worth emphasizing in this regard is the importance of the *topos* of the "virtues" *(aretai)*. Whether dealing with a person, a city or, indeed, a god, the encomium attempts to uncover, through deeds done, the virtues thus made manifest. The rhetoric of the encomium is the bearer of a morality with strong philosophic undertones.

The second treatise attributed to Menander approaches the encomium in a more practical and concrete spirit, enumerating the different types of epideictic orations. The material is not classified by subjects but by the situations in which the encomium is to be delivered. At the top comes the "imperial oration" *(basilikos logos)*, in principal a praise of a person, but not just any person: the emperor. Next to be considered are the orations dealing with travelers: "welcome speeches" *(epibatērios)*, whether spoken by an orator greeting an arrival (e.g., the governor upon his entry into a city) or by the new arrival himself saluting the city of his destination (e.g., upon his return home); "invitation oration" *(klētikos)*, inviting a governor, for example, to visit the city during a festival; "farewell oration" *(suntaktikos)*, for taking leave of a city; and *"bon voyage* oration" *(propemptikos)* on behalf of the traveler by those staying behind. Speeches dealing with family events constitute another category: "marriage oration" *(epithalamios, kateunastikos)*, "birthday oration" *(genethliakos)*, eulogy *(epitaphios* = "funeral oration"; *monōdia* = "lament"; *paramuthētikos* = "consolation"). These orations could be more or less solemn, depending on the status of the families concerned (from city bigwigs to the highest dignitaries and the imperial family). One further category is speeches set in political situations: "address to the governor" *(prosphōnētikos)*, here in a special case that appears to involve presenting a sword; "offer of a crown" *(stephanōtikos)* to the emperor; "embassy oration" *(presbeutikos)* in the emperor's presence on behalf of a city victimized by a natural catastrophe. The treatise closes with a solemn oration that is an appendage to the imperial speech, the "Sminthiac oration" *(Sminthiakos)*, in honor of Apollo Smintheus, meant for a great festival honoring this god at Alexandria in the Troad. It belongs to the class of "panegyrics" or speeches delivered at a religious festival *(panēguris)* and having for their subject, during the Empire, praise of the festival and all its appurtenances.

All these types of speeches consist principally of encomia and, while employing the commonplace lists, they combine them and adapt them to the situation. The orations delivered on the occasion of a journey, for example, combine praise of an individual (the traveler) with praise of a city (either the point of departure or the destination). Panegyrics combine praise of a god, a city, and sometimes a temple. Funeral orations combine praise of a person (the deceased) and other elements (expressions of sadness, consolation), while the embassy oration joins together praise of the emperor and an entreaty. And so on. Menander II thus furnishes formats for every occasion. He also indicates the appropriate length (not more than fifteen minutes for standard official compliments or for works whose emotional pull is wearying, more for more solemn works) and the appropriate style ("sustained" [*suntonos*] or "relaxed" [*anetos*]). The "relaxed" style is particularly suited to *lalia* (chatting, informal remarks), a type of flexible speech of varied content, which is used to praise, advise, or provide a lighthearted and amusing preamble to a declamation or the recitation of an oration or any literary work (when the *lalia* is sometimes called *prolalia*).

The majority of the types Menander II lists are, as rhetorical speeches, creations of the Imperial Age, and the terminology used to describe them is equally innovative. The Empire created new conditions, and they explain the rhetoric of praise and ceremony that clearly developed during the first centuries A.D. Peace, economic prosperity, urbanization, secure travel, multiplication of festivals, heightened role of municipal elites and imperial bureaucrats, reverence toward the emperor—all these developments presented new objects and new occasions for rhetorical praise, making it more necessary than it had ever been before. Thanks to Menander II (and to the orations, whether preserved or not, that correspond to the types he distinguishes), a world emerges where every important occasion has to be accompanied by rhetorical speeches, whether religious celebrations, political events, or affairs of the royal court (imperial or proconsular "entries," triumphs, jubilees, embassies, etc.), school ceremonies, or simple well-wishing in private homes. In each instance, the epideictic orator was there, as such, and no beautiful festival occurred without a beautiful speech.

It is necessary to augment Menander's list with some types he does not mention: the "ribbon cutting" speech (for a monument or neighborhood); the sports exhortation, encouraging athletes to compete courageously and fairly during festival contests; the motion of thanks (*gratiarum actio*) that consuls delivered before the Senate on the day they took office, to thank the emperor who had nominated them; and all the forms of thank-you in general. The mock encomium, around since the First Sophistic, continues on. Finally, a last category, which we know about from inscriptions, is the encomium delivered in artistic competitions. The first centuries A.D. were a period of intense activity, in the Greek world and even in the Roman, for sports and artistic contests organized under the banner of religious festivals. Alongside music, poetry, drama, and the like, these competitions regularly included a prose encomium contest, which generally had for its subject praise of the emperor or praise of the festival's eponymous god. It is worth noting that the encomium was the only rhetorical genre in competition, a privileged position that conveys its importance at the time.

Imperial society took the encomium seriously. An official oration, regulated by custom or law, delivered most often by an appointed speaker, who spoke on behalf of a group, it was a social rite affirming social values. In essence, the encomium proclaimed and maintained the social consensus, the adherence of all to recognized models and ways of thinking. It crystallized the ideas around which society wanted to see itself. As an instrument of consensus, the encomium came at a price: affirmation of a unanimity that was potentially a mere façade, support lent to the dominant ideology, stifling of opposition, flattery, and the cult of personality. The ancient rhetorical encomium, however, was never just cant, perhaps precisely because of its rhetorical nature. Rhetoric implied, as the ancients saw it, qualities of subtlety, intelligence, culture, and beauty, which went beyond what would have satisfied a purely totalitarian usefulness.

The encomium's ideological content comprised moral, political, and religious values beautifully expressed, with abundant historical and cultural references. Its first function (the "parainetic" function, from *parainesis* = "moral exhortation") was to extol these values, whose recall was not without use even though everyone was thought to subscribe to them. The epithalamium, for example, depicted for young spouses what their friends and family, as well as society at large, expected of their union. The encomium of concord recalled the need for order and alerted to the dangers of dissension. On top of its generic recommendations, the encomium grafted specific counsels and requests. Because it coaxes pleasingly, the encomium readies the reception for hard sayings. The encomia of Rome, for instance, provided a means for saying what was going well in the Roman Empire, what the subjects therefore favored, and what they wanted to continue. Praising a governor as he entered office offered the opportunity to provide the wish list of the province and, on occasion, to recall the grievances stored up against his predecessor. Praises of the gods sanctioned discussions on the meaning of myths, or on whether a sanctuary's decorative scheme was correct or not.

Bearing in mind the political and social conditions, it was a time for ceremonial, official ideology and the State religion. This fact explains the rise of the encomium, an oratorical form that explored the spaces open to persuasion in the imperial system, promoting carefully couched proposals as well as subtle exhortation. The reranking of the oratorical genres corresponded to the shifting of the stakes in the world of the time.

That explains why the invective never had the same importance as the encomium. Theoretically, blame is the inverse of praise. One can blame people and cities (the gods were not included) by taking the same *topoi* and reversing them. This happened in school as part of the preparatory exercises (example of the invective against the brigand Eurybatos). But in the society of the Imperial Age, invective had no official use, and so it remained restricted to the attacks found in judicial speeches, philosophers' admonitions, diatribes, and broadsides. It provided fertile ground for literature without ever becoming a rhetorical genre of public institutions.

The Roman Orators

Cassius Severus figures among the great names from the beginning of the principate. A highly gifted orator famous for his trenchancy and the author of courtroom speeches and declamations, he opposed the regime and was exiled under Augustus and Tiberius. Gnaeus Domitius Afer was born at Nimes. He was a great lawyer who ran political risks, but he had a successful career, attaining the consulate. He was Quintilian's teacher and in addition to his court orations published a treatise on witnesses. The works of these two men are lost. Thanks to epigraphy, on the other hand, we possess eulogies *(laudationes)* of two women, a grande dame called Turia, praised by her husband whom she had predeceased after forty-one years of marriage, and another illustrious lady, Murdia, praised by her son (Dessau, *Inscriptiones Latinae Selectae,* nos. 8393 and 8394, end of first century B.C. and beginning of first century A.D.; the *laudatio* of Turia has been edited and translated into English by E. Wistrand, *The So-Called "Laudatio Turiae"* [Lund, 1976]).

Pliny the Younger (61/62–113 A.D.), nephew of Gaius Plinius Secundus (Pliny the Elder, author of the *Natural History*), was nineteen when he embarked upon his legal career. His political career went on under Domitian and Trajan. Consul in 100, he was imperial legate in 111–13 A.D. in Pontus-and-Bithynia, when as a noteworthy part of his mission he had to hear the complaints lodged against Dio of Prusa. His oratorical masterpiece is the *Panegyric of Trajan,* an oration stemming from his motion of thanks delivered before the Senate upon his taking up the consulate, but reworked and lengthened for publication. The written version runs more than eighty modern pages, about four hours worth of speaking. Pliny read it to his friends in a public reading *(recitatio)* stretched out over three sessions on three consecutive days. In this ample speech, in a highly wrought style, Pliny praises Trajan, painstakingly going over the emperor's activity in the four years following Trajan's adoption by Nerva. He writes the chronicle of the start of the reign—a historical document of the highest importance—and through detailing the measures Trajan undertook, Pliny elicits the qualities he manifested, a man quite unlike some of his predecessors (a criticism of Domitian's tyranny). The oration therefore intends to be witness and homage and, at the same time, to trace in Trajan the portrait of the ideal ruler and to sum up the imperial ideology, seen from a Senatorial point of view.

Pliny's voluminous correspondence is important for the history of rhetoric because of the information it provides on literary and social life during the period, and so especially on the speeches delivered, the orators, and their public. It contains unique details about how Pliny and his correspondents prepared the texts of their speeches for publication, giving them out to their friends to read and criticize in private before submitting them to the test of public reading, itself a prelude to circulating written copies. This correspondence likewise spells out the author's esthetic and stylistic principles, which are in the Ciceronian tradition; many of his ideas, as well as his acuteness and good sense, accord with the conceptions of his master Quintilian. Pliny's lost works include poems, courtroom pleadings, an inaugural speech for the opening of the library at Como (founded by Pliny out of his own funds in his birthplace), and a eulogy of Vestricius Cottius.

Fronto (ca. 95–167 A.D.) enjoyed a great reputation as an orator in antiquity. Born at Cirta (present day Constantine) in Numidia, he was an attorney *(patronus)* and progressed through the *cursus honorum* to become consul and proconsul of the province of Asia, the last an office which illness prevented him from undertaking. During the final years of the 130s and the start of the 140s, he was the rhetoric master of the future emperor Marcus Aurelius, with whom he remained on good terms after Marcus's accession (161 A.D.). Granted an important and lasting position at court, Fronto was a literary personality of the first rank in Antonine Rome. Unfortunately, his speeches—courtroom pleadings and encomia of the emperors Hadrian and Antoninus, especially—have not been preserved. What we know of Fronto comes from his correspondence, which was discovered during the nineteenth century in two palimpsests (manuscripts reused to write a second text over an earlier original; Fronto's is the bottom and can be read only with great difficulty). Consisting of letters addressed to Antoninus, Marcus Aurelius, Lucius Verus, and other members of the imperial family, with replies by the addressees, and also containing some letters in Greek, this correspondence extends from 139 to 167 A.D. and touches on mostly literary and rhetorical topics. The information it provides on Fronto's archaism, as well as on his rhetoric classes with Marcus Aurelius and his conception of the emperor as orator, has been noted above. It also throws welcome light on the genre of the mock encomium, a Greek specialty, of which Fronto prided himself on being the first to do Latin crossovers, calling them "bagatelles" *(nugalia)*. Representative are an *Encomium of Smoke and Dust,* an *Encomium of Negligence,* and an *Encomium of Sleep* (this last text is lost, but we possess Marcus's rebuttal).

Apuleius (ca. 125 to after 170) was born at Madauros, not far from Fronto's birthplace. After studying rhetoric at Carthage, he traveled in Greece, where he received his training in philosophy and became an initiate of several cults. He must also have heard the sophists of the Second Sophistic there, whom he resembles in many ways. Upon his return to his own province, he carried on his writing career. Apuleius described himself as a philosopher, but his ideal of philosophy embraced all the literary and intellectual disciplines, including rhetoric, since the philosopher, in his eyes, had to have superior mastery of the spoken word. True to this conception, Apuleius wrote all sorts of works, philosophic, poetical, scientific, in Greek as well as in Latin. His best known is the novel *Metamorphoses* or the *Golden Ass,* which contains lovely oratorical passages, especially a long prayer to Isis (11.2).

The *Apology* is a courtroom oration that Apuleius delivered on his own behalf in a delicate case. After he had married a rich widow older than himself, the woman's family prosecuted him, alleging that he had literally bewitched her with magic to win her hand. The magic accusation was a serious charge, which could even lead to the death penalty. Apuleius answered it *con brio* with this oration full of verve and studded with numerous striking and erudite digressions (at least in the published version). In all probability he won the case. Besides this judicial speech, we possess an epideictic collection of his, called *Florida,* whose origin is unclear and which is composed of speeches and extracts of speeches delivered during the 160s. We see there the author in his greatness as celebrated orator and lecturer at Carthage. The collection is quite varied, with "informal remarks" (e.g., 9: encomium of the governor Severianus as he leaves the province), "introductory remarks" (e.g., 18: greeting the audience at the theater of Carthage and announcing the session's program, which would consist of a dialogue and a hymn to Aesculapius), as well as excerpts from different speeches containing character sketches, comparisons, and anecdotes. Ever on the lookout for the rare word and the unexpected effect, Apuleius wrote a Latin particularly remarkable for its inventiveness and sparkle.

For the century following Apuleius, the principal documents of Latin oratory are contained in the collection of epideictic speeches known as the *Panegyrici Latini* or *Latin Panegyrics*. The Younger Pliny's *Panegyric of Trajan* heads the collection, placed there by an ancient editor as the genre's ancestor and model. Then, after a leap of more than two hundred years, come eleven orations delivered by Gallic orators between 289 and 389 A.D., all encomia addressed to the emperors on the occasion of birthdays, marriages, jubilees, thanksgiving, congratulations after a victorious military campaign, invitation into a city, or entry into office as a new consul. The first four (numbered two thorough five, Pliny's being number one) fall within the chronological purview of the present chapter. Panegyrics Two and Three, by an orator named Mamertinus, delivered at Trier in 289 and 291, are encomia of the emperor Maximian, Diocletian's partner in power; one celebrates the anniversary of Rome's foundation, the other (called *genethliacus*) the emperor's birthday. Panegyric Four, by an anonymous author who served Maximian as secretary of state, was also delivered at Trier, in 297. It is an encomium addressed to Constantius Chlorus following his victories in Britain and spoken probably at the time of his being given the title Caesar. The fifth and most original of these panegyrics is the work of Eumenes, a native of Autun and grandson of an Athenian settled in Rome. He was a professor of rhetoric and then for four years a close associate of Constantius whom he served as private secretary. Back in Autun, where Constantius had named him director of the famous local schools, called "Maenian schools,"[3] Eumenes ascertained that the city,

---

3. So named, perhaps, after the style of gallery or balcony on the buildings housing them; cf. the *maeniana* on two large basilicas in the Forum Romanum used by spectators to observe activity in the Forum—WEH.

which barbarians and uncontrolled elements had devastated, was on the way to recovery, thanks to the aid furnished by the emperors, but that the schools still needed to be restored. Hence his speech, delivered in the forum of Autun in 298 before the governor of the Lyons province, and called *For the Restoration of the Schools*. Here he explains the reasons for the restoration and requests permission to authorize for this purpose the 600,000 sesterces salary that the emperors had allocated to him. This generous initiative recalls, in a way, Pliny's benefaction to the library at Como.

Scholars used to give the *Panegyrici Latini* a bad press, judging them empty toadyism. Recent research, of which Camille Jullian was a precursor, emphasizes how these texts, on the contrary, are written within the context of a precise political system and court ceremonial and how, if read correctly, they reveal rich information on the history (especially Gallic history) and ideology of the period. As for their workmanship, these orations of confirmed masters constitute important documents for the epideictic genre (typology, subject matter, style) and artistic Latin prose, which in this era evolves and nourishes itself on the models of Cicero, Pliny, and Fronto. They achieve a type of subtly refined political communication that simultaneously consolidates imperial authority in the civilian and military milieus touched by panegyric and brings to the attention of the emperor and court in return certain aspirations of these same milieus. No less than its art, coinage, and court ceremonies themselves, to which they are sometimes compared, the *Panegyrici Latini* represent an important element of the Roman world's political system in the Imperial Age.

The Second Sophistic

Rhetorical activity in the Greek world crystallized in the literary and social phenomenon called the "Second Sophistic."

It is so called with reference to the First Sophistic of Gorgias, Protagoras, Hippias, and the others; and just as in the fifth and fourth centuries B.C. sophists flourished in the Greek world, so in the first three centuries of the Empire a large number of men appeared with characteristics similar to those of their predecessors. To distinguish them from the "old sophists" (Lucian, *Herodotos* 4; Pseudo-Aelius Aristides, *Rhetoric* 2.50; Philostratos, *Lives of the Sophists* 590; Menander Rhetor I, 332.27), expressions were used like "sophists who lived only a little before our own time" (Lucian, *Lexiphanes* 23; *Mistaken Critic* 6), "contemporary sophists" (Hermogenes, p. 377, 13, Rabe ed.), "new sophists" (Menander Rhetor II, 411.32; *Prolegomena to Aelius Aristides* p. 119, 4; 155, 6, Lenz ed.), "New Sophistic" (Philostratos, *Lives of the Sophists* 481), and "Second Sophistic" (Ibid. and 507). A "second decade" was also created to parallel the canon of the ten Attic orators (the *Souda*, N 404). Such names conformed to the habits of a time that deliberately used titles of the type "New This, New That" to praise the present with reference to the past and to fit current trends into a continuum of past successes. In the present case, Classical Greece (hardly surprising, seeing how it was a fixation for Imperial Age culture), and within classicism, the sophists, were the standard as thinkers, teachers, and lecturers interested in the practice and theory of rhetoric and its ties with philosophy.

Between the Classical and Imperial Ages, there also existed men with such characteristics, like Potamon of Mytilene (*supra,* chapter 4), whom the *Souda* describes precisely as a "sophist." But these sophists of the intervening periods did not put a stamp on their time. It is only in the Imperial Age that the sophists became sufficiently numerous and important to form a movement and to serve as models, impressing a style on contemporary ideals. This sophistic renaissance was an aspect of a larger phenomenon, the renaissance of the Greek world, which manifested itself in a recovery of prosperity and splendor in all areas of activity of the Greek-speaking provinces.

Just as the First Sophistic, the Second presents problems of definition. It was not so much an organized movement as a multitude of individual initiatives, linked by a common spirit, a shared educational and intellectual practice, and numerous personal contacts. An official list, therefore, of the sophists of the Second Sophistic does not exist; the phenomenon was protean. On the other hand, the very word "sophist" *(sophistēs)* creates difficulty. Just as in the Classical period, the clear distinction between *rhētōr* and *sophistēs* did not exist under the Empire. Both words could be taken in the sense of "orator," "professional orator," "professor of rhetoric," so much so that their use overlapped and the first, the second, or both words at once could be applied to the same person, depending on how one looked at him and the particular implications of the context. The distinction between lawyer, political speaker, professor, and lecturing philosopher was theoretical, to the extent that these activities in fact most often went hand-in-hand. The word "sophist," moreover, was an occasion of complexity and frequent reservations because it was sometimes used in a laudatory way (it appears as an honorific in inscriptions) and sometimes pejoratively (with a critical viewpoint, as in the Platonic manner). Owing to the pejorative usage, some authors, who objectively belonged to the Second Sophistic and whom contemporaries considered to be sophists, refused to apply this term to themselves, preferring "orator" *(rhētōr)* or "philosopher" *(philosophos).*

The *Lives of the Sophists* by Philostratos (ca. 170–240 A.D.) describes the Second Sophistic best. The author, belonging to a family with several writers of the same name, was a professor of rhetoric who performed official duties at Athens, frequented imperial circles, and wrote various works. His *Lives,* composed around 230, contains a collection of fifty-eight biographies, divided into three groups:

1. The philosopher sophists (1.1–8): Philostratos introduces first eight authors who in his opinion were fundamentally philosophers but who were considered sophists because of their speaking ability (these include Dio of Prusa and Favorinus of Arles).

2. The First Sophistic (1.9–18): Philostratos continues with sophists properly so called, beginning with the sophists of the First Sophistic, to whom he devotes nine biographies. A tenth is given to Aiskhines, whom Philostratos considers to be the forefather of the Second Sophistic.

3. The Second Sophistic (1.19–2.33): after the foregoing preliminaries, the body of the work consists of forty biographies of sophists of the Imperial Age, from Niketes of Smyrna (second half of the first century A.D.) to Aspasios of Ravenna (beginning of the third century). These

are clearly not the only sophists Philostratos knew about; he has chosen here the forty most interesting to him. In the biographies devoted to them, he retraces their career, their ties with their teachers, students, and colleagues, and the role that they played in public life. He is particularly interested in describing their teaching and oratorical style and in recalling their most memorable contributions. The concluding lines of the work briefly mention sophists still living, whom Philostratos does not wish to discuss because they are his friends, notably Apsines.

As a historian, Philostratos is not above reproach. He has biases (for example, among the sophists' oratorical genres, he advances declamation over the rest), he aims to be neither exhaustive nor precise, and he likes to deck out his narrative with picturesque or sensationalist anecdotes. Yet despite these limitations, he is clearly well informed on the sophistic milieu, where he lived himself, and he bases himself on oral and written sources. The evidence we possess, moreover, generally tends to corroborate his information. So he is an irreplaceable witness. His *Lives of the Sophists* is all the more precious since the works he deals with are mostly lost: of the forty sophists, there are scarcely more than half a dozen whose texts we still have today (Polemon, Hermogenes, Aelius Aristides, Hadrian of Tyre, Pollux of Naukratis, Rufus of Perinthos, Aelian, maybe Herodes Atticus).

The work of Philostratos, as supplemented by contemporary sources (Lucian, Menander Rhetor, inscriptions, coins, etc.), allows us to define the essential characteristics of the Second Sophistic and even to restore thereby an important piece of the history of Greek rhetoric. Rhetorical activity, in fact, essentially defines the movement. The sophists were first and foremost teachers of rhetoric and orators. They held municipal and imperial chairs, made use of private schools and surrounded themselves with students, to whom they taught declamation. They gave lessons, wrote theoretical treatises, and practiced the three oratorical genres, judicial, deliberative, and epideictic. Virtuosity often marked their public displays, for the sophist was a star, expected to provide demonstrations that could go to strange and eccentric lengths, such as improvisation, sing-song delivery, wild theatrics, and so forth. All this mastery rested, after all, on unremitting toil, especially in attaining a pure Attic Greek and knowledge of the classics. The sophists most often used to publish their orations, and they practiced on occasion other literary forms (poetry, letter-writing, history, etc.).

Along with their rhetorical activity, the sophists performed political and social roles. They filled municipal and provincial offices (tax collector, "eirenarch" charged with maintaining law and order, high priest, etc.), and they were noted for their costly benefactions to society ("euergetism"). As spokesmen for their fellow citizens, they argued cases before Roman tribunals and led embassies to governors and emperors. They sometimes performed important functions in the Roman administration, such as "crown counsel" *(advocatus fisci)*, procurator, or *ab epistulis Graecis* (secretary of state for Greek language imperial correspondence). Some even knew the emperor personally.

For instance, when Domitian forbade extending viticulture in the province of Asia, the sophist Skopelian came as an ambassador to lobby the emperor on behalf of the grape-growing interests of his fellow Asians. His speech (Philostratos, *Lives* 520) succeeded in having the measure rescinded: not only was the planting of vines permitted, but those who did not plant any were fined! Polemon, Smyrna's leading official, obtained for his city in a single day a huge gift of ten million drachmas from Hadrian. When Antoninus Pius was governor of Asia, he lodged at Polemon's house while in Smyrna, and Polemon dared one day to show him the door (Ibid. 531, 534). Herodes Atticus, another sophist, was the leader of Athens, where he oversaw the construction of numerous monuments, and he became a Roman consul as well.

Modern scholarship has debated to what extent the sophists' social clout was tied to their rhetorical activity. Even if it is impossible to establish a mechanical cause and effect relationship, it is still clear that these two aspects are connected. The explanation hangs precisely on the nature of rhetoric, which in the ancient world was an instrument of political and social life. As a result, the sophist as a master of the oratorical art possessed an ability that made him socially influential. His linguistic, intellectual, and legal skills allowed him to be a "player" in all the areas where there was a premium on knowing how to speak, write, argue, persuade, and represent. Of course there were many sources of power in the Roman Empire (noble birth, wealth, military prowess, patronage, etc.: the sophists, who often came from aristocratic families, were also well provided for on these fronts too). Rhetoric was therefore one type of power among others, but a type of power it surely was. What the sophist knew as such made him powerful.

The sophists also exerted an influence of another order, as representatives of Greek culture in the face of Roman might. Since all their activity was based on Greek language, literature, history, and cultural values, the sophists were in some sense the representatives and guardians of Greek identity in the Empire's motley world. Their speeches incessantly recalled the glorious Greek past and proclaimed the existence of a Greek community formed of all those in the different Greek-speaking provinces who laid claim to the same language and the same roots. This affirmation of identity extended throughout the Mediterranean world, for the sophists were present in all the eastern provinces and also in the West, at Rome and Naples especially. Within the Empire the Second Sophistic thus played an important balancing role between Greeks and Romans, which as we saw above rested among other things on culture and rhetoric (the prizing of the Attic dialect, historical declamations, the myth of Classical Athens, orations analyzing and transposing Roman realities into Greek, encomia of Rome and the emperors, etc.).

A final characteristic of the Second Sophistic is its relation with philosophy. The sophists rubbed elbows with the philosophers and knew the philosophic doctrines, at least superficially. In their rhetorical speeches, they relied upon more or less popularized ethical and theological notions (as, for example, in the commonplaces of the encomium). In their treatises on rhetoric, they referred back to Platonic distinctions and doctrines (there are traces of Platonism in Hermogenes, Pseudo-Dionysios of Halikarnassos, Menander Rhetor). Illustrating this encounter within the Second Sophistic, a succession of authors, molded by rhetoric and laying claim to philosophy, advanced the fusion of the two disciplines.

Dio of Prusa (ca. 40 to after 110 A.D.) thought of himself as "a philosopher and hands-on politician" (*philosophos politeias hapsamenos*, Oration 48.14, WEH). This involvement necessarily occurred, in his eyes, as a result of the practice of oratory. Among his eighty works, around half, and the more important half, are public orations addressed to provincial cities (the *Bithynian Discourses* encountered above), to other cities, the objects of his reprimands and moral exhortations *(Discourses To Rhodes, Alexandria, Tarsus, Celenae),* to the Greeks assembled at the Olympic Games *(Olympian Oration),* or to the Emperor Trajan (the four discourses *On Kingship).* The corpus also contains two funeral orations (*Melancomas* 1 and 2) and a consolation *(Kharidemos).* Dio thought that the philosopher cannot be content with leading a solipsistic life of philosophy and abstract speculation: he has a duty to communicate his philosophy to someone else, to proclaim and incite. He needs oratory to do this; the philosopher's social and moral mission requires use of the spoken word, not only in private conversations, but also, and above all, in public speeches. Dio put this conception into action, multiplying his speaking endeavors and employing a trained eloquence that stopped at no paradox, no affectation, no daring in the service of his message as educator and political adviser. Rhetoric, something he knew amazingly well and could do with whatever he liked, was for him part of the pagan preacher's arsenal.

Favorinus of Arles (ca. 80 to mid-second century A.D.), a Gaul who wrote in Greek, was sometimes called a philosopher and at other times a sophist. He was famous, even notorious, in his day, not least because he was a hermaphrodite (owing to a birth defect) and declaimed his speeches in a high-pitched voice. He studied with Dio of Prusa and had numerous students of his own; he knew Aulus Gellius and was the sophist Polemon's enemy. His works, mostly lost, comprised treatises on ethics and philosophy, orations, mock encomia, and learned scientific and literary efforts.

Lucian (ca. 120–180 A.D.) was born in Samosata in Syria, and his native language was "barbarbian" (probably Aramaic). Thanks to his schooling, he learned Greek, using Attic with complete mastery and becoming thoroughly imbued with Hellenic culture. He was a lawyer, gave lecture tours, wrote declamations, *prolaliai,* and encomia (the celebrated *Praise of a Fly),* and taught rhetoric up until he was about forty. He then decided to devote himself to the dialogue, to a genre, that is, which antiquity considered the domain of criticism and philosophy. In fact, during this second part of his life, what he wrote was primarily satire. But that did not mean he forgot his rhetorical upbringing, for it profoundly marks all the works of the second period, in the themes treated, the manner of composition and argument, the language and style, and the general attitude of creative "imitation" *(mimēsis)* toward the Hellenic patrimony. In certain writings from this time, Lucian developed epideictic themes (encomium of the Emperor Lucius Verus's mistress, Pantheia, in *Essays in Portraiture* and *Essays in Portraiture Defended,* encomium of pantomime) and legal topics *(Double Indictment,* the *Fisherman).* Towards the end of his life, he went back on the lecture circuit with a new bag of *prolaliai.* In addition, he denounced in a succession of pamphlets the faults of the contemporary literary scene, showing that this area had not ceased interesting him. He targeted, among others, book collectors—silly bibliophiles—*(Ignorant Book-Collector),* word gatherers—hyper-Atticist pedants—*(Consonants at Law,* the *Solecist, Lexiphanes),* and in general bad sophists and rhetoric professors (the *Mistaken Critic,* the *Professor of Public Speaking).* Lucian's work thus offers a precious document of second-century rhetoric, both by way of illustration and counterpoint.

Cassius Longinus (ca. 200–272/73 A.D.) taught grammar, rhetoric, and philosophy at Athens and counted the philosopher Porphyry among his students. Towards the end of his life, he joined the entourage of Zenobia, the queen of Palmyra, whom he aided in her secessionist efforts against the Roman Empire. When the effort failed, Longinus was one of Zenobia's counselors whom the Emperor Aurelian had put to death. His numerous writings include treatises and philosophic commentaries of a Platonist cast, works of literary and textual criticism (especially on Homer), as well as works on meter and lexicography, a *Rhetoric,* and a eulogy of Zenobia's husband, Odaenathus. The *Rhetoric,* which is preserved, is rather traditional in conception, focused on the judicial genre, and divided according to the parts of rhetoric (invention, arrangement, style, delivery, memorization).

It is said of Cassius Longinus that he was "a living library and a walking National Archive" (Eunapios, *Lives of the Philosophers and*

Sophists 456, Loeb modified), so great was his learning, but this did not prevent him from engaging courageously in the events of his time. He is a good example of that broad conception of culture, frequently represented in antiquity, which did not separate philosophy, rhetoric, and literature and which did not erect barriers between study and real life. Additionally interesting as belonging to the third century, he demonstrates along with certain others (Pseudo-Aelius Aristides, *In Honor of the Emperor*, Kallinikos of Petra, Menander Rhetor, et al.) the continuity of Greek rhetoric during the crisis of the Empire.

SIXTH EXCURSUS

❧ *Aelius Aristides, Sophist by the Grace of Asklepios*

Aelius Aristides (117–after 180 A.D.) is a Greek author of the Second Sophistic. His life and his work, while embodying the major characteristics of the period's rhetoric, add to them a dimension of psychological and religious complexity.

Born in the region of Mysia in Asia Minor, Aristides belonged to a wealthy family and held Roman citizenship. He traveled in Egypt, Italy, and Greece, taught, and delivered orations. The climax of his life takes place around 178. That was when he scored a brilliant success lobbying the emperors after an earthquake had devastated Smyrna. Aristides wrote an *Epistle* to Marcus Aurelius and Commodus, soliciting their aid in reconstruction, and he won his case.

The corpus of Aristides contains fifty-three titles (not counting lost speeches and poems), which break out as follows:

— Encomia of people: especially funeral orations of his teacher Alexander of Kotiaion and of his student Eteoneus, two valuable pieces of evidence on the teaching of rhetoric in the second century.

— Encomia of cities: especially the *Panathenaic Oration,* which celebrates Athens as the home of Hellenic identity, and the *Roman Oration,* which paints an impressive picture of the Roman Empire.

— Encomia of the gods (hymns), a genre Aristides made his specialty and which he was one of the first to handle in prose, thus marking a new advance for rhetoric vis-à-vis poetry. Aristides is a great author of religious rhetoric.

— Deliberative orations: exhortations to concord.

— Declamations (cf. above).

— *Platonic Discourses,* voluminous discussion on the nature and usefulness of rhetoric, in response to Plato's accusations.

— *Sacred Tales,* a kind of autobiography or personal diary.

— Pamphlets and divers other works.

Aristides had, besides, pleaded in courts and was well aware of rhetorical theory (although the *Rhetoric* preserved under his name is not by him). He therefore covered the entire field of Imperial rhetoric, from teaching and declamation to each of the three oratorical genres (where he preferred epideictic). He made himself known in any number of settings and participated in public life. He tackled the cultural and political problems confronting rhetoric, like Atticism and the use of the Hellenic past, Greco-Roman relations, and replying to philosophy's challenge. For these reasons, Aristides deserves to be included, as Philostratos wishes, in the Second Sophistic, and he is a signal instance of it, even if he scarcely liked the word *sophistēs* and insisted on parting company with contemporary sophists, his adversaries and rivals.

The peculiar tone of Aristides's work derives from his personal history. In 143, during a voyage to Rome, he fell ill and, despairing of human medicine, repaired to the sanctuary of Asklepios at Pergamon to find a cure. The god, through the intermediary of dreams and omens, dispensed medical advice, which the priests and doctors attached to the shrine took responsibility for interpreting and applying. From this time on, Aristides suffered for the rest of his life multiple and recurring afflictions (with periods of remission), strongly suggestive of psychosomatic illness. He regularly returned to Pergamon in search of the god's care. These cures, minutely described in the *Sacred Tales,* convinced Aristides that Asklepios was protecting him. In his devotion, the valetudinarian considered himself as someone miraculously healed time and again, almost one of the elect.

Now Asklepios's concern did not stop at the physical, but extended to Aristides's oratorical activity and career. The god prescribed oratorical exercises for his patient, who was to deliver speeches, participate in ceremonies, and praise the gods. The god dictated subjects and suggested ways to develop them. Thus it came to pass that, throughout Aristides's life, rhetoric was entrusted to divine protection and inspiration. ". . . I had become ill through some divine good fortune, so that by my association with the god, I might make this improvement [in rhetoric]" (*Sacred Tales* 4.27, Behr trans.). An unusual psychological experience made rhetoric depend closely on medicine, religion, and the interpretation of dreams.

This is the source of Aristides's elevated idea of his art and his total commitment to its service:

> "I have honored this faculty [rhetoric] from the start and have valued it above all profit and all affairs, not so that I might be a flatterer of the people nor so that I might conjecture at the desires of the masses, nor for money . . . But guided by speech itself and believing that good oratory is a fitting possession for man, I work according to my ability." (*To Plato: In Defense of Oratory* 431, Behr)

> "But for me oratory means everything, signifies everything. For I have made it children, parents, work, relaxation, and all else. And for this purpose I invoke Aphrodite. This is my play, this is my work. In this I rejoice, this I admire, its doors I haunt. And though I could still say much else besides, I forbear, so that I may not appear boorish." (*To Those Who Criticize Him* 20, Behr)

These professions of faith show just how far, in certain exceptional situations, devotion to rhetoric could go during the Empire.

B. Keil (Berlin, 1898) has edited some of the works of Aelius Aristides, as have F. W. Lenz and C. A. Behr (Leiden, 1976–80). Behr has translated them all into English (Leiden, 1981–86). I have edited and translated into French the *Sicilian Orations* (*Les Discours siciliens d'Aelius Aristide,* 2nd ed. [Salem, NH, 1992]) and I have translated the *Roman Oration* (in *Eloges grecs de Rome* [Paris, 1997]).❦

Rhetoric and Literature

Some critics (e.g., V. Florescu, G. A. Kennedy) have used the Italian term *"letteraturizzazione"* or "literaturization" of rhetoric to designate the process by which forms and procedures belonging to rhetoric are transposed into literature. Rhetoric in this light no longer aims only at speeches but extends to all literary compositions (in the broad sense, including philosophical demonstrations, inscriptions, scientific treatises, etc.). Through this process, literature in turn opens itself to the techniques of speaking, so that the "literaturization" of rhetoric has as its corollary the "rhetorization" of literature. This phenomenon existed throughout antiquity, but it became particularly acute during the Empire. In the Imperial Age, it seems that rhetoric is everywhere and that it is expanding its realm to the point of leaving a quite noticeable mark, in substance and form, on the literary genres apart from it. Areas traditionally close to rhetoric remained more than ever under its influence, while new sectors opened up to it.[4]

Certainly the social value placed on rhetoric and its central place in teaching, a situation that made rhetoric a common foundation and an instrument of shared thought and expression, were causes for this development during the period. The practice of the "public reading" *(recitatio)*, where an author read his works before a sometimes large audience, contributed to bringing together literature and rhetoric by submitting all sorts of literary works to the test of oral performance, just as speeches were. In addition, many orators and sophists were writers and poets at times, and the majority of writers and poets, conversely, knew their rhetoric. Impregnable boundaries did not separate the genres, so that it seemed possible to essay, even outside of rhetoric strictly defined, a certain "eloquence" (*eloquentia:* cf. Quintilian, *Institutio Oratoria* 10.2.21–22). This could rely particularly upon forms of expression drawn from the preparatory exercises, on speeches inserted into a narrative, arguments, stylistic effects, and the resources of memory technique and delivery.

Ovid (43 B.C. to 18 A.D.) is a striking example of a poet disposed to rhetoric. He studied rhetoric in his youth and demonstrated considerable talent, according to the Elder Seneca (*Controversiae* 2.2.8–12). Then he turned to poetry but without compartmentalizing poetry from rhetoric. He wrote to Cassianus Salanus, who taught Germanicus rhetoric, "Our work differs, but it derives from the same sources" (*Ex Ponto* 2.5.65). Rhetoric indeed constitutes a key element of Ovidian poetry. The *Heroides* are a collection of letters (in verse) attributed to

4. The issue here is rhetoric's influence on literature. By the same token, literature is omnipresent in rhetoric, by way of language, content, models, and culture, as we saw earlier in this chapter under the headings "Literary Criticism" and "Archaism and Atticism."

mythological heroines, unhappy and deserted wives or lovers, who write entreaties or laments (Penelope to Odysseus, Dido to Aeneas, etc.), a type of composition that owes a great deal to the ethopoeia of the preparatory exercises and that uses at will *topoi* and the emotional figures. In the *Amores* and the *Metamorphoses,* there are a number of declamations using arguments structured for persuasive ends: a lover's begging a gatekeeper to let him enter the beloved's house (*Am.* 1.6); Apollo's address trying to keep Daphne (*Meta.* 1.504–24); Narcissus sweet talking a handsome youth—who is none other than himself (*Meta.* 3.441–73); Orpheus looking for Eurydice in the Underworld (*Meta.* 10.17–39); Ajax and Odysseus arguing rival claims over the arms of Achilles (*Meta.* 13.1–383); and so forth. In all these passages, which are, in short, speeches in verse, rich in argumentation and stylistic effects, Ovid displays an indisputable knowledge of rhetoric and the willingness to use it in his complex poetic enterprise. Often Ovid even makes fun of rhetorical art, using it in a willfully incongruous way, displaced and distanced, as, for example, when he depicts vanity and the failure of persuasion, the women of the *Heroides* talking in the void, the lover left at the door.

Ovid especially highlighted the theme of the lover's wooing, which aims at bending the love object's will and convincing it to give in. In this light, the poem called the *Art of Love* can be read in some sense as a pastiche of rhetorical treatises. Just as the art of rhetoric *(ars rhetorica)* gives advice on how to speak well, so the "art of love" *(ars amatoria)* gives advice on how to seduce well. The author humorously underlines the relationship between the two:

Learn noble arts, I counsel you, young men of Rome, not only that you may defend trembling clients: a woman, no less than populace, grave judge or chosen senate, will surrender, defeated, to eloquence. But hide your powers, nor put on a learned brow . . .

(*Ars Amatoria* 1.457–61)

This is one of rhetoric's essential themes. Peitho (Persuasion) was often associated with Aphrodite. In Homer, the encounter between Odysseus and Nausikaa had an erotic subtext. In Classical Greece, thinking about the spoken word was tied to thinking about love, in the *Helen* of

Gorgias and in the *Symposium* and *Phaidros* of Plato in particular. The alliance of rhetoric and love spotlights a fundamental kinship between the approach of the orator who wants to bend an audience to his reasoning and that of the lover who wants to seduce the object of his love. In both cases, there is conquest and sweet violence. This connection thus underlines persuasion's erotic component.

In addition to Ovid, Latin poetry of the Imperial Age clearly feels rhetoric's impact, as in Seneca's tragedies whose speeches are decked out with arguments, in the epics of Vergil and Lucan, in the epideictic themes of Statius's *Silvae,* in the declamatory aspects of Juvenal's *Satires,* and so on. We must avoid thinking of a mechanistic influence, as if the poets were actually composing with a rhetorical treatise in front of them, but must rather recognize that rhetoric, as an element of the culture and mental makeup of the time, infiltrated poems and combined with traditions and writing contexts proper to poetry. The speech cited above, for example, of the lover to the porter, combines rhetorical arguments with elegy's "lover's plaint at the doorstep" (in Greek, *paraklausithuron*).

Rhetoric likewise continued to influence the historians, both in inserted speeches and in narrative passages, as Livy, Tacitus, or the Greek historians Cassius Dio and Herodian show.

Philosophers, too, similarly continued to have recourse to modes of expression rooted in rhetoric. Plutarch on occasion did not disdain their use. The eclectic Platonist Maximus of Tyre (second century A.D.) delivered and published *Lectures (Dialexeis)* that were brilliant pieces in an extremely ornate style. The great names of Stoicism sought after discursive forms that were simultaneously artistic and persuasive, in order to meditate on their beliefs and to convey them to others, to the extent that one can talk of a Stoic rhetoric, as illustrated by Seneca, Epictetus, and Marcus Aurelius, great stylists all.

The consolation genre was an area, par excellence, for the interpenetration of rhetoric, philosophy, and literature. *Consolatio* in Latin, *paramuthia, paramuthētikos,* or *parēgoria* in Greek, the consolation sought to dissipate or at least moderate as much as possible the sorrow misfortunes aroused, or what current opinion thought to be misfortunes (decease, illness, exile, old age, etc.), by helping the individual receiving consolation to find spiritual tranquillity again. It took the form of a speech, poem, letter, or treatise. With a long and rich history (Antiphon; Athenian *epitaphioi;* the philosopher from the Academy, Krantor [fourth to third century B.C.]; Cicero; et al.), it encountered illustrious practitioners during the Empire.

The collection of *Letters* of Apollonios of Tyana contains two neo-Pythagorean consolations (55, 58). Seneca addressed consolations to Marcia (on the death of her son), to his mother Helvia (on his own exile), to Polybius (on the death of the latter's brother), and to Lucilius (*Epistles* 63, 93, 99). Plutarch wrote a *Consolation to His Wife* (a letter to his wife on the death of their granddaughter, Timoxena), a *Consolation to Apollonios* (to a certain Apollonios on the death of his young son; authorship uncertain), and a treatise *On Exile* (for a recently banished friend). Favorinus composed a treatise *On Exile* showing that exile was not an evil. These texts, written from a philosophic point of view, contained at the same time a rhetorical dimension, because they called upon logical and psychological arguments, *topoi,* and oratorical procedures (examples, citations, comparisons, prosopopeias presenting the deceased speaking, etc.). Medicine for the soul, considered especially in the Academy and the Stoa as a task of moral philosophy, came through speech:

As it is with our friends, so it is with the words we speak: best and most to be depended upon, we are told, are those which appear in adversity to some purpose and give help.

(Plutarch, *On Exile* 599A)

For its part, rhetoric was itself interested in the consolation, which, being advice, belonged to the deliberative genre. The preparatory exercises trained students in it (Theon, *Progymnasmata* 117), and the orators and theorists used it regularly, whether as an independent oration or as an obligatory part of the funeral oration (Aelius Aristides, Pseudo-Dionysios of Halikarnasssos, Menander Rhetor; cf. Fronto too). Rhetoric there developed philosophic themes.

The rhetorical or philosophical character of the consolation is therefore more a question of degree than the result of radical difference;

there is in fact a fundamental unity in the genre. Rhetoric is put to the service of philosophy, and vice versa. The commerce between philosophy and rhetoric is particularly noticeable, as might be expected, in the case of Dio of Prusa, author of a consolation on Kharidemos and consolatory passages in the two funeral orations for Melancomas (*Orations* 28–30). It is noteworthy that the consolation also attracted poets. Horace, for instance, wrote a consolation for Vergil on the occasion of the death of their mutual friend Quintilius Varus (*Odes* 1.24).

The consolation poses in an interesting way the problem of the commonplaces, for one of its chief characteristics is its traditional and repetitive cast. Confronted with always the same misfortunes and sorrows, the arguments could scarcely vary. And yet the consolation did not seem any the less necessary, from a moral and social point of view, whether it is a matter of simple courtesy or more deep condolences and the desire to help. At once conventional and essential, malleable too, consolatory eloquence aids in better understanding the value of the *topoi* in ancient rhetoric.

One final literary genre, and an innovation of the Imperial Age, is the novel. Novels are replete with passages recalling the preparatory exercises (fables, descriptions, etc.), and standard school topics, as well as actual speeches (court pleadings, addresses before popular assemblies and soldiers, encomia, laments). The novelists clearly knew rhetoric. Apuleius certainly did, and so did the Greek novelist Khariton of Aphrodisias, the author of *Khaireas and Kallirhoe* (first to second century A.D.), who introduces himself at the start of his work as secretary to a "lawyer" *(rhētōr)*. They like to have their characters speak, to lend them skillful, deceitful, or moving words, and to depict them in an oratorical guise. In so doing they were surely satisfying the tastes of their public and reflecting the character of an era where rhetoric reigned.

Conclusion

The Heritage of Greco-Roman Rhetoric

At the end of a survey covering more than a millenium, from Archaic Greece to the Late Roman Empire, ancient rhetoric appears simultaneously various and unified. It is various because it functioned in very diverse circumstances—in a Hellenic and in a Roman milieu, in Greek and in Latin, in democracies, aristocracies, and monarchies—and changed its fashions to suit each circumstance. And yet it is unified, because in this diversity of situations it constructed and preserved a fundamental identity. The components of this identity, or, to put it differently, the essential elements of a definition of ancient rhetoric, can be summed up as follows: norms of thought and writing, participation in the institutions of socio-political life, an intellectual system, a set of ongoing questions concerning ethics and philosophy, use of models as reference points, and reflection by its students on its own history.

One important theme was the connection between rhetoric and politics, or more precisely, rhetoric and liberty. Contrary to a commonly held view, noted at the beginning of this work, that associates rhetoric with the idea of manipulating others' minds, antiquity located rhetoric closer to debate and exchange and bound it up with freedom of expression in the search for persuasion and deliberation in common. This is not to say that there did not exist situations, as in all societies, when speeches put into play conflicting interests and power alignments; but channeling these interests and forces through rhetoric is precisely affirmed as the civil and humane way to handle them. Nor is any of this to say that there did not exist, in certain periods, political and religious propaganda, indoctrination, and cant; but even in these cases, he who spoke rhetorically spoke more than mere slogans or threats. When rhetoric came into play, no matter how totalitarian or absolutist the regime, it meant that the authorities wanted to act through the spoken word and persuasion, not by force alone. They took the risk of seeing this word get away from them (in its being relayed) and seeing different, indeed dissident opinions and discourses take shape or indirect criticisms materialize and opposing exchanges occur. Without any misplaced innocence, and without covering up the harshness of ancient societies as judged by the political and moral criteria of present-day Western democracies, one can say that rhetoric, as antiquity used it, that is, as simultaneously historical reality and ideological model, weighed in on the side of liberty, because it was tied by its very definition to argument, persuasion, and debate, as well as to teaching and culture. Rhetoric could not possibly have been present in a society that at the same time was devoid of the signature values rhetoric encouraged.

Rhetoric may also have been an element in individual liberty, as an educative discipline fostering mental power and as an art seeking to better nature. It gave its practitioners the wherewithal to use their intelligence better, as well as their personality and physical presence, to defend their point of view, and to communicate their ideas while avoiding the determinism of received opinions, pre-judged situations, and even unattractive looks. Through oratory, someone, no matter how ugly and lacking in natural grace, can persuade with the inflections of his voice and the play of his features.

The liberty thus acquired by the orator is not arbitrary, but set within norms. These norms do not come down to the simple criterion of momentary success or failure with listeners. According to most ancient authors, immediate efficacy did not measure a speech's worth (or not only, since it was not advisable to lose every case either), so much as did higher considerations of a technical, moral, and aesthetic order.

Greco-Roman rhetoric, in all its defining traits, was therefore a circumscribed entity subject to exacting standards. And then all of a sudden it came into contact with another culture, another rhetoric. It encountered Christianity.

The Conversion of Rhetoric

Christianity necessarily has its place in a history of ancient rhetoric, because it is a religion of the Word. The spoken word, accordingly, has theological importance. It was also important in the propagation of the new religion, for which the intermediary of persuasive language was the notable and perhaps principle means. Jesus delivered many speeches; after his death, the Gospel was preached in a thousand ways. As a result, there is a real Christian rhetoric. But what kind of rhetoric?

Christian rhetoric differs essentially from that of the Greco-Roman tradition (hereafter called pagan rhetoric for short). It was the heir of the Jewish tradition (via the Old Testament or the synagogue preaching of the Hellenistic Age), which had forms of expression uniquely its own. It spread in the most humble social strata, among people who had not been to school and had not learned to speak according to the rules of the craft (from this point of view, Christian rhetoric filled a gap in pagan rhetoric and occupied a space the latter had left vacant). Finally, at its core, the Gospel message set itself apart from the usual endeavor of Greek and Latin discourse: it announced a revealed truth, relying less upon rational persuasion and intellectual proofs than on an empowered "proclamation" *(kērugma)*. It proceeded through absolute affirmations, paradoxes, images (narratives, parables), and Biblical citations, rather than through the classical procedures of pagan rhetoric.

This special character of Christian discourse is noticeable in the New Testament. Even if one encounters there literary forms familiar from paganism (narrative, encomium, prayer, anecdote or *"khreia,"* etc.), even if St. Luke, in particular, seems schooled and educated in Greek culture, the overall impression is one of great linguistic and literary difference, compared to contemporary pagan texts. In their speeches, Jesus and his disciples do not at all conform to the rhetorical guidelines (of which undoubtedly many among them were ignorant). The oratorical ideal of the New Testament is on the contrary that of the truly spoken word, artless, directly inspired by the Holy Ghost, in accordance with the prescription Jesus gave to his first four apostles:

But when they shall lead you, and deliver you up, take no thought beforehand what ye shall speak, neither do ye premeditate: but whatsoever shall be given you in that hour, that speak ye: for it is not ye that speak, but the Holy Ghost.

(Mk 13.11, AV)

Paul, surely one of the greatest orators of antiquity, strenuously stressed this opposition between his inspired word as Christian preacher and the ordinary "wisdom" (*sophia,* the word signifying as well "knowledge" and "ability") of human persuasion:

And I, brethren, when I came to you, came not with excellency of speech or of wisdom, declaring unto you the testimony of God. For I determined not to know any thing among you save Jesus Christ, and him crucified. And I was with you in weakness, and in fear, and in much trembling. And my speech and my preaching was not with enticing words of man's wisdom, but in demonstration of the Spirit and of power: that your faith should not stand in the wisdom of men, but in the power of God.

(1 Cor 2.1–5, AV)

New message, new rhetoric; for a divine message, a superhuman rhetoric. Yet contacts were inevitable, and they occurred.

As Christianity developed in the Greco-Roman world, it could not help but expose itself to the culture of this world and, hence, among other things, to this world's rhetoric. This opening was not only pragmatic, compelled by the need for educational and intellectual tools. Anthropological reasons justified it (all men, even pagans, have souls of divine origin and God is capable of having put a spark of the truth in them), and so did theological ones (paganism is a phase of salvation history and so there is no call to ignore it totally). Christians purposely quoted on this point the passage from Exodus (12.35–36, AV) in which it is said "the children of Israel . . . borrowed of the Egyptians jewels of silver, and jewels of gold, . . . and they spoiled the Egyptians." Israel's despoiling of the Egyptians provided the Christians with the model of their own desired appropriation of Greco-Roman culture. It meant recycling paganism to make it serve the expression of Christian values and to work profoundly the conversion of ancient culture, just as one converted individuals.

There was, at first, some distaste and resistance on the part of Christians, since pagan rhetoric was viewed as contrary to the simple, indeed rustic model set forth in the Scriptures; pagan stylistic niceties appeared idle and the pleasure aroused by beautiful speeches dangerous. The very idea of a technique of the spoken word was questionable for believers who wanted to give witness to the truth in the sparest way possible. On the other hand, pagan rhetoric had proved its worth as an educational method, as an instrument for language mastery, as an art of persuasion, and as a force for culture and beauty. In a neighboring field, exegesis based on philosophy, great thinkers like Clement of Alexandria (140/50 to 220/30) and Origen (ca. 185 to 252) who had Philon (20 B.C. to 41 A.D.) as a forerunner in the Jewish tradition, exemplified the fertile assimilation of Greco-Roman culture. Progressively throughout the second and third centuries, authors consequently turned toward pagan rhetoric. Apologists built solid cases on behalf of the new religion; among them, Tatian (second century) in Greek was particularly influenced by the Second Sophistic, while Tertullian (ca. 155 to 225) in Latin displayed a deep rhetorical background and richness of style and argumentation. Melito of Sardis wrote his *Easter Homily* in Asianist style (ca. 160 to 170), and Gregory Thaumaturgus was the author of the first preserved Christian epideictic oration (the *Thanksgiving to Origen,* delivered in 238, in a farewell ceremony upon the author's departure from Origen's school).

When Christianity became the official religion, Christian rhetoric supplanted pagan. The decisive turning point occurred in the fourth century, one of the most brilliant periods in the history of ancient rhetoric, which witnessed a kind of culmination of the Greco-Roman tradition coincident with the triumph of the Fathers of the Church. Greek paganism experienced such a flowering that modern scholars sometimes speak of it as a "Third Sophistic," represented by the orators and professors Libanios and Himerios, the orator-philosopher Themistios, the Emperor Julian, and the theorist of the *progumnasmata,* Aphthonios. In Latin, the panegyric tradition continued (*Panegyrici Latini* 6–12); Symmachus delivered official orations; Marius Victorinus wrote a commentary on Cicero's *De inventione.* A line of truly great names, however, sheds luster on Christian rhetoric. In Greek, there were Eusebios of

Caesarea; the Cappadocian Fathers, Gregory of Nanzianzus, called the "Christian Demosthenes," Gregory of Nyssa, and Basil of Caesarea; and John Chrysostom. As for Latin, there were Lactantius (the "Christian Cicero"); Ambrose; and then, at the turn of the fourth to fifth century, Augustine. Christian rhetoric was now using numerous genres: formal sermons, simple homilies, funeral orations, panegyrics of the saints and martyrs, consolations, polemics, and refutations of heresies, divers kinds of speeches necessitated by the functioning of ecclesiastical institutions and the like. Soon Augustine added a theoretic treatise to the list when, in the *De doctrina christiana,* he created the theory of Christian culture and in the fourth book defined the very rules of a Christian eloquence.

It is essential, furthermore, to see clearly that for a long time nothing walled off paganism from Christianity concerning rhetoric. Some Christian orators were students of pagan rhetors. Conversions happened, and so did apostasies. Some orations eluded classification, because they were religiously circumspect or because they proposed doctrines so vague as to be equally compatible with a pagan philosophic monotheism or Christianity. Hence there was a trafficking in themes and ideas, added to which was the fact that invariables exist in rhetoric: forms and themes that, by the nature of things, are just the same no matter the religious context. All these reasons facilitated Christianity's absorption of pagan rhetoric.

As to how pagan specialists in rhetoric thought of the Jewish and Christian tradition (here the Jewish), we have a piece of evidence whose date (first century) makes it precious, as does its originality, in Pseudo-Longinus. When he is defining "thoughts" as sources of the sublime, apropos of texts portraying the gods, the author quotes some passages in Homer, and then introduces a new example:

So, too, the lawgiver of the Jews, no ordinary man, having formed a worthy conception of divine power and given expression to it, writes at the very beginning of his *Laws:* "God said"—what? "Let there be light," and there was light, "Let there be earth," and there was earth.

> (*On the Sublime* 9.9: the syntax of this sentence is debated, but the overall sense is not in doubt; cf. Genesis 1.3, 9–10)

This is the first time, so far as we know, that a pagan rhetor took an interest in the Bible, and he did it in an open-minded and sympathetic spirit extraordinary for the time. Pseudo-Longinus puts the Bible on the same level as Homer, indeed above him, and uncovers the sublime in the majestic simplicity of the *Fiat lux*. Such an approach looked to the future in that it announced the later rapprochement between pagan and Christian rhetoric. That is why this short passage of an anonymous author so vividly impressed modern scholars who saw in it a mysterious and prophetic encounter. At the turn of the seventeenth to the eighteenth century, the comment of Pseudo-Longinus was the object of a long rhetorical and theological controversy between Pierre-Daniel Huet, bishop of Avranches and a great Hellenist and Hebraicist, and Boileau, translator of the treatise, who took this occasion to clash over the definition of the sublime style and the very possibility of a rhetoric of God. (Cf. the *Préface* of Boileau's translation and his *Réflexions critiques sur quelques passages du rhéteur Longin*, X, as well as the *Lettre à Monsieur le Duc de Montausier* of Huet.)

From the End of Antiquity to Modern Times

After the fourth century, rhetoric remained part of the framework of civilization, in educational, political, religious, and literary realms. The end of antiquity saw the fulfillment of particularly important work in compilation and interpretation relating to theory. In the Greek East, the treatises of Hermogenes and Aphthonios became a canon, probably as the fifth century passed to the sixth, and they were the object of endless commentaries (some were by neo-Platonist philosophers, as once again in its history rhetoric encountered philosophy). At the same time, in the Latin-speaking world, there was a flowering of "manuals" *(artes)* and "epitomes" *(compendia)*. Boethius (sixth century) did a commentary on Cicero, and the encyclopedists of the fifth to seventh centuries (Martianus Capella, Cassiodorus, Isidore of Seville) all accorded space to rhetoric. This at times remarkable production was destined to exert a large influence on medieval rhetoric. The end of the ancient world chose and hallowed the doctrines that eventually prevailed: those of Aphthonios and Hermogenes in Constantinople, Cicero's in the Latin West.

The Middle Ages, as much in the medieval West as in the Byzantine Empire, preserved and transmitted the textual and intellectual heritage of ancient rhetoric, all the while reinterpreting it in the light of new contexts.

In modern Europe, ancient rhetoric has constituted, more perhaps than one imagines, a reference point and a source of inspiration. We have encountered various examples of this above, discussing the political model of the Athenian democracy, the history of teaching (the long-term influence of ideas of Isokrates, Cicero, and Quintilian, as well as the preparatory exercises), the persistence of Greek and Latin rhetorical terminology in modern languages, or the seventeenth- and eighteenth-century discussions of the sublime. Recall as well the continuing work over the centuries on Greek and Latin texts; the ever-present problem of religious eloquence; the rediscovery during the Renaissance of the Greco-Roman heritage; the royal panegyric in France of the Ancien Régime inspired by ancient models; the oratory of the French Revolution invoking Rome and Sparta; the line of great English and American orators influenced by Demosthenes and Cicero in the eighteenth and nineteenth centuries, like Pitt, Lord Brougham, John Quincy Adams, and Rufus Choate; Nietzsche's rehabilitation of the sophists; Péguy, molded by ancient culture, analyzing "the authority of the oratorical commandment" of Jaurès; Malraux rediscovering the inspiration of Asianism. One could go on.

Greco-Roman Rhetoric Today

Rhetoric has become today an important research topic in the field of ancient studies, an importance explained by the general movement of ideas. Some milestones may facilitate a better understanding of the increasing role of ancient rhetoric in the thought of the twentieth and now the twenty-first centuries.

In the United States, from the end of the 1950s, George Kennedy methodically explored ancient rhetoric in all its guises, from Homer to the dawn of the Middle Ages, and even beyond in some of his works. The author has recounted, in the foreword of *Greek Rhetoric under Christian Emperors* ([Princeton, 1983], p. xvi), how when he was starting out, rhetoric was scarcely thought about in Classics departments, and how the great scholar Werner Jaeger (who did not share the common prejudice) said to him one day, "I have written *Paideia;* you must write *Peitho.*" Kennedy successfully followed up on this advice, and his highly influential books relaunched the study of ancient rhetoric, which has now become a recognized discipline in the American university world, meaningfully engaging any number of researchers.

To explain ancient rhetoric's favorable reception, it is necessary to consider the context. A tide that was lifting rhetoric in general sustained the labors of American scholars on ancient rhetoric. Contributions concerning antiquity struck a responsive chord because they harmonized with a larger movement of ideas.

The twentieth century, in fact, witnessed a revival in the study of rhetoric in the English-speaking world. Beginning from very different sets of issues, authors became interested in the art of the spoken word and language criticism. I. A. Richards, in *The Philosophy of Rhetoric,* placed at the center of his thought the notion of "misunderstanding" and saw in rhetoric, both as compositional technique and analysis of discourse, the way to remedy lack of comprehension, to communicate appropriately, and to avoid conflicts. The many works of Kenneth Burke, dealing notably with art, literature, communication, or religious language, made of rhetoric an especially valuable critical tool. One could say that Burke, throughout all his work, conducted an "unending conversation" with rhetoric, to use a celebrated expression he himself employed in another context.

Two universities were active in the revival of rhetoric during the 1920s and 1930s, Columbia and Cornell. At the former, C. S. Baldwin wrote his three books devoted to rhetoric and poetics in antiquity, the Middle Ages, and the Renaissance, while Cornell in those years had the only graduate program in rhetoric. The University of Chicago, where

R. M. Weaver was an important faculty member, likewise played a leading role. Similarly, at Cambridge University, specialists in the philosophy of language were at work on research destined to have a large impact. S. E. Toulmin analyzed speech's demonstrative power. J. L. Austin recognized in speech activity in general an element that he called "illocution," defining it as what happens in issuing an utterance, by virtue of issuing an utterance. According to this theory, the "performative" dimension of the utterance does not constitute an assertion, which could be true or false. It reports nothing; rather, it does something, is in itself an act. Austin opened up a field of inquiry that has given birth to the whole movement studying "speech acts" and to "pragmatics."

The work of such thinkers created an overall climate where ancient texts especially stood out as foundations, models, and sources of inspiration. R. McKeon, a friend of Burke, is a case in point. Coming from philosophy at Chicago, McKeon recognized the importance of both rhetoric and Cicero.

In addition, Speech departments in a number of American universities kept up an ongoing interest in ancient rhetoric, whose rules were valuable for teaching public speaking.

Turning to the French-speaking world, the thought of some writers, like Paul Valéry, Raymond Queneau and Jean Paulhan, gave rise to one kind of interest in rhetoric, for they were curious about language and desirous of understanding the functioning and structure of a work of literature better. A linguist like Roman Jakobson, for his part, put metaphor and metonymy at the center of his research. In this setting, ancient rhetoric appeared likely to provide not only approaches for thought but even tools directly applicable to the semiotic and stylistic analysis of texts. The highly influential work of Roland Barthes explored in this direction, as did that of Gérard Genette and the Groupe μ (a research group naming itself after the Greek letter *mu,* the first letter of the word *metaphora* or "metaphor").

Among philosophers, Paul Ricœur played an important role by basing on Greek texts his thought about rhetoric and poetics, insofar as they concerned metaphor, narrative, history, and politics.

In Belgium, another leading light, Chaïm Perelman, a jurisprudent and philosopher, followed by L. Olbrechts-Tyteca, took a personal interest in argumentation. Perelman felt the need for thinking about justice and the functioning of the judicial system in Europe after the end of the Second World War. Formal logic, it seemed to him, provided inadequate methods of reasoning in a realm where value judgments were necessarily approximate and labile. So it was that he turned to the methods of rhetorical argument, as more appropriate to defining the terms for persuading both before chance audiences who were not "clean slates" (but animated by human emotions and prejudices) and on issues that did not lend themselves to absolutely conclusive proofs. For working out his *Traité de l'argumentation,* Perelman found no better guide than Aristotle. His "new rhetoric" was a return to the sources and held the ancient patrimony in esteem.

In the last years of the twentieth century, as structuralism was running out of discoveries, Marc Fumaroli reintroduced rhetoric into literary studies under a new guise. "Restrained rhetoric" was no longer the issue, that is, rhetoric reduced to figures and presented as an abstract and timeless intellectual tool, but rhetoric in its history, as a branch of history in general. This approach not only offered fresh insights on the evolution of ideas, literary and artistic forms, and society, but also regenerated the very notion of "literature." Studied in its historical relations with "eloquence," "discourse," the *"res literaria,"* "literature" emerged as something infinitely more rich and complex than certain modern, frozen senses of the term. Amid this complexity, the thinking of the Greco-Roman heritage was crucial. The approaches Fumaroli opened and numerous scholars subsequently pursued illuminated how the presence of ancient rhetoric was hardly anecdotal in the history of French and European letters.

In a completely different area, there was no want of practitioners of the spoken word who were fascinated as much by the technique as by the ethical and philosophical reflections of the ancients on rhetorical matters. We have the example of Jean-Denis Bredin and Thierry Lévy and Gilbert Collard, celebrated lawyers and authors of recent books on the subject.

The general movement of ideas therefore provoked a renaissance of studies on rhetoric in the twentieth century, a renaissance in which ancient rhetoric, in particular, played an important part. The observations made above on the English- and French-speaking worlds could be extended, were space to permit, to still other cultural settings. The activity of the International Society for the History of Rhetoric, founded in 1977 by M. Fumaroli, A. D. Leeman, A. Michel, J. J. Murphy, H. Plett, and B. Vickers, with its five official languages and membership on five continents, is a witness to the breadth of the phenomenon.

The communication sciences and technologies, which have assumed such great importance in our own time, do not ignore—or should not—that they have had in rhetoric a kind of forerunner. Rhetoric can still be useful to them by providing a cultural background, a memory, and by encouraging them to consider "ethics," another notion that has taken on renewed importance and which lay at the very core of ancient rhetoric's concerns.

Thinking about ancient rhetoric clearly prompts consideration about work still to be done. Topics await research; texts await basic translating and explicating. Perspectives, too, await broadening, so that research on rhetoric may benefit more than itself by contributing to a better understanding of other areas of ancient civilization. One may ask, for example, if there exists a rhetoric of scientific discourse, or explore more deeply the question of rhetoric's connection with the figurative arts, or with religion. The emerging area, finally, of "comparative rhetoric" (G. A. Kennedy) is promising. It juxtaposes the usage and forms of discourse from civilizations not only different from one another but sometimes far removed in time and space, at the risk of running into startling differences and even more startling similarities.

It is not only a matter of fields lying open but of a new way of working. Rhetoric, indeed, is a subject that breaches certain traditional boundaries between disciplines and periods. It simultaneously calls upon linguistics, aesthetics, philosophy, textual history, literary history, history, period. For students and scholars, rhetoric offers a modern, because comprehensive methodology and an original angle of approach with which to confront antiquity.

Thesaurus
The System of Rhetoric

Ancient rhetoric does not present conceptions and technical terms in isolation, but as part of a network taking the form of a multitude of lists. Each list means to be as complete a description as possible of one sector or aspect. It aims to detail the constitutive elements of the topic being considered, following the method of division into genera and species in order to cover it completely and to define it by enumerating its parts.

The different lists are juxtaposed, superimposed, and mesh with one another. Bringing these lists together, when they are all looked at as an ensemble, forms the system of ancient rhetoric. It is a prodigious intellectual construct, capable of almost infinite subdivision, which aims to render a full accounting of the art of the spoken word.

This system was built in stages over the course of history and, as it continually enriched itself, gradually imposed itself during the Hellenistic and Imperial Ages. Spread far and wide, conveyed particularly by teaching, it represented a kind of shared possession for all those—and they were many—who had been educated in rhetoric. That is why it is important to know this system today, the better to understand the ancient texts. Furthermore, many of the notions thus defined have remained current in modern languages and thought.

The overall coherence of the system, however, did not prevent unflagging research and constant rearranging—the lists were endlessly modified, abridged, lengthened, debated. Nor did it prevent numerous divergences on points of detail among authors, not to mention actual contradictions between one list and another.

We provide here a panorama of the system, presenting the most important lists. This is a synchronic overview, and we do not seek to retrace the history of the different lists (some observations on this topic have been made along the way in the body of the book). We cite each list, as much as possible, in the most currently accepted form, from a representative source within the chronological limits of the present work (i.e., from the very beginnings to the third century A.D.). We indicate with "cf." supplementary references, contained within the same chronological limits; the choice has had to be very selective, given the wealth of material. Technical Greek and Latin terms, chosen among the best attested, are drawn from the sources.

List of Abbreviations

Alex.: Alexander, 2nd cent. A.D. (ed. Spengel, *Rhetores Graeci,* III)
  Fragments
  Fig.: On the Figures

Anon. Seg.: Anonymous Seguerianus, 2nd–3rd cent. A.D., *The Art of Political Speech* (ed. Dilts-Kennedy, *Two Greek Rhetorical Treatises from the Roman Empire*)

Apsines, 3rd cent. A.D.
  Rhet.: Rhetoric (ed. Dilts-Kennedy, op. cit.)
  Probl. Fig.: On Figured Problems (ed. Patillon)

Aquil. Rom.: Aquila Romanus, 3rd cent. A.D., *On the Figures of Thought and Diction* (ed. Halm, *Rhetores Latini Minores*)

Arist.: Aristotle, 4th cent. B.C.
  Rhet.: Rhetoric (ed. Loeb, Freese)
  Top.: Topics (ed. Loeb, Forster)

Cic.: Cicero, 1st cent. B.C.
  Brut.: Brutus (ed. Loeb, Hendrickson)
  De or.: On the Orator (ed. Loeb, Rackham)
  Inv.: On Invention (ed. Loeb, Hubbell)
  Or.: Orator (ed. Loeb, Hubbell)
  Part.: On the Classification of Rhetoric (ed. Loeb, Rackham)
  Top.: Topica (ed. Loeb, Hubbell)

Demetr.: Demetrios, 2nd–1st cent. B.C. (?), *On Style* (ed. Loeb, Innes)

D. Hal.: Dionysios of Halikarnassos, 1st cent. B.C., *Critical Essays* (ed. Loeb, Usher)
  Lys.: Lysias
  Dem.: Demosthenes

Diog. L.: Diogenes Laertios, 3rd cent. A.D., *Lives of Eminent Philosophers* (ed. Loeb, Hicks)

Gell.: Aulus Gellius, 2nd cent. A.D., *Attic Nights* (ed. Loeb, Rolfe)

Hermag.: Hermagoras I, 2nd cent. B.C. (ed. Matthes)

Hermog.: Hermogenes, 2nd–3rd cent. A.D. (ed. Rabe)
   Id.: Forms of Style
   Inv.: Invention
   Prog.: Preparatory Exercises
   Stat.: Questions at Issue
Isokr.: Isokrates, 4th cent. B.C. (ed. Loeb, Norlin and Van Hook)

Longin.: Cassius Longinus, 3rd cent. A.D., *Rhetoric* (ed. Patillon-Brisson)

Men. Rhet.: Menander Rhetor I, 3rd cent. A.D., *Division of Epideictic Orations,* and II, 3rd cent. A.D., *On Epideictic Orations* (ed. Russell-Wilson)

Minuc.: Minucianus, 3rd cent. A.D., *On Epicheiremes* (ed. Spengel-Hammer, *Rhetores Graeci* I, 2)

Philod.: Philodemos, 1st cent. B.C., *Rhetoric* (ed. Sudhaus)

Plat.: Plato, 4th cent. B.C., *Phaidros* (ed. Loeb, Fowler)

Ps.-Aristides: Pseudo-Aelius Aristides, 2nd cent. A.D., *Rhetoric* (ed. Patillon)

Ps.-D. Hal.: Pseudo-Dionysios of Halikarnassos, 3rd cent. A.D., *Rhetoric* (ed. Usener-Radermacher)

Quint.: Quintilian, 1st cent. A.D., *Institutio Oratoria* (ed. Loeb, Russell)

Rhet. Alex.: Pseudo-Aristotle, 4th cent. B.C., *Rhetoric to Alexander* (ed. Loeb, Rackham)

Rhet. Her.: 1st cent. B.C., *Rhetorica ad Herennium* (ed. Loeb, Caplan)

Rufus, 2nd cent. A.D., *Rhetoric* (ed. Patillon)

Rut. Lup.: Rutilius Lupus, 1st cent. A.D., *On the Figures of Thought and Diction* (ed. Brooks)

Sen. Rhet.: Seneca the Elder, 1st cent. B.C.–1st cent. A.D., *Controversiae and Suasoriae* (ed. Loeb, Winterbottom)

Tac., *Dial.:* Tacitus, 1st cent. A.D., *Dialogus* (ed. Loeb, Winterbottom)

Theon: Ailios Theon, 1st–2nd cent. A.D., *Preparatory Exercises* (ed. Patillon)

Tiber.: Tiberios, 3rd–4th cent. A.D., *The Figures in Demosthenes* (ed. Ballaira)

Tryph.: Tryphon, 1st cent. B.C., *On the Tropes* (ed. Spengel, *Rhetores Graeci* III)

The Art of Rhetoric: General Categories

1. The **Components of Rhetoric:** Greek, *rhētorikēs merē,* Latin, *rhetorices partes* (also called **Tasks of the Orator:** Greek, *rhētoros erga,* Latin, *oratoris opera*)

Invention: Greek, *heuresis,* Latin, *inventio* ("discovery" of the arguments)

Arrangement: Greek, *taxis, oikonomia,* Latin, *dispositio* (arranging the arguments found, plan of the speech)

Expression: Greek, *lexis, hermēneia, phrasis,* Latin, *elocutio* (putting arguments into words and sentences, diction and style)

Memory: Greek, *mnēmē,* Latin, *memoria* (fixing the speech in the mind so as to recall it from memory)

Delivery: Greek, *hupokrisis,* Latin, *actio, pronuntiatio* (delivering the speech)
(*Rhet. Her.* 1.3. Cf. Cic., *Inv.* 1.9; *De or.* 1.142, 2.79; Quint. 3.3)

The list of the "components of rhetoric" constitutes the framework of some rhetorical treatises (for example, Cicero's *On the Orator* [books 2 and 3] and Cassius Longinus's *Rhetoric*). Others are divided according to the "parts of the speech" (cf. below, section 9: e.g., the *Rhetorics* of the Anonymous Seguerianus, Apsines, and Rufus). Still others try to combine the two systems (e.g., the *Rhetorica ad Herennium* and the *Institutio Oratoria* of Quintilian).

2. The **Duties of the Orator:** Latin, *oratoris officia*

To Instruct, Inform: Latin, *docere* (or **To Prove:** Latin, *probare*)

To Delight: Latin, *delectare* (or **To Win Over:** Latin, *conciliare*)

To Move: Latin, *movere, permovere* (or **To Prevail Upon:** Latin, *flectere*) (Cic., *On the Best Type of Orators* 3. Cf. Cic., *De or.* 2.115, 128; *Brut.* 185, 276; *Or.* 69; Quint. 3.5.2)

One can compare the division *logos/ēthos/pathos* in Aristotle (cf. below, section 12), but the two triads do not overlap exactly.

3. The Sources of Oratorical Ability

Natural gifts: Greek, *phusis*, Latin, *natura, ingenium*

Learning (or "Art," "Science"): Greek, *epistēmē, mathēsis,* Latin, *doctrina, artificium, ars*

Practice: Greek, *meletē, askēsis,* Latin, *exercitatio*
(Plat., *Phaidros* 269D. Cf. Isokr., *Against the sophists* 14–17; *Antidosis* 187; Cic., *Inv.* 1.5; *Brut.* 25; Quint. 7.10.14)

Some added **Imitation:** Greek, *mimēsis,* Latin, *imitatio* (*Rhet. Her.* 1.3; Quint. 3.5.1).

Types of Speech

4. The **Preparatory Exercises:** Greek, *progumnasmata,* Latin, *praeexercitamina, praeexercitamenta*

Fable: Greek, *muthos,* Latin, *fabula*

Narrative: Greek, *diēgēma,* Latin, *narratio*

Anecdote: Greek, *khreia,* Latin, *chria, usus*

Maxim: Greek, *gnōmē,* Latin, *sententia*

Refutation/Confirmation: Greek, *anaskeuē/kataskeuē,* Latin, *refutatio/confirmatio*

Commonplace: Greek, *koinos topos,* Latin, *communis locus*

Praise: Greek, *enkōmion,* Latin, *laus* (and **Invective:** Greek, *psogos,* Latin, *vituperatio*)

Comparison: Greek, *sunkrisis,* Latin, *comparatio*

Ethopoeia or **Prosopopoeia:** Greek, *ēthopoiia, prosōpopoiia,* Latin, *adlocutio, sermocinatio*

Description: Greek, *ekphrasis,* Latin, *descriptio*

Theme: Greek, *thesis*, Latin, *thesis, positio*

Law Proposal: Greek, *nomou eisphora*, Latin, *legis latio* (Hermog., *Prog.* [translated into Latin by Priscian of Caesarea in the 5th–6th cent. A.D.]. Cf. Quint. 1.9; 2.4; Theon)

5. The Two Types of **Question:** Greek, *zētēma*, Latin, *quaestio*

General Theme: Greek, *thesis*, Latin, *quaestio infinita, propositum* (a speech dealing with a subject in the abstract and in general, without taking into account individual "circumstances" [cf. below, section 14]); subdivided into:

> **Theoretical:** Greek, *theōrētikē*, Latin, *scientiae, cognitionis*
> **Practical:** Greek, *praktikē*, Latin, *actionis*

Specific Theme: Greek, *hupothesis*, Latin, *quaestio finita, causa* (a speech bearing on a concrete subject and referring to "circumstances") (Quint. 3.5.5–18. Cf. Hermag., fr. 6; Cic., *Inv.* 1.8; *De or.* 2.65–68; *Part.* 61–63; *Top.* 79–81; Theon 121.6–14; Hermog., *Prog.* 25.3–12)

6. The **Genres of Rhetorical Speeches** or **Rhetorical Genres:** Greek, *tōn logōn tōn rhētorikōn genē, rhētorikēs genē,* Latin, *causarum genera, rhetorices genera* (in place of "Genres" the word **Forms** is also used: Greek, *eidē*, Latin, *species*)

Deliberative: Greek, *sumbouleutikon*, Latin, *deliberativum* (to advise for or against)

Judicial: Greek, *dikanikon*, Latin, *iudiciale* (to prosecute or to defend)

Epideictic: Greek, *epideiktikon*, Latin, *demonstrativum* (to praise or to blame; this genre is also called **Encomiastic:** Greek, *enkōmiastikon*, Latin, *laudativum;* and **Panegyric:** Greek, *panēgurikon*, Latin, *panegyricum*) (Arist., *Rhet.* 1.3. Cf. *Rhet. Her.* 1.2; 2.1; Philod. 1.212; D. Hal., *Lys.* 16.2; Theon 61.21–23; Alex., *Fragments* 1.3–2.7; Diog. L. 7.42)

On the question of knowing whether this list of the three genres takes into account the full diversity of oratorical forms, or whether it is appropriate to insert supplementary genres, cf. the discussions of Cic., *De or.* 2.43–64; Quint. 3.4.

7. The Two Types of **Declamation:** Greek, *melētē,* Latin, *declamatio*

Suasoria: a declamation on a deliberative topic

Controversia: a declamation on a legal topic
(Tac., *Dial.* 35.4. Cf. Sen. Rhet., books 1–9 and book 10; Ps.-D. Hal., chap. 10)

8. The Types of **Figured Speech:** Greek, *eskhēmatismenos logos,* Latin, *figuratus sermo, figurata oratio*

Color: Greek, *khrōma;* also **Allusion:** Greek, *kat'emphasin* (saying what one means but gingerly, or being content to suggest indirectly)

Innuendo: Greek, *plagios, plagiōs* (saying something obliquely, intending something else)

The Contrary: Greek, *ta enantia, kata to enantion* (saying one thing but intending its contrary)

Subsidiary Types:
Claiming to express the same opinion as the preceding speaker, but speaking with a different meaning
Claiming to express an opinion contrary to the preceding speaker's, but actually supporting it
Deferring frank discussion of a topic
(Ps.-D. Hal. 8.2–4. Cf. Demetr. 287–98; Quint. 9.2.65–99; Hermog., *Inv.* 4.13; Apsines, *Probl. Fig.;* Ps.-D. Hal. 9)

Plan and Parts of the Oration

9. The **Parts of the Oration:** Greek, *logou merē,* Latin, *orationis partes*

Exordium, Introduction: Greek, *prooimion,* Latin, *exordium, principium, prooemium*

Narration: Greek, *diēgēsis,* Latin, *narratio*

Outline, Division: Greek, *prothesis, prokataskeuē,* Latin, *propositio, partitio, divisio* (sets forth the points to be treated, comes either before or after the narration)

Argumentation: Greek, *pisteis, agōnes,* Latin, *argumentatio,* usually divided into:
Proof: Greek, *pistis, apodeixis,* Latin, *probatio, confirmatio*

Refutation: Greek, *lusis*, Latin, *refutatio, confutatio* (refutation of the opposing side's arguments, whether they have been already expressed or in anticipation of their being expressed)

Peroration: Greek, *epilogos*, Latin, *peroratio, conclusio*
(*Rhet. Her.* 1.4. Cf. Plat., *Phaidros* 266D–267D; Arist., *Rhet.* 3.13; Cic., *Inv.* 1.19; *Or.* 122; D. Hal., *Lys.* 17–19; Quint. 3.9; Diog. L. 7.43. Cf. also above, section 1)

This paradigm is meant principally for the judicial genre. The other genres (deliberative and epideictic) keep a tripartite division from this outline (exordium, body of the speech, peroration), but they present a different organization that is based on specific *topoi* for the body of the speech: cf. below, sections 16 and 18.

10. The Functions of the Exordium

To Clarify the Case for the Listeners: Greek, *tou pragmatos dēlōsis, eumatheian apergasasthai*, Latin, *docilem facere*

To Catch the Listeners' Attention: Greek, *epi to prosekhein parakalesai, prosokhēn apergasasthai*, Latin, *attentum facere*

To Win Their Goodwill: Greek, *eunous poiēsai, eunoian apergasasthai*, Latin, *benivolum facere*
(*Rhet. Alex.* 29.1. Cf. Arist., *Rhet.* 3.14.1415a34–b1; *Rhet. Her.* 1.7; Cic., *Inv.* 1.20; *De or.* 2.82; *Top.* 97; D. Hal., *Lys.* 17.9; Quint. 4.1.5; *Anon. Seg.* 8)

11. Virtues of the Narration: Greek, *diēgēseōs aretai*, Latin, *narrationis virtutes*

Clarity: Greek, *saphēneia*, Latin, *dilucida, lucida, aperta, perspicua*

Succinctness: Greek, *suntomia*, Latin, *brevis*

Plausibility: Greek, *pithanotēs*, Latin, *veri similis, probabilis, credibilis*
(*Rhet. Her.* 1.14. Cf. *Rhet. Alex.* 30.4–5; Cic., *Inv.* 1.28; *De or.* 2.83; D. Hal., *Dem.* 34.7; Theon 79.20–21; Quint. 4.2.31; *Anon. Seg.* 63)

12. Categories of Proof

Ready-made: Greek, *atekhnos*, Latin, *artis expers, inartificialis* (proofs not of the orator's making, but which already exist: evidence, confessions obtained under torture, written documents, etc.)

Custom-made: Greek, *entekhnos,* Latin, *artificialis* (proofs worked up by the orator), deriving from:

The **Character** of the orator, as it is presented in the speech: Greek, *ēthos*

The **Attitudes** the orator creates in the listeners, the **Emotions** he inspires: Greek, *pathos*

The **Oration** itself (through the weight of its arguments): Greek, *logos*

(Arist., *Rhet.* 1.2.1355b35–1356a20. Cf. Cic., *De or.* 2.116; *Part.* 6–7; D. Hal., *Lys.* 19; Quint. 5.1; *Anon Seg.* 145–47; Minuc. 1)

13. The Functions of the Peroration

Summation: Greek, *anakephalaiōsis,* Latin, *enumeratio*

Amplification, "Build Up": Greek, *auxēsis,* Latin, *amplificatio* (aiming especially to arouse **Indignation:** Greek, *deinōsis,* Latin, *indignatio*)

Appeal to Pity: Greek, *eleos,* Latin, *commiseratio, conquestio*

(*Rhet. Her.* 2.47. Cf. Arist., *Rhet.* 3.19; Apsines, *Rhet.* 10.1)

The last two functions can be grouped together, in which case the list has only two components:

Factual: Greek, *praktikos,* Latin, *in rebus* (corresponding to "Summation")

Emotional: Greek, *pathētikos,* Latin, *in adfectibus* (corresponding to both "Amplification-indignation" and "Appeal to Sympathy")

(*Anon. Seg.* 203. Cf. Cic., *Part.* 52; Quint. 6.1.1)

"Commonplaces" Related to Argumentation in the Speech

The **commonplaces** (Greek, *topoi,* Latin, *loci*) are the means of finding ideas. They consist of lists of predefined rubrics to which the orator turns when he wants to handle a given subject and which suggest arguments to him, with the stipulation that he adapt these general suggestions to the individual case he is arguing. sections 14 and 15 are lists meant for general use and apply to all types of speeches, while the subsequent lists apply principally (but not exclusively) to a specific oratorical genre: section 16 to the deliberative genre, 17 to the judicial, 18 to the epideictic.

14. The **Circumstances** or **Essential Components of the Situation:** Greek, *peristasis, persistaseōs moria, peristatika moria, stoikheia,* Latin, *negotium, circumstantia, circumstantiae partes* (or also **Elements,** Greek, *stoikheia,* Latin, *elementa*)

Person: Greek, *prosōpon,* Latin, *persona.* **Who?** Greek, *tis,* Latin, *quis*

Deed: Greek, *pragma,* Latin, *factum, actum.* **What?** Greek, *ti,* Latin, *quid*

Place: Greek, *topos,* Latin, *locus.* **Where?** Greek, *pou,* Latin, *ubi*

Time: Greek, *khronos,* Latin, *tempus.* **When?** Greek, *pote,* Latin, *quando*

Manner: Greek, *tropos,* Latin, *modus.* **How?** Greek, *pōs,* Latin, *quemadmodum*

Cause: Greek, *aitia,* Latin, *causa.* **Why?** Greek, *dia ti,* Latin, *cur* (Hermog., *Stat.* 45.20–46.3. Cf. Hermag., fr. 7; Quint. 3.5.17; 3.6.25–28; Hermog., *Inv.* 140.16–141.3; Men. Rhet. I, 366.5–13)

Some added **Material:** Greek, *hulē,* Latin, *materia,* to the list, or the **Means, Instrument, Opportunity,** et al.

Among other uses, this list serves a particular function as a list of *topoi* in the narration, whence its occasional designation **Parts or Components of the Narration:** Greek, *diēgēseōs moria, diēgēseōs stoikheia,* Latin, *narrationis elementa.* Cf. Theon 78.16–20; Quint. 4.2.55; *Anon. Seg.* 90.

15. The Standard "Commonplaces" for Argumentation (logical methods as a basis for reasoning; these rhetorical lines of argument are often called an **enthymeme:** Greek, *enthumēma,* or an **epicheireme:** Greek, *epikheirēma*)

Definition: Greek, *horos,* Latin, *finis, finitio*

Division: Greek, *diairesis,* Latin, *divisio, partitio*

Parallel, Comparison: Greek, *parathesis,* Latin, *adpositum, comparativum, comparatio*

Conjugation: Greek, *sustoikhia,* Latin, *coniugatum, coniunctum* (reasoning drawing support from a shared designation, as with etymologically related words; e.g., a "commons" may clearly be grazed "in common")

Implication: Greek, *periokhē* (line of argument showing that a notion contains within itself one or several other notions)

Similarity: Greek, *ek tōn homoiōn,* Latin, *ex similibus*

Concomitance, Attendant Circumstance: Greek, *to parepomenon,* Latin, *ab adiunctis* (reasoning drawing support from something previous to, concomitant with, or after the action)

Conflict, Contradiction: Greek, *makhē,* Latin, *ex pugnantibus*

Motive: Greek, *dunamis, hulē,* Latin, *causa, materia* (argument based on motivations for actions)

Judgment: Greek, *krisis,* Latin, *iudicium, iudicatio* (argument based on the opinion of an authority)
(*Anon. Seg.* 171–81. Cf. Arist., *Rhet.* 2.23–24; *Top.;* Cic., *De or.* 2.166–73; *Top.;* Quint. 5.10–11; Theon 107.24–108.32; 122.13–123.2; 124.23–125.19; Minuc. In this highly technical area, the variations among authors are particularly pronounced.)

16. The **Rubrics Relating to Ends:** Greek, *telika kephalaia,* Latin, *finalia capitula* (this name, attested from the Empire, signifies that these rubrics concern the "end" in the sense of **purpose** [Greek, *telos*] of acts: they bring together the criteria for evaluating the grounds of an action)

Justice: Greek, *to dikaion,* Latin, *iustum*

Legality: Greek, *to nomimon,* Latin, *legitimum*

Expedience: Greek, *to sumpheron,* Latin, *utile*

Morality: Greek, *to kalon* (also **Honorableness, Appropriateness:** Greek, *to endoxon, to prepon*), Latin, *honestum*

Pleasure: Greek, *to hēdu,* Latin, *iucundum*

Ease: Greek, *to rhadion,* Latin, *facile*

Possibility: Greek, *to dunaton,* Latin, *possibile*

Necessity: Greek, *to anankaion,* Latin, *necessarium*
(*Rhet. Alex.* 1.4. Cf. Cic., *Inv.* 2.157–76; Theon 116.27–32; Quint. 3.8.16–35; Hermog., *Prog.* 14.6–8; 25.22–26.2; *Stat.* 76.4–79.16; Apsines, *Rhet.* 9; [Longin.], App. 2, 233–34; Men. Rhet. I, 358.19–31)
Some added **Result:** Greek, *to ekbēsomenon;* **Piety:** Greek, *to hosion,* Latin, *pium;* and other criteria.

17. The **Questions at Issue:** Greek, *staseis,* Latin, *status, constitutiones* in **Rational or Logical Inquiries:** Greek, *logika zētēmata,* Latin, *rationale genus* (a courtroom speech dealing with an act, the most frequent case)

Conjecture: Greek, *stokhasmos,* Latin, *coniectura.* Question: **Did it happen?** Latin, *An sit.* Line of argument (for the defense, the opposite for the prosecution): **I did not do it.** Latin, *Non feci.*

Definition: Greek, *horos, horismos,* Latin, *finis, finitio.* Question: **What, strictly speaking, happened?** Latin, *Quid sit.* Line of argument: **I did this, but I am charged with something else.** Latin, *Feci, sed aliud.*

Circumstances, "Accidents": Greek, *kata sumbebēkos,* Latin, *per accidentia,* or, more often, **Quality, Qualification:** Greek, *poiotēs,* Latin, *qualitas, genus.* Question: **How is the act to be understood?, What sort of thing is it?** Latin, *Quale sit.* Line of argument: **I did it, but was right to do it.** Latin, *Feci, sed iure* (or *recte*).

Standing: Greek, *metalēpsis, paragraphē,* Latin, *translatio, praescriptio.* Line of argument: **I did the deed** (or **I did not do it**), **but the case against me is not in accord with the law.** Latin, *Feci* (or *Non feci*) *sed actio non iure intenditur.*

(Hermag., fr. 12–13. Cf. *Rhet. Her.* 1.18–2.26; Cic., *Inv.* 1.10–16; 2.14–115; *De or.* 2.104–13; Quint. 3.6; 7; Hermog., *Stat.* Here again the variations among authors are many.)

18. The **"Commonplaces" of the Encomium:** Greek, *enkōmiastikoi topoi;* **Encomium of an emperor:** Greek, *basilikos logos*

Nationality: Greek, *patris,* Latin, *patria*

Ancestry: Greek, *genos,* Latin, *genus*

Birth: Greek, *genesis* (circumstances surrounding birth)

Nature: Greek, *phusis,* Latin, *natura* (this commonplace in the chapter of Menander covers the physical qualities as they are manifested at birth; in other theorists, the issue is, for a child or adult, the **Body's Physical Endowment** or **Natural Advantages:** Greek, *sōmatos phusis, sōmatos agatha,* Latin, *corporis forma, corporis bona, corporis commoda*)

Nurture: Greek, *anatrophē* (way the subject was raised in childhood)

Upbringing, Formation: Greek, *paideia,* Latin, *disciplina, educatio, institutio* (some of these Latin terms can be applied to the previous commonplace)

Character Traits: Greek, *epitēdeumata* (characteristics manifested in youth before adult deeds)
Accomplishments: Greek, *praxeis,* Latin, *facta, res gestae*
   In War: Greek, *ta kata polemon,* Latin, *bello*
   In Peace: Greek, *ta kat'eirēnēn,* Latin, *pace*
This division war/peace is combined with the much more important division by **Virtues:** Greek, *aretai,* Latin, *virtutes* (moral virtues manifested in deeds done):
   Courage: Greek, *andreia,* Latin, *fortitudo*
   Justice: Greek, *dikaiosunē,* Latin, *iustitia*
   Moderation: Greek, *sōphrosunē,* Latin, *temperantia, continentia*
   Prudence: Greek, *phronēsis,* Latin, *prudentia*
Praise of virtues manifested in wartime, one after another, precedes praise of virtues manifested in accomplishments during peacetime.

Luck: Greek, *tukhē,* Latin, *fortuna* (or **Good Luck:** Greek, *eutukhia,* Latin, *felicitas*)
(Men. Rhet. II, 369.17–376.31. Cf. Arist., *Rhet.* 1.9.1366a33–b34; 1367b27–35; *Rhet. Alex.* 35.3–16; *Rhet. Her.* 3.10–15; Cic., *De or.* 2.45–46, 342–47; *Part.* 74–82; Theon 111.12–112.8; Quint. 3.7.10–18; Alex., *Fragments* 2.19–20; Hermog., *Prog.* 15.18–17.4; Ps.-D. Hal. 268.4–269.11; 274.8–275.11.)
In the case of the funeral eulogy, **Death** is added: Greek, *thanatos, teleutē,* Latin, *mors, finis.*

Style

19. The **Stylistic Virtues or Qualities:** Greek, *lexeōs aretai,* Latin, *elocutionis virtutes*

Correctness: Greek, *hellēnismos,* Latin, *latinitas, purus sermo*

Clarity: Greek, *saphēneia,* Latin, *explanatio, perspicuitas*

Appropriateness: Greek, *prepon,* Latin, *quid deceat, decorum, aptum*

Ornamentation: Greek, *kataskeuē,* Latin, *ornatus*
(Cic., *Or.* 79 [quoting Theophrastos]. Cf. Cic., *De or.* 1.144; 3.37; Quint. 1.5.1; 8.1.1; 11.1.1)

The Stoics added a fifth quality, **Succinctness:** Greek, *suntomia,* Latin, *brevitas* (Diog. L. 7.59).

20. The **Stylistic Genres:** Greek, *logou kharaktēres,* Latin, *dicendi genera*

Grand, Elevated, Grave, Full: Greek, *hadros, hupsēlos, megaloprepēs,* Latin, *uber, gravis, grandis*

Middle: Greek, *mesos,* Latin, *mediocris, modicus, medius* (sometimes also **Florid:** Greek, *anthēros,* Latin, *floridus*)

Simple, Thin, Slender: Greek, *iskhnos, litos,* Latin, *extenuatus, attenuatus, tenuis, gracilis, subtilis*
(*Rhet. Her.* 4.11. Cf. Cic., *De or.* 3.177, 199, 212; *Or.* 20–21; D. Hal., *Dem.* 1–3; Quint. 12.10.58–72; Gell. 6.14. The system varies slightly in Demetr.)
Cic., *Or.* 69, and Quint. 12.10.59 correlate this list with the list of the orator's duties (above, section 2), according to the following outline:

> Grand style = to move
> Middle style = to delight
> Simple style = to instruct

21. The **Stylistic Forms:** Greek, *logou ideai,* Latin, *dicendi genera sive orationum formae*

Clarity: Greek, *saphēneia,* Latin, *claritas, aperta oratio*
   Purity: Greek, *katharotēs,* Latin, *puritas*
   Distinctness: Greek, *eukrineia,* Latin, *perspicuitas*

Grandeur: Greek, *megethos,* Latin, *magnitudo* (similarly, **Pomp, Dignity:** Greek, *onkos, axiōma,* Latin, *tumor, amplitudo*)
   Solemnity: Greek, *semnotēs,* Latin, *gravitas*
   Asperity: Greek, *trakhutēs,* Latin, *asperitas*
   Vehemence: Greek, *sphodrotēs,* Latin, *acrimonia et vehementia*
   Brilliance: Greek, *lamprotēs,* Latin, *splendor*
   Ripeness, Strength: Greek, *akmē,* Latin, *vigor*
   Abundance: Greek, *peribolē,* Latin, *circumducta sive exaggerata oratio* (similarly, **Fullness:** Greek, *mestotēs,* Latin, *plena sive referta oratio*)

Beauty: Greek, *kallos,* Latin, *pulchritudo* (also, **Carefulness:** Greek, *epimeleia,* Latin, *accurata dicendi forma*)

Liveliness: Greek, *gorgotēs,* Latin, *celeritas, velox oratio*

Character: Greek, *ēthos,* Latin, *mores*

    Simplicity: Greek, *apheleia,* Latin, *simplicitas*

    Sweetness: Greek, *glukutēs,* Latin, *suavitas* (also, **Pleasure, Charm:** Greek, *hēdonē, hōra,* Latin, *laeta oratio, venusta oratio*)

    Sharpness: Greek, *drimutēs,* Latin, *acris oratio* (also, **Subtlety:** Greek, *oxutēs,* Latin, *acuta oratio*)

    Modesty: Greek, *epieikeia,* Latin, *moderatio, mitigatio*

    Truthfulness: Greek, *alētheia,* Latin, *veritas*

    Indignation: Greek, *barutēs,* Latin, *gravitas quae est in obiurgando*

Forcefulness: Greek, *deinotēs,* Latin, *eloquentia, apta oratio* (Hermog., *Id.;* the Latin translations here are those of the great humanist Jean Sturm [1571]. Cf. Ps.-Aristides)

22. The **Tropes:** Greek, *tropoi,* Latin, *tropi* (stylistic effects concerning, strictly speaking, an isolated word and consisting in replacing the literal word by another)

    Metaphor: Greek, *metaphora,* Latin, *translatio, tralatio* (replacing the literal word by an image, acknowledging an implied comparison)

    Catachresis: Greek, *katakhrēsis,* Latin, *abusio* (use of a word in a figurative sense, in the absence of a literal word)

    Allegory: Greek, *allēgoria,* Latin, *inversio, permutatio* (use of a word with a double meaning)

    Enigma: Greek, *ainigma,* Latin, *aenigma* (use of a deliberately obscure expression)

    Metalepsis: Greek, *metalēpsis,* Latin, *transumptio* (use of word that, in another context, is a synonym)

    Metonymy: Greek, *metōnumia,* Latin, *denominatio* (substitution, e.g., of the name of the inventor for that of the invention, or vice versa)

    Synecdoche: Greek, *sunekdokhē,* Latin, *intellectio* (e.g., the part for the whole, or vice versa)

    Onomatopoeia: Greek, *onomatopoiia,* Latin, *nominis fictio, nominatio* (word coinage)

Periphrasis: Greek, *periphrasis,* Latin, *circuitio, circumlocutio* (use of several words instead of just one)

Anastrophe: Greek, *anastrophē,* Latin, *reversio* (inversion of normal word order)

Hyperbaton: Greek, *huperbaton,* Latin, *transgressio, transcensus* (placing a word out of normal word order; this and the previous procedure are sometimes included among the tropes, sometimes among the stylistic figures, depending on whether they are thought to affect the sense of the words or only their order)

Pleonasm: Greek, *pleonasmos,* Latin, *pleonasmus* (redundancy)

Ellipsis: Greek, *elleipsis,* Latin, *ellipsis* (omission of a part of a word, a contraction: at the beginning of the word, "aphaeresis"; in the middle, "syncope"; at the end, "apocope")

(Tryph. [after this first list, the author adds a supplementary series of twenty-five entries]. Cf. *Rhet. Her.* 4.42–46; Cic., *De or.* 3.155–69; *Or.* 92–94; Quint. 8.6)

N.B. The definitions given here for the tropes and the figures can only be brief and generalized.

23. The **Figures of Thought:** Greek, *dianoias skhēmata,* Latin, *sensus figurae, sententiarum figurae* (stylistic effects involving several words and obtained by use of terms taken literally and affecting the content, no matter how the content is expressed; the figure remains even should other words be employed)

Question: Greek, *erōtēma, pusma,* Latin, *interrogatio* (commonly called "rhetorical question")

Response: Greek, *hupophora,* Latin, *subiectio* (answering one's own question)

Anticipation: Greek, *prolepsis,* Latin, *praesumptio* (foresee an objection, answer in advance)

Aporia: Greek, *aporia, diaporēsis,* Latin, *dubitatio* (feigned hesitation or being at a loss)

Anacoenosis: Greek, *koinōnia, anakoinōnēsis,* Latin, *communicatio* (to pretend to consult the audience)

Surprise: Greek, *paradoxon, para prosdokian,* Latin, *inopinatum* (to add something unexpected)

Epitrope: Greek, *epitropē,* Latin, *permissio* (pretending to defer to the judges' decision, as if contrary to one's interest)

Bluntness: Greek, *parrhēsia,* Latin, *licentia* (to insist on "speaking freely" and frankly)

Prosopopoeia: Greek, *prosōpopoiia,* Latin, *personae fictio* (giving voice to a dead person, an abstraction, anything inanimate)

Apostrophe: Greek, *apostrophē,* Latin, *aversio* (turning from the audience to address someone else)

Hypotyposis: Greek, *hupotupōsis,* Latin, *evidentia* (evocation, vivid sketch)

Irony: Greek, *eirōneia,* Latin, *dissimulatio, simulatio, ironia* (different sorts of feigning)

Synchoresis: Greek, *sunkhōrēsis,* Latin, *concessio* (admission of some unfavorable facts, with no damage to one's case, as a sign of confidence)

Aposiopesis: Greek, *aposiōpēsis,* Latin, *reticentia, obticentia, interruptio* (breaking off a sentence prior to its conclusion out of consideration, moderation, etc.)

Characterization: Greek, *ēthopoiia, mimēsis,* Latin, *morum imitatio* (imitation or description of the character of other persons)

Hint: Greek, *emphasis,* Latin, *significatio* (suggestion of a hidden meaning)

(Quint. 9.2.6–64 [I abbreviate the list a little]; from "Hint" Quintilian moves on to the related but not identical issue of figurative speech (above, section 8). Cf. *Rhet. Her.* 4.47–69; Cic., *De or.* 3.202–5; *Or.* 136–39; Rut. Lup.; Alex., *Fig.* 1; Aquil. Rom. 1–16; Tiber. 1–22, 43–45)

24. Figures of Diction or **Expression, Figures of Words:** Greek, *lexeōs skhēmata,* Latin, *elocutionis* (or *dictionis*) *figurae, verborum figurae* (stylistic effects involving several words, achieved through the use of terms taken in a literal sense and affecting the very fabric of the diction, i.e., the words' position and form; the figure disappears if other words are used)

Epanalepsis, Repetition, Reprise: Greek, *anadiplōsis, palillogia, epana-lēpsis,* Latin, *conduplicatio, reduplicatio, iteratio, repetitio* (resumption or repetition of a word)

Anaphora: Greek, *epanaphora,* Latin, *repetitio, relatio* (repetition of the same word or phrase at the beginning of successive clauses)

Antistrophe: Greek, *antistrophē,* Latin, *conversio;* similarly, **Epiphora:** Greek, *epiphora,* Latin, *desitio* (repetition of the same word at the end of successive clauses)

Symploce: Greek, *sumplokē, sunthesis,* Latin, *complexio, conexus* ("stitching," beginning and ending successive clauses with the same word: brings together the two previous entries)

Synonymy: Greek, *sunōnumia,* Latin, *nominis communio* (use of synonyms)

Return: Greek, *epanodos,* Latin, *regressio* (a form of repetition consisting in the reprising of two previously spoken words)

Climax: Greek, *klimax,* Latin, *gradatio, ascensus* (linking or "laddering" clauses through repetition, with the last word of each clause also the first word of the succeeding clause)

Clarification: Greek, *prosdiasaphēsis* (insertion of a clarifying word)

Periphrasis: Greek, *periphrasis,* Latin, *circuito, circumlocutio* (already encountered above, section 22, among the tropes: an illustration of the overlapping among the different series of tropes and figures)

Pleonasm: Greek, *pleonasmos,* Latin, *pleonasmus* (same remark as in the preceding entry)

(Alex., *Fig.* 2 [I am giving only the first ten figures here out of a total of twenty-seven]. Cf. *Rhet. Her.* 4.18–41; Cic., *De or.* 3.206–7; *Or.* 135; Rut. Lup.; Quint. 9.3; Aquil. Rom. 22–47; Tiber. 23–42, 46–48)

Oratorical Delivery

25. The Components of **Delivery:** Greek, *hupokrisis,* Latin, *actio, pronuntiatio*

Voice: Greek, *phōnē,* Latin, *vox*

Body Movement: Greek, *sōmatos kinēsis,* Latin, *corporis motus*
Gesture: Latin, *gestus*
Facial Expression: Latin, *vultus*
(*Rhet. Her.* 3.19–27. Cf. Cic., *De or.* 3.213–27; *Or.* 55–60; Quint. 11.3; Longin., fr. 48, 370–439)

Chronological Table

	Greek World	Latin World
	ARCHAIC AGE	
8th cent. B.C.	Homer	753: Rome founded
	CLASSICAL AGE	ROMAN REPUBLIC
5th cent. B.C.	Empedokles	494: Fable of Menenius
	Protagoras, Prodikos,	Agrippa
	Hippias	470: Trial of Appius
	427: Gorgias on embassy	Claudius
	to Athens	
	Euripides, Aristophanes,	
	Thucydides	
	Antiphon, Andokides	
4th cent. B.C.	Antisthenes, Alkidamas	
	Plato	
	Lysias, Isokrates, Isaios,	
	Demosthenes,	
	Aiskhines, Hyperei-	
	des, Lykourgos,	
	Deinarkhos	
	Rhetoric to Alexander,	
	Aristotle	
	HELLENISTIC AGE	
	Theophrastos,	
	Demokhares, Khari-	
	sios	Appius Claudius Caecus
3rd cent. B.C.	Kleokhares, Kineas, He-	Cato the Elder
	gesias	

	Greek World	Latin World
2nd cent. B.C.	Hermagoras, Athenaios	**161:** Senatusconsultum against philosophers and rhetors
		155: Embassy of Karneades, Kritolaos, and Diogenes of Babylon to Rome
		Institution of standing juries
		The Gracchi
	Aretology of Maroneia	M. Antonius, L. Licinius Crassus
1st cent. B.C.	Demetrios, *On Style* (?)	L. Plotius Gallus
	Apollonios Molon, Gorgias the Younger, Tryphon, Metrodoros of Skepsis, Diophanes of Mytilene, Philodemos	**92:** Edict against *Rhetores Latini* *Rhetorica ad Herrenium* Hortensius, Cicero, Cato the Younger, Pompey, Caesar
	Hybreas, Potamon	**44:** Marc Antony's funeral oration of Caesar
	Inscription of Antiochus of Kommagene	Brutus, Licinius Calvus, Hortensia
		Asinius Pollio
	ROMAN EMPIRE	ROMAN EMPIRE
	Dionysios of Halikarnassos, Caecilius, Apollodoros, Theodore	Vergil, Livy, Seneca the Elder, Ovid, Cassius Severus
		Laudatio Turiae
1st cent. A.D.		Domitius Afer, Rutilius Lupus
	Ps.-Longinus	*Tabula Claudiana*
	Niketes, Skopelian	Seneca, Quintilian
2nd cent. A.D.	Dio of Prusa	Tacitus, Pliny the Younger
	Theon	
	Favorinus, Polemon	Suetonius
	Herodes Atticus	Fronto
	Lucian, Aelius Aristides	Aulus Gellius, Apuleius

	Greek World	Latin World
	Phrynikhos, Pollux Maximus of Tyre, Marcus Aurelius	

3rd cent. A.D.	Hermogenes, Apsines
	Philostratos
	Anonymous Segueri-
	    anus, Ps.-Dionysios of
	    Halikarnassos,
	    Menander Rhetor
	Kallinikos of Petra, Cas-
	    sius Longinus
		Aquila Romanus

		Panegyrici Latini 2–5

Bibliography

Collections of Sources

Carey, C., et al. *Greek Orators.* Warminster, England, 1985– .

Diels, H., and W. Kranz. *Die Fragmente der Vorsokratiker.* 6th ed. Berlin, 1951.

Gagarin, M., ed. *The Oratory of Classical Greece.* Austin, TX, 1998– .

Halm, C. *Rhetores Latini minores.* Leipzig, 1863.

Jander, K. *Oratorum et rhetorum Graecorum noua fragmenta.* Bonn, 1913.

Kirk, G. S., J. E. Raven, and M. Schofield. *The Presocratic Philosophers.* 2nd ed. Cambridge, 1983.

Kunst, K. *Rhetorische Papyri.* Berlin, 1923.

Malcovati, E. *Oratorum Romanorum fragmenta liberae rei publicae.* 2nd ed. Turin, 1955.

Malherbe, A. J. *Ancient Epistolary Theorists.* Atlanta, GA, 1988.

Rabe, H. *Prolegomenon sylloge.* Leipzig, 1931.

Radermacher, L. *Artium scriptores (Reste der voraristotelischen Rhetorik).* Vienna, 1951.

Russell, D. A., and M. Winterbottom. *Ancient Literary Criticism: The Principal Texts in New Translations.* Oxford, 1972.

Spengel, L. *Rhetores Graeci.* Leipzig, 1853–56; 2nd ed. of vol. 1, 2, by C. Hammer. Leipzig, 1894.

Sprague, R. K., ed. *The Older Sophists.* Columbia, SC, 1972.

Walz, C. *Rhetores Graeci.* Stuttgart and Tübingen, 1832–1836.

Winterbottom, M. *Roman Declamation: Extracts Edited with Commentary.* Bristol, 1980.

N.B.: Because the list would be too long, editions, translations, commentaries, and lexica bearing on individual authors and texts are not included here. They may be found by reference to the usual bibliographies dedicated to Greek and Latin literature, e.g., *L'Année Philologique.* See also the "List of Abbreviations" in the "Thesaurus" above.

General Works

Achard, G. *La Communication à Rome.* Paris, 1991.

Albaladejo, T. *Retórica.* Madrid, 1989.

Anderson, R. D., Jr. *Glossary of Greek Rhetorical Terms.* Leuven, 2000.

Bizzell, P., and B. Herzberg, eds. *The Rhetorical Tradition: Readings from Classical Times to the Present.* Boston, MA, 1990.

Clark, D. L. *Rhetoric in Greco-Roman Education.* New York, 1957.

Conley, T. M. *Rhetoric in the European Tradition.* Chicago, 1990.

Desbordes, F. *La Rhétorique antique.* Paris, 1996.

Ernesti, J. C. G. *Lexicon technologiae Graecorum rhetoricae.* Leipzig, 1795.

———. *Lexicon technologiae Latinorum rhetoricae.* Leipzig, 1797.

Hadot, P. "Philosophie, dialectique, rhétorique dans l'Antiquité." In *Etudes de philosophie ancienne,* 159-93. Paris, 1998. Originally published in 1980.

Kennedy, G. A. *The Art of Persuasion in Greece.* Princeton, NJ, 1963.

———. *The Art of Rhetoric in the Roman World, 300 B.C.–A.D. 300.* Princeton, NJ, 1972.

———. *Greek Rhetoric Under Christian Emperors.* Princeton, NJ, 1983.

———. *A New History of Classical Rhetoric.* Princeton, NJ, 1994 (a condensed version, in one volume, of the three preceding works).

———. *Classical Rhetoric and Its Christian and Secular Tradition from Ancient to Modern Times.* Chapel Hill, NC, 1980.

———, ed. *The Cambridge History of Literary Criticism.* Vol. 1, *Classical Criticism.* Cambridge, 1989.

Kroll, W. "Rhetorik." In *Paulys Realencyclopädie der classischen Altertumswissenschaft,* Suppl. 7, 1940, col. 1039–1138.

Landfester, M. *Einführung in die Stilistik der griechischen und lateinischen Literatursprachen.* Darmstadt, 1997.

Lanham, R. A. *A Handlist of Rhetorical Terms.* 2nd ed. Berkeley and Los Angeles, 1992.

Lausberg, H. *Handbook of Literary Rhetoric.* Trans. M. T. Bliss, A. Jansen, and D. E. Orton. Leiden, 1998.

Leeman, A. D. *Orationis Ratio: The Stylistic Theories and Practices of the Roman Orators, Historians, and Philosophers.* Amsterdam, 1963.

López Eire, A. *Poéticas y Retóricas griegas.* Madrid, 2002.

Marrou, H.-I. *A History of Education in Antiquity.* Trans. G. Lamb. New York, 1956.

Martin, J. *Antike Rhetorik: Technik und Methode.* Munich, 1974.

Meyer, M., ed. *Histoire de la rhétorique des Grecs à nos jours.* Paris, 1999.

Bibliography 239

Michel, A. *La Parole et la Beauté: Rhétorique et esthétique dans la tradition occidentale.* Paris, 1982.

Murphy, J. J., and R. A. Katula, eds., with F. I. Hill and D. J. Ochs. *A Synoptic History of Classical Rhetoric.* 3d ed. Mahwah, NJ, 2003.

Norden, E. *Die antike Kunstprosa vom VI. Jahrhundert v. Chr. bis in die Zeit der Renaissance.* 3d ed. Leipzig and Berlin, 1918. Trans. ital. B. Heinemann Campana with a "Nota di aggiornamento" by G. Calboli. Rome, 1986.

Patillon, M. *Eléments de rhétorique classique.* Paris, 1990.

Pennacini, A. *Forme del pensiero: Studi di retorica classica.* Alessandria, 2002.

Porter, S. E., ed. *Handbook of Classical Rhetoric in the Hellenistic Period, 330 B.C.–A.D. 400.* Leiden, 1997.

Russell, D. A. *Criticism in Antiquity.* London, 1981.

Sloane, T. O., ed. *Encyclopedia of Rhetoric.* Oxford, 2001.

Ueding, G., ed. *Historisches Wörterbuch der Rhetorik.* Tübingen, 1992– .

Vickers, B. *In Defence of Rhetoric.* Oxford, 1988.

Volkmann, R. *Die Rhetorik der Griechen und Römer.* 2nd ed. Leipzig, 1885.

Walker, J. *Rhetoric and Poetics in Antiquity.* Oxford, 2000.

Proceedings, *Mélanges*, and Collections

Abbenes, J. G. J., S. R. Slings, and I. Sluiter, eds. *Greek Literary Theory after Aristotle . . . in Honour of D. M. Schenkeveld.* Amsterdam, 1995.

Ars rhetorica antica e nuova. Genoa, 1983.

Association Guillaume Budé: Actes du XIᵉ congrès. Paris, 1985 (Theme: Rhetoric).

Bonnafous, S. et al., eds. *Argumentation et discours politique.* Rennes, 2003.

Calboli Montefusco, L., ed. *Papers on Rhetoric.* Bologna-Rome, 1983– .

Cassin, B., ed. *Le Plaisir de parler.* Paris, 1986.

Chevallier, R., ed. *Colloque sur la rhétorique.* Paris, 1979.

Cresci, L. R., F. Gazzano, and D. P. Orsi. *La retorica della diplomazia nella Grecia antica e a Bisanzio.* Rome, 2002.

Dangel, J., ed. *Grammaire et rhétorique.* Strasbourg, 1994.

Döpp, S., ed. *Antike Rhetorik und ihre Rezeption: Symposion zu Ehren von Professor Dr. Carl Joachim Classen.* Stuttgart, 1999.

Dominik, W. J., ed. *Roman Eloquence.* London, 1997.

Flashar, H., ed. *Le Classicisme à Rome aux Iᵉʳˢ siècles avant et après J.-C.* Vandœuvres and Geneva, 1979.

Fortenbaugh, W. W., and D. C. Mirhady, eds. *Peripatetic Rhetoric after Aristotle.* New Brunswick, NJ, 1994.

Freyburger, G., and L. Pernot, eds. *Recherches sur les rhétoriques religieuses.* Turnhout, 2000– .

Fumaroli, M., pres., and L. Pernot, ed. *Actualité de la rhétorique.* Paris, 2002.

Galy, J.-M., and A. Thivel, eds. *La Rhétorique grecque.* Nice, 1994.

Heuzé, P., and J. Pigeaud, eds. *Chemins de la re-connaissance. En hommage à Alain Michel.* Helmantica 50. Salamanca, 1999.

Innes, D., H. Hine, and C. Pelling, eds. *Ethics and Rhetoric: Classical Essays for Donald Russell.* Oxford, 1995.

Kieffer, R., ed. *Parole sacrée, parole profane . . . De la religion à l'éloquence.* Luxembourg, 1991.

Kirby, J. T., ed. *Landmark Essays on Roman Rhetoric.* Davis, CA, 1994.

Lardinois, A. P. M. H., and L. McClure, eds. *Making Silence Speak: Women's Voices in Greek Literature and Society.* Princeton, NJ, 2001.

Lévy, C., and L. Pernot, eds. *Dire l'évidence.* Paris, 1997.

Neumeister, C., and W. Raeck, eds. *Rede und Redner.* Möhnesee, 2000.

Pennacini, A., ed. *Studi di retorica oggi in Italia.* Bologna, 1987 and 1998.

————, ed. *Retorica della comunicazione nelle letterature classiche.* Bologna, 1990.

Pernot, L., ed. *Rhétoriques de la conversation.* Rhetorica, 11, 4. Berkeley, CA, 1993.

Schirren, T., and G. Ueding, eds. *Topik und Rhetorik.* Tübingen, 2000.

Schröder, B.-J. and J.-P. Schröder, eds. *Studium declamatorium. Untersuchungen zu Schulübungen und Prunkreden von der Antike bis zur Neuzeit.* Munich and Leipzig, 2003.

Sutherland, C. M., and R. Sutcliffe, eds. *The Changing Tradition: Women in the History of Rhetoric.* Calgary, 1999.

Vickers, B., ed. *Rhetoric Revalued.* Binghamton, NY, 1982.

Wooten, C. W., ed. *The Orator in Action and Theory in Greece and Rome: Essays in Honor of G. A. Kennedy.* Leiden, 2001.

Worthington, I., and J. M. Foley, eds. *Epea and Grammata: Oral and Written Communication in Ancient Greece.* Leiden, 2002.

Specialized Journals

Logo: Revista de retórica y teoría de la comunicación. Salamanca.

Philosophy and Rhetoric. State College, PA.

Rhetorica: A Journal of the History of Rhetoric. Berkeley (http://www.ucpress.edu/journals/rh). Journal of the International Society for the History of Rhetoric (http://ishr.ticdavis.edu).

Rhetorical Review: The Electronic Review of Books on the History of Rhetoric. Denmark (http://www.nnrh.dk/RR/index.html).

Rhetorik: Ein internationales Jahrbuch. Tübingen.

Thematic and Diachronic Studies

Alonso del Real, C., ed. *Consolatio.* Pamplona, 2001.

Bonner, S. F. *Roman Declamation in the Late Republic and Early Empire.* Liverpool, 1949.

Cairns, F. *Generic Composition in Greek and Roman Poetry.* Edinburgh, 1972.

Calboli, G. "Rhétorique et droit romain." *Revue des études latines* 76 (1998): 158–76.

Calboli Montefusco, L. *La Dottrina degli "status" nella retorica greca e romana.* Bologna, 1984.

———. *Exordium narratio epilogus: Studi sulla teoria retorica greca e romana delle parti del discorso.* Bologna, 1988.

Cassin, B. *L'Effet sophistique.* Paris, 1995.

Celentano, M. S. "La codificazione retorica della comunicazione epistolare nell'*Ars rhetorica* di Giulio Vittore." *Rivista di filologia e di istruzione classica* 122 (1994): 422–35.

———. "Comicità, umorismo e arte oratoria nella teoria retorica antica." *Eikasmos* 6 (1995): 161–74.

Crook, J. A. *Law and Life of Rome.* London, 1967.

———. *Legal Advocacy in the Roman World.* London, 1995.

Gross, N. P. *Amatory Persuasion in Antiquity.* Newark, DE, 1985.

Gunderson, E. *Staging Masculinity: The Rhetoric of Performance in the Roman World.* Ann Arbor, MI, 2000.

Heldmann, K. *Antike Theorien über Entwicklung und Verfall der Redekunst.* Munich, 1982.

Kassel, R. *Untersuchungen zur griechischen und römischen Konsolationsliteratur.* Munich, 1958.

Katsouris, A. G. *Rhêtorikê hupokrisê.* Ioannina, 1989.

Kierdorf, W. *Laudatio funebris.* Meisenheim am Glan, 1980.

Koster, S. *Die Invektive in der griechischen und römischen Literatur.* Meisenheim am Glan, 1980.

Laurens, P. *L'Abeille dans l'ambre. Célébration de l'épigramme, de l'époque alexandrine à la fin de la Renaissance.* Paris, 1989.

Montiglio, S. *Silence in the Land of Logos.* Princeton, NJ, 2000.

Moretti, G. *Acutum dicendi genus: Brevità, oscurità, sottigliezze e paradossi nelle tradizioni retoriche degli Stoici.* Bologna, 1995.

Norden, E. *Agnostos Theos: Untersuchungen zur Formengeschichte religiöser Rede.* Leipzig and Berlin, 1913. Trans. ital. with an introduction by C. O. Tommasi Moreschini. Brescia, 2002.

Ochs, D. J. *Consolatory Rhetoric.* Columbia, SC, 1993.

Ong, W., S.J. *Orality and Literacy: The Technologizing of the World.* London and New York, 1982.

Parodi Scotti, F. *Ethos e consenso.* Bologna, 1996.

Pernot, L. "Lieu et lieu commun dans la rhétorique antique." *Bulletin de l'Association Guillaume Budé* (1986): 253–84.

——. *La Rhétorique de l'éloge dans le monde gréco-romain.* Paris, 1993.

——. "*Periautologia*: Problèmes et méthodes de l'éloge de soi-même dans la tradition éthique et rhétorique gréco-romaine." *Revue des études grecques* 111 (1998): 101–24.

Rispoli, G. M. *L'ironia della voce.* Naples, 1992.

——. *Dal suono all'immagine: Poetiche della voce ed estetica dell'eufonia.* Pisa and Rome, 1995.

Romilly, J. de. *Magic and Rhetoric in Ancient Greece.* Cambridge, MA, 1975.

Russell, D. A. *Greek Declamation.* Cambridge and New York, 1983.

Schouler, B. "Le Déguisement de l'intention dans la rhétorique grecque." *Ktèma* 11 (1986): 257–72.

Spina, L. *L'Oratore scriteriato: Per una storia letteraria e politica di Tersite.* Naples, 2001.

Vernant, J.-P. "Langage religieux et vérité." In *Religions, histoires, raisons,* 55–62. Paris, 1979. Originally published in 1969.

Wisse, J. *Ethos and Pathos from Aristotle to Cicero.* Amsterdam, 1989.

Yates, F. A. *The Art of Memory.* Chicago, 1966.

Archaic and Classical Greece (Chapters 1 to 3)

Blass, F. *Die attische Beredsamkeit.* 2nd ed. Leipzig, 1887–98.

Butti de Lima, P. *L'inchiesta e la prova.* Turin, 1996.

Buxton, R. G. A. *Persuasion in Greek Tragedy: A Study of peitho.* Cambridge and New York, 1982.

Canfora, L. "L'agorà: Il discorso suasorio." In *Lo spazio letterario della Grecia antica,* I, 1, 379–95. Rome, 1992.

——. "Le collezioni superstiti. 4. Gli oratori." In *Lo spazio letterario della Grecia antica,* II, 164–84. Rome, 1995.

Carawan, E. *Rhetoric and the Law of Draco.* Oxford, 1998.

Carlier, P. *Démosthène.* Paris, 1990.

Chiron, P. "La Période chez Aristote." In P. Büttgen, S. Diebler, and M. Rashed, eds., *Théories de la phrase et de la proposition*, 103–30. Paris, 1999.

Clavaud, R. *Le Ménexène de Platon et la rhétorique de son temps*. Paris, 1980.

Cole, T. *The Origins of Rhetoric in Ancient Greece*. Baltimore, MD, 1991.

Conacher, D. *Euripides and the Sophists*. London, 1998.

Consigny, S. *Gorgias: Sophist and Artist*. Columbia, SC, 2002.

De Jong, I. J. F. Character-text (speeches). Chap. 5 in *Narrators and Focalizers: The Presentation of the Story in the Iliad*. Amsterdam, 1987.

De Meyer, L. *Vers l'invention de la rhétorique*. Louvain-la-Neuve, 1997.

Demont, P. *La Cité grecque archaïque et classique et l'idéal de tranquillité*. Paris, 1990.

———. "Die *Epideixis* über die *Techne* im V. und IV. Jh." In W. Kullmann and J. Althoff, eds., *Vermittlung und Tradierung von Wissen in der griechischen Kultur*, 181–209. Tübingen, 1993.

Detienne, M. *The Masters of Truth in Archaic Greece*. Trans. J. Lloyd. New York and Cambridge, MA, 1996.

Diès, A. *Autour de Platon*. Paris, 1927.

Enos, R. L. *Greek Rhetoric Before Aristotle*. Prospect Heights, IL, 1993.

———, and L. P. Agnew, eds. *Landmark Essays in Aristotelian Rhetoric*. Mahwah, NJ, 1998.

Erickson, K. V., ed. *Plato: True and Sophistic Rhetoric*. Amsterdam, 1979.

Gagarin, M. *Antiphon the Athenian*. Austin, TX, 2002.

Gondros, E. A. *Auf dem Weg zur rhetorischen Theorie: Rhetorische Reflexion im ausgehenden fünften Jahrhundert v. Chr.* Tübingen, 1996.

Grimaldi, W. *Studies in the Philosophy of Aristotle's Rhetoric*. Wiesbaden, 1972.

Hansen, M. H. *The Athenian Democracy in the Age of Demosthenes*. Trans. J. A. Crook. Oxford and Cambridge, MA, 1991.

Hellwig, A. *Untersuchungen zur Theorie der Rhetorik bei Platon und Aristoteles*. Göttingen, 1973.

Hubbell, H. M. *The Influence of Isocrates on Cicero, Dionysius and Aristides*. New Haven, CT, 1913.

Jarratt, S. C. *Rereading the Sophists*. Carbondale, IL, 1991.

Johnstone, C. L., ed. *Theory, Text, Context: Issues in Greek Rhetoric and Oratory*. New York, 1996.

Jouan, F. "Euripide et la rhétorique." *Les études classiques* 52 (1984): 3–13.

Jouanna, J. "Rhétorique et médecine dans la Collection Hippocratique: Contribution à l'histoire de la rhétorique au Ve siècle." *Revue des études grecques* 97 (1984): 26–44.

Kerferd, G. *The Sophistic Movement.* Cambridge, 1983.

Lavency, M. *Aspects de la logographie judiciaire attique.* Louvain, 1964.

Leclerc, M.-C. *La Parole chez Hésiode.* Paris, 1993.

Lloyd, M. *The Agon in Euripides.* Oxford, 1992.

Loraux, N. *The Invention of Athens: The Funeral Oration in the Classical City.* Trans. A. Sheridan. Cambridge, MA, 1986.

McClure, L. *Spoken like a Woman: Speech and Gender in Athenian Drama.* Princeton, NJ, 1999.

Martin, R. P. *The Language of Heroes: Speech and Performance in the Iliad.* Ithaca, NY, 1989.

Navarre, O. *Essai sur la rhétorique grecque avant Aristote.* Paris, 1900.

Noël, M.-P. "Lectures, relectures et mélectures des sophistes." *Noesis* 2 (1998): 19–36.

———. "Gorgias et' 'invention' des *Gorgieia skhemata.*" *Revue des études grecques* 112 (1999): 193–211.

———. "De la sophistique à la néosophistique: Sur quelques 'lectures' modernes des sophistes." In J. Leclant, pres., and A. Michel, dir., *Tradition classique et modernité: Actes du 12ᵉ colloque de la Villa Kérylos,* 43–53. Paris, 2002.

Nouhaud, M. *L'Utilisation de l'histoire par les orateurs attiques.* Paris, 1982.

Ober, J. *Mass and Elite in Democratic Athens.* Princeton, NJ, 1989.

O'Sullivan, N. *Alcidamas, Aristophanes and the Beginnings of Greek Stylistic Theory.* Stuttgart, 1992.

Pearson, L. *The Art of Demosthenes.* Meisenheim am Glan, 1976.

Perceau, S. *La parole vive: Communiquer en catalogue dans l'épopée homérique.* Leuven, 2002.

Pernot, L. "Demostene allievo di Platone?" *Seminari romani di cultura greca* 1 (1998): 313–43.

———. "Le serment du discours *Sur la couronne* (Dém., XVIII, 208) dans la critique littéraire et rhétorique de l'Antiquité." *Revue des études grecques* 114 (2001): 84–139.

———. "Aristote et ses devanciers: Pour une archéologie du genre délibératif." *Ktèma* 27 (2002): 227–35.

Poulakos, J. *Sophistical Rhetoric in Classical Greece.* Columbia, SC, 1995.

Poulakos, T. *Speaking for the Polis: Isocrates' Rhetorical Education.* Columbia, SC, 1997.

Prinz, K. *Epitaphios logos.* Frankfort, 1997.

Ramírez Vidal, G. *La retórica de Antifonte.* Mexico City, 2000.

Romilly, J. de. *Histoire et raison chez Thucydide.* Paris, 1956.

————. *The Great Sophists in Periclean Athens*. Trans. J. Lloyd. Oxford and New York, 1992.

Ruzé, F. *Délibération et pouvoir dans la cité grecque de Nestor à Socrate*. Paris, 1997.

Schiappa, E. *Protagoras and Logos*. Columbia, SC, 1991.

————. ed. *Landmark Essays on Classical Greek Rhetoric*. Davis, CA 1994.

————. *The Beginnings of Rhetorical Theory in Classical Greece*. New Haven, CT 1999.

Spina, L. *Il Cittadino alla tribuna*. Naples, 1986.

Stadter, P. A., ed. *The Speeches in Thucydides*. Chapel Hill, NC, 1973.

Too, Y. L. *The Rhetoric of Identity in Isocrates*. Cambridge and New York, 1995.

Trédé, M. *Kairos, l'à-propos et l'occasion*. Paris, 1992.

Usher, S. *Greek Oratory: Tradition and Originality*. Oxford, 1999.

Velardi, R. *Retorica, filosofia, letteratura*. Naples, 2001.

Wardy, R. *The Birth of Rhetoric*. London, 1996.

Worthington, I., ed. *Persuasion: Greek Rhetoric in Action*. London, 1994.

————, ed. *Demosthenes: Statesman and Orator*. London and New York, 2000.

Yunis, H. *Taming Democracy*. Ithaca, NY, 1996.

The Hellenistic Greek World (Chapter 4)

Blass, F. *Die griechische Beredsamkeit in dem Zeitraum von Alexander bis auf Augustus*. Berlin, 1865.

Chiron, P. *Un rhéteur méconnu: Démétrios (Ps.-Démétrios de Phalère)*. Paris, 2001.

Luzzatto, M. T. "La Cultura nella città e le scuole: la retorica." In S. Settis, ed., *I Greci: Storia, cultura, arte, società*, 2, III, 483–502. Turin, 1998.

Wooten, C. W. *A Rhetorical and Historical Study of Hellenistic Oratory*. Chapel Hill, NC, 1972 (unpublished dissertation, distributed on microfilm; parts have appeared in *Quarterly Journal of Speech*, 1973, *American Journal of Philology*, 1974, and *Revue des études grecques*, 1975).

Republican Rome (Chapter 5)

Achard, G. *Pratique rhétorique et idéologie politique dans les discours "optimates" de Cicéron*. Leiden, 1981.

Cavarzere, A. *Oratoria a Roma*. Rome, 2000.

Craig, C. P. *Form as Argument in Cicero's Speeches*. Atlanta, GA, 1993.

Dangel, J. "Parole et écriture chez les Latins: Approche stylistique." *Latomus* 58 (1999): 3–29.

David, J.-M. *Le Patronat judiciaire au dernier siècle de la République romaine.* Rome, 1992.

Enos, R. L. *Roman Rhetoric: Revolution and the Greek Influence.* Prospect Heights, IL, 1995.

Grimal, P. *Cicéron.* Paris, 1986.

Lévy, C. *Cicero Academicus: Recherches sur les Académiques et sur la philosophie cicéronienne.* Rome, 1992.

————. "Rhétorique et philosophie: La monstruosité politique chez Cicéron." *Revue des études latines* 76 (1998): 139–57.

López, A. "La Oratoria femenina en Roma a la luz de la actual." In *La oratoria en Grecia y Roma,* 97–115. Universidad de Verano de Teruel, 1989.

Ludwig, W., ed. *Eloquence et rhétorique chez Cicéron.* Vandœuvres and Geneva, 1982.

May, J. M., ed. *Brill's Companion to Cicero: Oratory and Rhetoric.* Leiden, 2002.

Michel, A. *Rhétorique et philosophie chez Cicéron: Essai sur les fondements philosophiques de l'art de persuader.* Paris, 1960.

————. "Rhétorique et philosophie chez Cicéron." *Aufstieg und Niedergang der Römischen Welt* I, 3 (1973): 139–208.

Narducci, E. *Cicerone e l'eloquenza romana.* Rome and Bari, 1997.

Nicolet, C. *The World of the Citizen in Republican Rome.* Trans. P. Falla. Berkeley, CA, 1980.

Pina Polo, F. *Contra arma verbis. Der Redner vor dem Volk in der späten römischen Republik.* Stuttgart, 1996.

Steel, C. E. W. *Cicero, Rhetoric, and Empire.* Oxford, 2002.

Wooten, C. *Cicero's Philippics and Their Demosthenic Model.* Chapel Hill, NC, 1983.

Roman Empire (Chapter 6)

Albaladejo, T., and E. del Río Sanz, eds. *Quintiliano.* Logroño and Madrid, 1998.

Anderson, G. *Philostratus.* London, 1986.

————. *The Second Sophistic.* London, 1993.

Aubrion, E. *Rhétorique et histoire chez Tacite.* Metz, 1985.

Behr, C. A. *Aelius Aristides and the Sacred Tales.* Amsterdam, 1968.

Billault, A., ed. *Lucien de Samosate.* Lyon, 1994.

————. *L'Univers de Philostrate.* Brussels, 2000.

Bompaire, J. *Lucien écrivain.* Paris, 1958.

Boulanger, A. *Aelius Aristide et la sophistique dans la province d'Asie au IIe siècle de notre ère.* Paris, 1923.

Bowersock, G. W. *Greek Sophists in the Roman Empire.* Oxford, 1969.

Bowie, E. L. "Greeks and Their Past in the Second Sophistic." In M. I. Finley, ed., *Studies in Ancient Society,* 166–209. London and Boston, MA, 1974. Originally published in 1970.

Champlin, E. *Fronto and Antonine Rome.* Cambridge, MA, 1980.

Dangel, J. *La Phrase oratoire chez Tite-Live.* Paris, 1982.

Desideri, P. *Dione di Prusa.* Messina and Florence, 1978.

Fairweather, J. *Seneca the Elder.* Cambridge, 1981.

Fontaine, J. *Aspects et problèmes de la prose d'art latine au IIIe siècle.* Turin, 1968.

Gamberini, F. *Stylistic Theory and Practice in the Younger Pliny.* Hildesheim, 1983.

Gleason, M. W. *Making Men: Sophists and Self-Presentation in Ancient Rome.* Princeton, NJ, 1995.

Harrison, S. J. *Apuleius: A Latin Sophist.* Oxford, 2000.

Heath, M. *Hermogenes on Issues.* Oxford, 1995.

Heuzé, P. *L'Image du corps dans l'œuvre de Virgile.* Rome, 1985.

Jones, C. P. *The Roman World of Dio Chrysostom.* Cambridge, MA, 1978.

———. *Culture and Society in Lucian.* Cambridge, MA, 1986.

Kennedy, G. A. *Quintilian.* New York, 1969.

———. "Some Recent Controversies in the Study of Later Greek Rhetoric." *American Journal of Philology* 124 (2003): 295–301.

Korenjak, M. *Publikum und Redner: Ihre Interaktion in der sophistischen Rhetorik der Kaiserzeit.* Munich, 2000.

L'Huillier, M.-C. *L'Empire des mots: Orateurs gaulois et empereurs romains.* Besançon, 1992.

Marache, R. *La Critique littéraire de langue latine et le développement du goût archaïsant au IIe siècle de notre ère.* Rennes, 1952.

Michel, A. *Le Dialogue des orateurs de Tacite et la philosophie de Cicéron.* Paris, 1962.

Milazzo, A. M. *Un dialogo difficile: La retorica in conflitto nei Discorsi Platonici di Elio Aristide.* Hildesheim, 2002.

Nicosia, S. *Elio Aristide nell' Asclepieio di Pergamo e la retorica recuperata.* Palermo, 1979.

Patillon, M. *La Théorie du discours chez Hermogène le rhéteur.* Paris, 1988.

Pernot, L. "La rhétorique de l'Empire, ou comment la rhétorique grecque a inventé l'Empire romain." *Rhetorica* 16 (1998): 131–148.

————. "L'art du sophiste à l'époque romaine: Entre savoir et pouvoir." In C. Lévy, B. Besnier, and A. Gigandet, eds., *Ars and Ratio*, 126–42. Brussels, 2003.

Puech, B. *Orateurs et sophistes grecs dans les inscriptions d'époque impériale.* Paris, 2002.

Quet, M.-H. "Rhétorique, culture et politique: Le fonctionnement du discours idéologique chez Dion de Pruse et dans les *Moralia* de Plutarque." *Dialogues d'histoire ancienne* 4 (1978): 51–117.

Reardon, B. P. *Courants littéraires grecs des IIe et IIIe siècles après J.-C.* Paris, 1971.

Rees, R. *Layers of Loyalty in Latin Panegyric, A.D. 289–307.* Oxford, 2002.

Rutherford, I. *Canons of Style in the Antonine Age.* Oxford, 1998.

Sandy, G. *The Greek World of Apuleius.* Leiden and New York, 1997.

Schmid, W. *Der Atticismus in seinen Hauptvertretern.* Stuttgart, 1887–97.

Schmitz, T. *Bildung und Macht: Zur sozialen und politischen Funktion der zweiten Sophistik.* Munich, 1997.

Swain, S. *Hellenism and Empire.* Oxford, 1996.

————, ed. *Dio Chrysostom.* Oxford, 2000.

Tellegen-Couperus, O., ed. *Quintilian and the Law.* Leuven, 2003.

Van der Stockt, L., ed. *Rhetorical Theory and Praxis in Plutarch.* Leuven, 2000.

Veyne, P. "L'Identité grecque devant Rome et l'empereur." *Revue des études grecques* 112 (1999): 510–67.

N.B.: Detailed bibliographies on most of the authors studied in this chapter appear in *Aufstieg und Niedergang der Römischen Welt*, II, vol. 30ff.

The Heritage of Greco-Roman Rhetoric (Conclusion)
Fourth to Sixth Centuries

Bouffartigue, J. *L'Empereur Julien et la culture de son temps.* Paris, 1992.

Dagron, G. *L'Empire romain d'Orient au IVe siècle et les traditions politiques de l'hellénisme: Le témoignage de Thémistios.* Paris, 1968.

Kaster, R. A. *Guardians of Language: The Grammarian and Society in Late Antiquity.* Berkeley and Los Angeles, 1988.

MacCormack, S. *Art and Ceremony in Late Antiquity.* Berkeley and Los Angeles, 1981.

Pernot, L. "Rhetoric." In G. Bowersock, P. Brown, and O. Grabar, eds., *Late Antiquity: A Guide to the Postclassical World*, 669–70. Cambridge, MA, 1999.

Schouler, B. *La tradition hellénique chez Libanios.* Lille and Paris, 1984.

Whitby, M., ed. *The Propaganda of Power: The Role of Panegyric in Late Antiquity.* Leiden, 1998.

Rhetoric and Christianity

Brown, P. *Power and Persuasion in Late Antiquity.* Madison, WI, 1992.

Cameron, A. *Christianity and the Rhetoric of Empire.* Berkeley and Los Angeles, 1991.

Classen, C. J. *Rhetorical Criticism of the New Testament.* Boston and Leiden, 2002.

Fredouille, J.-C. *Tertullien et la conversion de la culture antique.* Paris, 1972.

Kennedy, G. A. *New Testament Interpretation through Rhetorical Criticism.* Chapel Hill, NC, 1984.

Meynet, R. *L'Analyse rhétorique: Une nouvelle méthode pour comprendre la Bible.* Paris, 1989.

Watson, D. F., and A. J. Hauser. *Rhetorical Criticism of the Bible: A Comprehensive Bibliography.* Leiden, 1994.

Winter, B. W. *Philo and Paul among the Sophists.* Cambridge, 1997.

The Middle Ages

Camargo, M. "Rhetoric." In D. L. Wagner, ed., *The Seven Liberal Arts in the Middle Ages,* 96–124. Brooklyn, NY, 1983.

Curtius, R. *European Literature and the Latin Middle Ages.* Trans. W. R. Trask. Reprint with new epilogue. Princeton, NJ, 1990.

Dagron, G. *Empereur et prêtre: Etude sur le "césaropapisme" byzantin.* Paris, 1996.

Hunger, H. Rhetorik. Chap. 2 in *Die hochsprachliche profane Literatur der Byzantiner.* Munich, 1978.

Irigoin, J. "La tradition des rhéteurs grecs dans l'Italie byzantine (X^e–XIIe siècle)." In *La Tradition des textes grecs,* 581–92. Paris, 2003. Originally published in 1986.

Kustas, G. *Studies in Byzantine Rhetoric.* Thessaloniki, 1973.

Longère, J. *La prédication médiévale.* Paris, 1983.

Michel, A. *Théologiens et mystiques au Moyen Age.* Paris, 1997.

Murphy, J. J. *Rhetoric in the Middle Ages.* Berkeley and Los Angeles, 1974.

———, ed. *Medieval Eloquence.* Berkeley, CA, 1978.

Zink, M. *La Prédication en langue romane avant 1300.* Paris, 1976.

The Modern Period

For this immense area, we refer the reader to:

Fumaroli, M., dir. *Histoire de la rhétorique dans l'Europe moderne, 1450–1950.* Paris, 1999.

Additional bibliographic information may be found, in particular, in G. A. Kennedy, *Classical Rhetoric and Its Christian and Secular Tradition from Ancient to Modern Times,* and T. M. Conley, *Rhetoric in the European Tradition* (cited above).

The Heritage of Greco-Roman Rhetoric Today (in the English- and French-Speaking Worlds)

Austin, J. L. *How to Do Things with Words.* Oxford, 1962.

Baldwin, C. S. *Ancient Rhetoric and Poetic.* Westport, CT, 1924.

———. *Medieval Rhetoric and Poetic (to 1400).* New York, 1928.

———. *Renaissance Literary Theory and Practice.* New York, 1939.

Booth, W. C. *The Rhetoric of Fiction.* Chicago, 1961.

———. *Modern Dogma and the Rhetoric of Assent.* Notre Dame, IN, 1974.

Bredin, J.-D., and T. Lévy. *Convaincre: Dialogue sur l'éloquence.* Paris, 1997.

Burke, K. *A Rhetoric of Motives.* New York, 1950.

———. *The Rhetoric of Religion.* Boston, MA, 1961.

Carpenter, R. *History as Rhetoric.* Columbia, SC, 1995.

Collard, G. *L'Art de s'exprimer en toutes circonstances.* Paris, 1999.

Corbett, E. P. J. *Classical Rhetoric for the Modern Student.* New York, 1965.

———, J. L. Golden, and G. F. Berquist, eds. *Essays on the Rhetoric of the Western World.* Dubuque, IA, 1990.

Detienne, M. Des pratiques d'assemblée aux formes du politique. Chap. 5 in *Comparer l'incomparable,* Paris, 2000.

Florescu, V. *La Rhétorique et la néorhétorique.* Bucharest and Paris, 1982.

Foss, K. A., S. K. Foss, and R. Trapp. *Contemporary Perspectives on Rhetoric.* Prospect Heights, IL, 1985.

Foucault, M. *L'Ordre du discours.* Paris, 1971.

Fumaroli, M. *L'Âge de l'éloquence: Rhétorique et "res literaria" de la Renaissance au seuil de l'époque classique.* Geneva, 1980.

———. *Leçon inaugurale,* Collège de France, Chaire de rhétorique et société en Europe (XVIᵉ–XVIIᵉ siècles). Paris, 1987.

———. *Héros et orateurs: Rhétorique et dramaturgie cornéliennes.* Geneva, 1990.

———. *The Poet and the King: Jean de la Fontaine and His Century.* Trans. J. M. Todd. Notre Dame, IN, 2002.

———. *Chateaubriand: Poésie et Terreur.* Paris, 2003.

Genette, G. *Figures of Literary Discourse.* Trans. A. Sheridan, intro. M.-R. Logan. New York, 1982.

Groupe μ. *A General Rhetoric.* Trans. P. B. Burrell and E. M. Slotkin. Baltimore, MD, 1981.

Hagège, C. *L'homme de paroles.* Paris, 1985.

Horner, W. B., ed. *The Present State of Scholarship in Historical and Contemporary Rhetoric.* Columbia, MO, 1983.

Johnson, N. *Nineteenth Century Rhetoric in America.* Carbondale, 1991.

Kennedy, G. A. *Comparative Rhetoric.* Oxford, 1998.

McCloskey, D. N. *The Rhetoric of Economics.* Madison, WI, 1985.

McKeon, R. P. *Rhetoric: Essays in Invention and Discovery.* Ed by M. Backman. Woodbridge, CT, 1987.

Nelson, J. S., A. Megill, and D. N. McCloskey, eds. *The Rhetoric of the Human Sciences.* Madison, WI, 1987.

Perelman, C. *The Realm of Rhetoric.* Trans. W. Kluback, intro. C. C. Arnold. Notre Dame, IN, 1982.

———, and L. Olbrechts-Tyteca. *Rhétorique et philosophie.* Paris, 1952.

———. *The New Rhetoric: A Treatise on Argumentation.* Trans. J. Wilkinson and P. Weaver. Notre Dame, IN, 1969.

Recherches rhétoriques Communications, 16. Paris, 1970 (contributions by R. Barthes, G. Genette, and the *Groupe μ*).

Richards, I. A. *The Philosophy of Rhetoric.* New York and London, 1936.

Ricœur, P. *The Rule of Metaphor.* Trans. R. Czerny, with K. McLaughlin and J. Costello. Toronto and Buffalo, NY, 1977.

———. *Time and Narrative.* Trans. K. McLaughlin and D. Pellauer. Chicago, 1984–88.

———. *Lectures.* Paris, 1991–94.

Sloane, T. O. *On the Contrary: The Protocol of Traditional Rhetoric.* Washington, D.C., 1997.

Toulmin, S. E. *The Uses of Argument.* Cambridge, 1958.

Valesio, P. *Novantiqua: Rhetorics as a Contemporary Theory.* Bloomington, IN, 1980.

Wallace, K. R., ed. *History of Speech Education in America.* New York, 1954.

———. *Understanding Discourse.* Baton Rouge, LA, 1970.

Weaver, R. M. *The Ethics of Rhetoric.* Chicago, 1953.

Welch, K. E. *The Contemporary Reception of Classical Rhetoric.* Mahwah, NJ, 1990.

White, H. V. *The Content of the Form: Narrative Discourse and Historical Representation.* Baltimore, MD, 1987.

Index of Proper Names

Index of Subjects

Index of Greek Words

Index of Latin Words

Rhetoric in Antiquity was designed and composed in Garamond with Requiem display type by Kachergis Book Design of Pittsboro, North Carolina. It was printed on sixty-pound Natural Offset and bound by McNaughton & Gunn, Inc., Saline, Michigan.